Glove Stories

Glove Stories

The Collected Baseball Writings of Dave Kindred

To Grandma Lena, who sent me to the train station
on Sunday mornings to buy the Chicago papers,
And to all the sportswriters now and then
who know we go to games to have fun
and read to have that fun again

Contents

Acknowledgements

The columns and handful of features in this book were written for *The Sporting News* beginning in October of 1991. They are collected here at the generous insistence of Steve Meyerhoff, the company's Book Division Editorial Director. Production artist Christen Sager designed the book. Archivist Jim Meier tracked down the words and made them reappear.

Like first basemen who catch every short-hop throw, TSN's editors have saved me a hundred embarrassments. Thanks to Bob Hille, Dale Bye, Steve Gietscher, Jim Gilstrap, Ron Smith, Dennis Dillon, Joe Hoppel, Larry Wigge, Leslie McCarthy, Anna Jones, and Kathy Sheldon.

Jim Nuckols and John Rawlings, the big bosses, have given me every freedom a journalist should want. When those freedoms just weren't enough, Editorial Coordinator Lesley Hunt has said, "Dave, go walk your dogs. I'll get it done." Which she did, bless her.

Introduction

JOHN D. RAWLINGS

EDITOR, THE SPORTING NEWS

When I met Dave Kindred, I was a young sports editor and he was established as the preeminent sports voice in the nation. Although we were separated in age by only a few years, it felt to me as though we were divided by eons professionally. Introduced in a press box at Soldier Field by a mutual friend, we chatted amiably, Dave answering questions as fast as I could pepper them at him. He acted as though I were every bit his equal, even though I had nothing to offer him in return for his wisdom.

That is the essence of why Dave is such a wonderful columnist: he sees worth in every life, grace in every life.

Whether writing about Mark McGwire—a man among children—or Charlie Brown—a child among children—Dave makes us see life in a way we never did before.

Dave has won all sorts of awards in his career, not the least of which is one named for Red Smith, who many of us believe is the best writer our business has ever seen. Dave does not write to win awards; they come to him because of what he sees. The first collection of his writing was named "Heroes, Fools and Other Dreamers," and that tells you something about Dave right there.

Dave, in turn, has delighted and enraged readers of The Sporting News for a decade now. "During the Gulf War, I wrote several columns with war themes. I didn't like the overheated patriotism I saw at the Super Bowl. Nor did I like the Seton Hall story in which the Italian basketball player, Marco Lokar, was basically run out of the country because he wouldn't wear an American flag. On those issues, I was in a minority so small as to be invisible. Even my wife, my best friend, asked why I wrote columns that ran so directly against public sentiment. I had to do them, I told her, because sports is more than just games. It's a real part of our lives and we need to understand what sports tells us about ourselves."

Dave will make you care about Kenny Krahenbuhl as much as you care about Mark McGwire. That's what makes him great.

Foreword

JOHN FEINSTEIN

If you are a student of the rather narrow topic of sports literature, you are no doubt aware that legend has it the very best writing on sports is almost always produced by those writing on two subjects: baseball and boxing.

If you study this legend further, you will find that those who have written at length about the so-called "sweet science," rarely write at great length about the sport itself. One can only spend so much time explaining hooks and jabs and there was only one Ali Shuffle. They write, instead, about the cast of characters surrounding the sport because they are often the stuff of great storytelling.

Baseball is different. There are more ways to write about baseball than any sport on the planet with the possible exception of politics, which actually is a combination of all sports rolled into one very dirty and colorful package. Last season, a friend of mine wrote an entire column on why a manager had decided to send in a pinch-runner for a pinch-runner. Baseball writers range from those who spill thousands of words breaking down the game statistically to those who spend just as many words explaining the deep spiritual meaning of the game, conjuring up emerald chess boards and the secret of life itself being found somewhere on the base paths.

Somewhere in the middle of all this lies the best of baseball.

Which brings us to Dave Kindred.

What Kindred brings to baseball writing is a unique sense of why we love the game. Once, several hundred years ago, he played the game with some measure of skill, well enough to be a small college second baseman. Granted, spending your adult life telling people that, "I was half of a double-play combination in college with Doug Rader," isn't going to get you on a Hall of Fame ballot, but it does indicate a feel for the game that goes beyond Little League and the bleacher seats in Chicago, or, in Kindred's case, St. Louis.

Kindred has an understanding of what it is like to try to play the game well; what it is like to be on the field with players who are far better than you (his double-play partner, among others) and what it means to work at the game because you want desperately to play it well.

Beyond that, Kindred has a feel for words that HAS put him on numerous writing Hall of Fame ballots. With no offense intended to Rader, where Kindred has gone as a writer goes well beyond the level Rader reached in baseball. Kindred isn't just a student of the game, he is a student of people. He does one thing better than almost anyone I have met in journalism (myself included): he LISTENS. Which is why he is such a wonderful story-teller. He hears other people's stories and then finds the words to tell those stories with an eloquence that makes readers laugh and cry and, most important, keep reading.

Kindred is one of the few people who can write about his relationship with a baseball glove and make the effort not only worthwhile, but gratifying. He has known many of the game's great players and managers well and his writing reflects that, without falling into the name-dropping parlance so many of our colleagues today are guilty of. You will never read the following from Kindred: "The other night while I was having dinner with Mark McGwire ..." Chances are though, if you read Kindred on Mark McGwire you will learn more about McGwire than you will from any 10 people who will claim to have had dinner with him.

In conclusion, there are only two reasons to read this book:

If you love baseball.

If you love great writing.

Those are the two reasons I always read Kindred on baseball. Even when he's writing about that 50-year-old glove.

CHAPTER 4

Prologue

Mom

One day when the world was young, Mom came home with a typewriter for me. It was a clunky amalgamation of iron pieces that weighed a pound or two less than Dad's '48 Ford pickup. At our kitchen table, I rolled a piece of paper into the machine. Then, as I would do for the rest of the 20th century and into the 21st, I sat before the typewriter not knowing what to write.

I wanted the words to be memorable, my first typed words. Finally, I began pecking at the keyboard. Here's what came out ...

S-t-a-n-l-e-y F-r-a-n-k M-u-s-i-a-l.

All these years later, my mother, Marie, still works at that kitchen table in the house my father built. It's on First Street in the small central Illinois town of Atlanta. First Street runs alongside a raised railroad bed. On the other side of the railroad tracks are tar-patched remnants of U.S. Route 66. In the famous highway's glory days, we'd drive three hours north and be at Wrigley Field. Three hours south, Sportsman's Park and Stan Musial. Like living in the middle of heaven.

I was a baseball kid. I'm still a baseball kid, as I hope this collection of Sporting News columns shows. From our house in Atlanta, it's six blocks to the town's ball diamond. I walk there now, out to shortstop, to remind myself how good it felt to be in a place where being in that place was all mattered.

A small world, the ball diamond, and I love it.

Before organization made children into regimented and uniformed athletes, we were blue-jeaned kids who knew that if we wandered to the ball diamond we'd find someone there. We came with broken bats held together by black friction tape. (Bats beyond repair were used on the railroad bed where you tossed up white stones and whacked them until the bat's barrel became a mush of splinters.) We brought baseballs, some coming apart at the seams, some made leaden by a night in the yard in the rain. Any ball hit out of the infield on the fly was declared a home run by urchins imagining themselves to be Stan The Man or Ernie Banks.

In the summer of 2001, as I rose from the kitchen table where Mom had given me that typing machine, she asked, "Where are you going?"

"To the ball diamond," I said, and I realized then that I use those words only in Atlanta.

There are hundreds of "baseball fields" and "ballparks" and dozens of mighty "baseball stadiums." But only one ball diamond. I have kept faith with that black-dirt infield and the four rows of wooden bleachers and the tin-roofed barn in left center and the cow-pasture wire fence at 272 feet down the left field line. Never mind that the barn is gone and the wire fence is gone. Never mind that the wooden bleachers have yielded to progress (if cold aluminum seats are progress). Never mind any change. If you allow yourself to be a kid, you can walk on that rich, black, magical, farm country dirt to shortstop and you can look into left field and there you can see the old barn. Yes, you can. There is in the magic dirt a crack in time and you can leap through it and you're a kid ...

... and Mom is driving three hours north on Route 66 to Aunt Rosie's house in Evergreen Park, a suburb of Chicago.

From Aunt Rosie's we rode a streetcar to Wrigley Field. Mom said of the trip, "You were 6 years old and you looked at all the big buildings. The conductor asked, 'Would you like to live in Chicago?' You said, 'No, people live all stacked on top of one another, and where would I ride my bike?'"

Another time, at Comiskey Park, Mom said Aunt Rosie had seats for us near the Yankee dugout. "Mickey Mantle struck out six or seven times in a doubleheader," Mom said. "So Aunt Rosie, who'd say anything, hollered, 'Mickey, what's wrong with you today?' Mickey took his bat and knocked over all the other bats. Aunt Rosie got a kick out of that."

Mom and Dad taught me the game, took me to games, watched me play games from grade school through college. "Down in Mississippi once," Mom said, "the kids in the bleachers were shouting, 'Yankee, go home.' I laughed and told them, 'But we just got here.' They got friendly after that."

They were always together, Mom and Dad. He coached my kids' teams; she kept score. They drove that old pickup past cornfields all over central Illinois to see their son get dirty at shortstop. Dad, a carpenter, built a trophy case for the high school; then, with a jigsaw, he made a wooden "A" with wings on it because we were the Atlanta Redwings. Mom painted the "A" in the school colors, red and white.

At our spot along Route 66 in the middle of heaven, you chose sides: Cardinals or Cubs. Mom said, "I needed to aggravate you," so she chose the Cubs against my Cardinals. In afternoons she listened to the Cubs by radio, the broadcaster Bert Wilson insisting, "I don't care who wins—as long as it's the Cubs." Nights belonged to the Cardinals and Harry Caray shouting into his mike, "It's way back, it might be … it could be … it IS," another home run for Stanley Frank Musial.

I have tried to grow up, I really have.

But then I walk through a mall.

And I see a sports store.

So I go in.

Not to buy anything, but to find the baseball gloves. Not to put a glove on my hand, but to smell the leather.

Aluminum bats, yikes. Melt them down, make them into safety pins. But baseball gloves are forever.

On the first page of his wonderful book, "Baseball," historian Robert Smith says he long justified obsession with baseball by praising the game's "essential simplicity and goodness and its offering its rewards without regard to station in life." But even as he sang the game's praises, he came to recognize the lyrics as self-delusion: "I know as well as you do that in order to fret over who wins a baseball game or to find Greek tragedy in the careers of its heroes, a man has to be two parts bereft of his good sense."

So Smith, being sensible, decided baseball is a "mere game" with "no relation to the basic verities of human faring." Worse, its most famous practitioners often were stuffed-shirt robber barons, "self-important and self-indulgent young fatheads, men on fire with cruel egotism, and swaggering roisterers whom no one can bear to live with once the fame and the money have been used up."

Well, there is that, and it's as true in the 21st century as when Smith wrote it in 1947. Intellectually true, that is. The heart is another matter. And the evidence of his own work is testimony that the "mere game" owns Robert Smith's heart: "Baseball" opens with those three paragraphs of dyspepsia and follows with 428 pages of delights.

A "mere game." And Everest is a hill. Red Smith saw such beauty inside the lines that he wrote, "Ninety feet between bases is the nearest to perfection that man has yet achieved." The great truth is, if we do baseball well and faithfully, the game's power reaches outside the lines, connecting every mom and dad and son and daughter.

Ever hit a thrown corn cob? Dad discovered that new form of batting practice, the corn cobs doing air tricks knuckleballs only dreamed of. Ever throw a strike inside twine? Dad built a wooden frame, defined the strike zone with twine, then caught pitches until dark. And in the week of his dying, when I was 22 and didn't know how to say what needed to be said, I spoke the language we shared. "I'll teach my son," I said, "everything you taught me about baseball."

And there came a soft night in May of 1998 when Mom and I went to a ball game, 51 years after our first one.

My sister, Sandra, drove our mother from Atlanta to St. Louis, not on Route 66, which exists today only in ghostly patches, but on I-55. From our 12th-floor hotel room, Mom looked down onto Busch Stadium. The hotel bellman told her, "Stand right here, Mark McGwire might hit one to you."

Mom had a different idea. She pointed at a spot close to the stadium and said to me, "On our way to the ballpark, let's go see Stanley."

There stands in front of Busch Stadium a heroic bronze statue of Stanley Frank Musial. He's in uniform, body coiled in that boy-peeking-around-a-corner stance, the barrel of the bat straight up. Mom's scouting report: "Looks like he's ready to hit a home run."

For two hours and maybe three—it could have been four or five for all we cared—Mom sat near enough the Cardinals' on-deck circle to say, "That Mark McGwire, his arms are bigger around than my waist used to be."

Came the seventh inning, she softly sang along, "Take me out to the ball game, buy me some peanuts and Cracker Jack …"

The next morning, we drove north to Atlanta. As we passed the ballpark, Mom saw the Musial statue again. She said, "Goodbye, Stanley."

CHAPTER 1

Child's Play

Child's play

May 24, 1993

On a Friday after school in a small Southern town, we're at the county ball fields.

Mothers and fathers bring the kids here. You can buy Cokes and hot dogs at a shed run by the Memorial United Methodist Church. Five ball fields are busy with a couple hundred boys and girls from 5 to 12 years old. Light towers lean in different directions. The infield dirt is red clay and the outfield grass is tall enough that you can't see everyone's feet.

It's getting on to sundown and the air is made golden by the dying light. On a Friday in one small town, grownup voices shout to the kids:

"Boys, you gotta know what you're going to do with it."

"You gotta call it, Stacy, you gotta call it."

"Attaway to charge that ball, big man, yessir!"

We're watching boys and girls 7 and 8 years old in a game that is a step above T-ball.

They swing at pitches thrown to their liking by their coaches. There is a five-run rule (once a team scores five runs in an inning, the other side gets to bat). When defenders throw the ball back to the pitcher, all baserunners must stop.

Everybody gets to play, and at game's end, everybody lines up to trade high-fives. Then they get a can of pop and maybe a brownie from the coaches.

"Hey, infield, touch any base."

"Quit trying to kill the ball."

"Hit the ball, David, and run fast."

Two real estate firms, a tree-cutting service and an insurance agent have signs on the outfield fence. There's an electric scoreboard in right field with so many burnt-out light bulbs that 9s come out looking like 3s.

We're sitting on wooden bleachers watching kids play ball when a boy named DeMarcus Miller hits a line drive to right center that rolls so far he turns it into a home run.

Miller celebrates by coming to the second row of the wooden bleachers behind third base. His mom and dad are all smiles and DeMarcus says to his mother, "A bite?"

So mom, in this small Southern town on a Friday after school, gives her ballplayer son a bite of her church-bought, mustard-and-onions hot dog.

"Lindsay, put that cap up where you can see the ball."

"You gotta swing level, not uppercut it."

"Let's hear some chatter. Chatter up, guys, gotta hear some chatter."

Chris Davison is a shortstop whose freckles dance on his nose as light leaps from his eyes. On this Friday after school, he hits two home runs. Another time he scores with a head-first slide into home plate. In the field, he makes plays that show he knows where the ball should go when it comes to him. He moves with a ballplayer's instincts. He is 8 years old.

There's a can of orange pop in his glove and he nibbles at a brownie while a grown-up asks him questions.

Why does he like baseball? "It's fun to play."

What does he like most? "Hitting the ball."

Besides that? With a smile: "It's nice to get away from home."

Where'd he learn that head-first slide? "David Justice."

Marva Davison, the ballplayer's mother, says he has played since he was old enough to hold a ball. His grandfather and grandmother hit 300 groundballs a day to him. Not long ago, she says, Chris made an unassisted triple play.

How'd he do that? "I caught the ball, tagged the runner going to second and ran to third before that runner could get back."

Just like that. Nothing to it. Eight years old and a triple-play maker.

"C'mon, Katy, that's way too low, hon."

"Taylor, a ball on the ground in front of you, you stop. In the air, stay. On the ground over there, come here."

"You outfielders, quit taking a bite out of that ball before you get it back in."

The games are done. Night shadows own the ball fields. The big boys 7 and 8 years old have gone home.

Now a little guy gets a chance. His name is Carson Carroll, he is 3 years old and he wears a batting helmet. His dad is lobbing him pitches and his mom is standing where a little guy's first base might be.

Carson, who swings from the heels, hits the ball hard, tosses down the bat and takes off running. He has been hitting, his dad says, since just before his second birthday.

"Hit one more and we're going home," dad says.

Carson thinks not.

"This many," he says, holding up his right hand -- all five fingers.

The boy hits the one more and then dad gives in, saying, "OK, one more and we're going."

"This many," Carson says again, again spreading out his little hand.

"They gotta lock up the ball field now," mom says. "We gotta go."

"Mommy," Carson says, "this many."

One more is all the boy got.

The one was a line drive past dad. And when the boy ran to first base, he must have wanted to go back and hit some more because we heard his mom say, there on the ball field in a small town, "Ballplayers don't cry."

Carson walks off the ball field with mom and dad. He carries his bat on his shoulder, just in case somebody gives in and pitches him one more.

Thanks, Mr. Bogar

OCTOBER 18, 1999

This father-and-son adventure begins when they take their baseball gloves to the ballpark. Gary is 39, once a sportswriter, now an author/teacher, always a baseball fan. Ross is 10. He's a Little Leaguer who plays for the Orioles, sometimes wears a Mark McGwire jersey and wants to be a big-leaguer.

They're in Atlanta at Turner Field for the Astros and Braves. Their mission: Get a baseball.

The boy carries his glove to every game. But neither the father nor the son has ever caught a ball in a big-league park. This day the father has a plan.

As they arrive, the father thinks, "Great," they've beaten the crowd. For a 4 o'clock start, they're at the ballpark by 2. They walk to the center field bleachers and stand two rows behind the wall, shaded toward right-center.

From there they can talk to Astros idling in the outfield. The father has a program with the players' names and numbers. If you're going to ask for favors, he figures, better to do it by calling names than shouting, "Hey, you, NUMBER 16."

So the father eventually sees Stan Javier, an Astros outfielder, and calls out, "HEY, STANNNN." Javier looks up. "Stan, you can make my 10-year-old son's dream come true if you'd give him a ball."

Javier nods and goes back to his throwing when he hears, "Stan, my son's almost the same age I was when I watched your dad in the 1968 World Series."

Bingo. From 70 feet away, Stan Javier, the son of Julian Javier, the Cardinals' second baseman of that time long ago, throws a strike to the father.

The father says, "STANNNN, you're the MANNNN."

Five minutes in center field after 39 years without a ball, the father now has a genuine major league baseball that he hands to his son. His bedazzled son. His son with eyes this big. Eyes that should they in years to come see all of the world's wonders will judge them against this greatest of all wonders, a baseball.

Now the father notices Jose Cruz. Once a good hitter and now an Astros coach, Cruz stands behind second base with a fungo bat, popping fly balls toward center field. So the father shouts, "JOSE, HIT ONE OUT HERE!"

Cruz hears the voice, half-waves, and here it comes. A baseball in the high, blue sky. Floating, floating. Toward the fence. Over the fence. Into the second row. "My God," the father says, and puts his glove in front of his face just in time to save his teeth. "JOSE, YOU'RE THE MAN."

Now the son has two baseballs, one for himself, one for his younger brother Winnie.

"We need one for Leigh," Ross says. She's his sister.

So he checks his program. He sees the catcher Randy Knorr. The father says, "Go ahead, Ross, ask him if you can have a ball."

"Mr. Knorr, can I please have a ball?"

Knorr tosses a ball.

The father thinks this is incredible, three balls in 30 minutes, and hears his son say, "What about Mommy?"

"What about her?"

"A ball for Mommy?"

Tim Bogar is an Astros infielder. At the moment, he's taking throws near the warning track as if the track is the sideline on a football field and he's a wide receiver trying to make a catch and keep both feet inbounds.

"Hey, Tim," the father says, "don't worry about it, this is SEC country. One foot in is enough. Welcome to the real South."

"Thank you," Bogar says. And a little-boy voice says, "Mr. Bogar, could I have that baseball when you're done with it?"

Bogar nods and indicates he'll throw him the ball.

"Dad," the boy says, "what if I drop it?"

He catches it. He catches the big-league ball thrown by a big-league player. "Thanks, Mr. Bogar."

The player smiles, turns away and then turns back. "Hey," Bogar says, and points to the starburst on his Astros jersey, "how about rooting for us today?"

Four balls in 45 minutes, and Ross is ready to go home and show off the baseballs to his buddy, Nate. But the father and son stay for the game, baseballs in their gloves, and that evening, as the boy puts on his pajamas for bed, he tells his father, "I want to write Tim Bogar a letter."

"Fine, after school tomorrow."

"No, now."

So Ross gets a lined sheet of fifth-grade theme paper and writes:

"Dear Tim Bogar,

"You may not remember me, but my name is Ross Pomerantz. You threw me a ball before Game 1 of the Division Series in Atlanta. I asked you to throw me the ball when you were done throwing with your teammates.

"It was the first time anyone has thrown me the ball at a major league game. You made my dream come true. Now you are my favorite player.

"I hope to meet you when you come back to Atlanta with the Astros. I was wondering if you would autograph my ball, but I'm afraid to send it because it might get lost in the mail.

"Could you send me an autographed picture? What advice would you give a 10-year-old like me wanting to play major league baseball?

"I will follow your box scores every game. I wish you good luck.

"From Ross."

The next morning, as the father woke the son for school, the boy reached under his pillow and brought out his baseball. That afternoon, his new favorite player autographed it.

Perspectives from right field

There's a reserved bleacher seat in heaven for anyone who loves ballfields on a summer night. Happy to say, then, that an old friend and my grandson both played ball the other night.

She's softball, he's baseball. She's antique, he's shiny new. They both play right field for their safety and the greater good of their teams. Let's hear first from the fortysomething friend ...

"Oh, my poor young body is hurting," she said the morning after a long night that began with her getting to the ballfield late. She had run errands because she didn't figure to be playing early. She even left her glove at home.

Her games usually are frolics designed for no purpose more serious than rendering everyone thirsty. But this night's opponent turned out to be the seriously serious city champion.

"As I walked up to the field, I knew we were in trouble," she said, "because I heard our coach and pregnant second baseman having not-nice words, like him saying, 'It looks like amateur night out there already.'" She hadn't stayed at second to take a relay from left on a ball over the fielder's head.

"I'm hearing this and I'm thinking, 'We don't need this seriousness of

29

making the right play.' Hey, for 17 years the main reason we've been playing together is to have a beer after. What's this seriousness thing?

"Suddenly the coach tells me, 'Warm up.' Whoa. I borrow a friend's glove, and the thing is all hot and sweaty. Putting my hand in it is like putting my feet into my son's tennis shoes after he has been playing outside all day. I go, 'Yukkkk.'

"Two minutes later I'm out in right center. Next thing I know, they're killing the ball my way."

Six hundred miles away, my grandson also was sent into right field exile. There, the little guy slouched and tugged his cap bill down and dug at dandelions with his cleats. Some days are bad days, even for a kid.

He has become afraid of pitches. Every pitch by a 12-year-old causes him to lean away from the plate. In the batting cage before the full practice started, he swung at two dozen pitches and hit none. In the evening's practice game, another two dozen pitches, he never swung. Finally he ducked out of the way of a pitch—except that by ducking, he stuck his head right where the ball was.

The scary hollow clunk against the batting helmet ended his at-bat. He went to sit in the dugout, no one else there. Didn't put on his favorite red Beech-Nut cap. Some tears. Drew his knees up to his chin. After a while, a coach said, "You're OK. Go to right."

There, the boy stood alone, as if cast out, kicking at weeds.

My aging friend, on the other hand, had too much to do in right field. "The first four balls came right at me. The first one was bobbled by the second baseman and I backed her up, fortunately, because I didn't want the coach coming down on me. That's all I was thinking: 'Just let me do good and get me off this field fast.'

"The next ball, I would have caught if I were really, really hustling. But I got it on the first bounce. The third one, I got lucky and caught it just before it went over my head. The fourth one was a hard-hit groundball that somehow stuck in my icky glove, and I threw it to third.

"Pretty good for an old girl, but ooooh, I was out of breath, out of energy and hurtin' for certain."

My grandson, on the ride home from the ballfield, had a complaint. "The coach makes me stand real, real close to the plate, like one inch, and when pitches come inside and I jump back, he calls them strikes."

What you might do, I said, is move back from the plate a little, then step toward the pitcher to hit the ball.

"But every time I back up, the coach makes me get closer."

"He's just trying to help you. Maybe tomorrow we should go to practice early and I'll throw you lots of pitches to hit. Want to?"

Of the many things that scare kids, most of them unsuspected by adults, few scare them more certainly than a baseball that they think might hit them in the face. This day a pitch clunked off my grandson's hat, and later a bad-hop grounder banged against his throat. What would the boy say to an old man who now proposed to throw balls at him?

"Sure," he said. "That sounds fun."

Wow.

My creaky, antique friend, wrung out by her inning's work, then came to bat. "I got lucky, got a single. On a grounder, I slowly made it to second. Our next hitter, unfortunately for me, hit one that was kicked around and made me think about trying to score from second. Oh, no.

"Could I go all the way? Should I go all that way? I was soooooo tired, I didn't even hear what the coach was telling me to do. I stopped at third and later found out that's what he wanted me to do. Thank heaven."

She scored her team's last run in a 17-4 defeat. "The good news is, our coach redeemed himself after all the complaining. He brought out a cooler of Bud Light. Sprawled out on the ground, too tired to get up, I thought, 'This is what it's all about.'"

Two beers later, my friend heard her 7-year-old son's voice. He interrupted her sweet reverie to deliver a message, timidly.

"Mommy," said he, "I locked the keys in the car."

If we care enough

Steve Bandura did marketing for a bank until he realized he cared more about kids than money. Doesn't happen often, such an epiphany. Nor does it happen often to a young white guy in South Philly, a hard city's hardest place. But one day his boss asked Bandura to look at a recreation center nearby with the idea the bank might help out.

So Bandura, once an athlete himself, walked down the street to the Marian Anderson Recreation Center. What he found there disappointed him. No, wait. Disappointment is not near strong enough. "I was appalled," he says. "There was no baseball, no football, no basketball. There was nothing down here while in Northeast Philly there's a Boys' Club on every corner."

Well, what's a guy to do?

Change the world?

OK.

Bandura quit his job and went on unemployment so he could work at the rec center.

In the first year of baseball there, he had 180 kids playing. In 1993 he started the Jackie Robinson Baseball League. He returned to school to get a master's in education, the better to cut his bank salary in half by becoming first a teacher and then a recreation leader. Now his baseball team of 12-year-olds, the Anderson Monarchs, is the very model of what can be done if we care enough.

They know their roots. They do homework on Negro league history. Last summer they barnstormed across America in a 1947 model bus, driving 3,300 miles in 13 days. Next spring Bandura hopes to make a two-week trip to Africa called "Rounding Third and Heading for Home."

"Everybody kept saying baseball wasn't 'their' game," Bandura says in graceful allusion to the current notion that blacks are born to basketball. "The only way I could see that baseball wasn't 'their' game was that they'd never been given the opportunity when they needed it—at an early age, at 5, 6, 7."

Yes, kids play baseball today. Even black kids. In Atlanta they play. In Washington they play. In Philadelphia they play out of a recreation center named for a black opera singer. They play under the name of the most famous Negro league team ever, the Monarchs.

In addition to games in their Jackie Robinson league, the Monarchs travel to that other world of Northeast Philly to compete in the Devlin League, where their faces are the only black faces, where children can learn about differences for themselves.

"You know what's best about those boys?" says Gene Benson, once a Negro league star in Philadelphia, a piece of living history befriended by Steve Bandura on behalf of his Monarchs. "The boys they play against, they're almost all white. Teaches everybody something that way."

Gene Benson always thought we all ought to get along together. A little big man at 5-8, 185 pounds—think Kirby Puckett in the 1930s—he'd been a frozen-rope .300 hitter and basket-catching center fielder for the Philadelphia Stars.

"Lefthanded all the way," Benson says, "but I could hit lefthanders. Never knew why except I didn't know I wasn't supposed to be able to. And Satchel Paige, I hit him like I owned him. Never could figure that out, either, until Satch told me, 'Ben, you hit me because you don't try to hit me. You just put the bat out there and it goes.' Satch had it right, I imagine."

Benson is 84 and can tell you what he said to the young firebrand Jackie Robinson 53 winters ago.

They were roommates during the 1945-46 winter season in Venezuela. Though only five years older than Robinson, Benson had been a professional ballplayer 15 years. Robinson had signed with the Dodgers in 1945.

"Felton Snow, our manager, said, 'Ben, everybody likes you, you've got the right temperament to teach Robinson something.' Robinson was a very hard fellow to get along with in this respect: He had a temper and he'd fight at the drop of a hat.

"So we weren't such great friends at first. One night in the room, he got loud with me and I told him, 'Jackie, I'm trying to help you, temper-wise. You can't just fight every time you get mad. But if you want to fight me, you should know I'm a better boxer than my stepfather and he fought the champion Tiger Flowers to a draw.

" 'I'm telling you this because you're getting mad, and I want you to know you're going to get hurt as much as, and possibly more than, you're going to hurt me. I have no fear of you, Jackie. I'm here only to help you make the major leagues.'

"That took his nerve away. He calmed down and from then on we became the best of friends. Two or three days before he died, I went to see him and he looked awful. Snow white hair. He said, 'Ben, I'd have never made it if it weren't for you.' "

Because his heart is giving him trouble, Gene Benson doesn't get around much any more. Still, he came to the Anderson rec center's ballpark at 18th and Fitzwater streets the other day. The Monarchs asked him to throw out the first ball for their Little League season. Then they retired two uniform numbers. Jackie Robinson's 42 and Gene Benson's 16.

A good man, that Charlie Brown

JANUARY 10, 2000

By scores such as 63-0, 40-0, 41-0, 48-0, 200!!!-0, 123-0, 184-0, 57-0, 293!!!-0 and another 123-0, Charlie Brown's sandlot baseball team one year lost all 40 of its games to unseen opponents whose line drives up the middle kept Charlie in a constant state of undress. His ERA was 80.00. His team once made 12 errors in an inning, though not the same inning when he walked 35 straight hitters. His center fielder, Lucy Van Pelt, once refused to catch a fly ball because her glove already was full of tapioca pudding.

What a know-it-all grouch, Lucy. She marched to the mound every inning or so to counsel poor Charlie (and to draw within kissing distance of Schroeder, the concert pianist/catcher who preferred Beethoven).

One day, Lucy told Charlie that good pitchers had nicknames: "You should be Catfish, or Babe, or Doc, or something." Back in center field, she shouted, "Throw it in there, Cementhead!"

Lucy's brother, Linus, wasn't much help, either. "I got it," he shouted on a popup. "At least I think I've got it! Who knows? Actually, who cares? When you've lost at love, you've lost at everything. Nothing matters! Who's got it? That's a good question! I've got it! You've got it! Nobody's got it! We all lose in the end!"

As the ball bonked down, Charlie Brown, his cap twisted sideways, stood on the mound muttering, "I can't stand it! I just can't stand it!"

Nor can we stand the recent revoltin' developments. Charlie Brown's creator, the cartoonist Charles Schulz, has done a Jordan/Elway/Gretzky thing. At the top of his game, Schulz has retired. Y2K didn't get us, but Charlie Brown did, for this truly is the End of the World as We Have Come to Love It.

No more Charlie Brown? Think what that means. No more Charlie trying and trying and trying to kick a football or win a Stanley Cup. This is terrible. Because if you love sports for what sports can be, you had to love good ol' Charlie Brown. In 1993, after 43 years of trying, Charlie cartwheeled his way home shouting, "I hit a home run in the ninth inning and we won! I was the hero!" His sister, Sally, looked at him and said, "You?!"

He'd never quit trying, and he knew that trying was all that mattered, as on the occasion of that 184-0 squeaker when he asked, "How can we lose when we're so sincere?"

The real world sneaked into Charlie Brown's games. There was a gambling scandal (Rerun Van Pelt, Lucy's baby brother, bet a nickel on a game). There was talk of moving the franchise (but who would have such a team?). And Snoopy, the power-hitting beagle at shortstop, once came to the mound with his supper dish clamped between his teeth, causing Charlie to mumble, "I hate these salary disputes."

But if Charlie's team lost games, that never made Charlie a loser. No adversity could discourage a warrior whose hero and role model was Joe Shlabotnik, the .004 hitter who played in the Green Grass League and was famous for making a spectacular catch of a routine fly ball. "After all," Charlie said, "it's not the winning that counts. ... The fun is in the playing!"

Well, most times. My favorite Peanuts strip begins with Linus in front of a TV set, his arms raised, shouting, "FANTASTIC!" He runs outside to Charlie, who's holding a football, and he says, "Charlie Brown, I just saw the most unbelievable football game ever played ... What a comeback! The home team was behind 6-0 with only 3 seconds to play. ... They had the ball on their own 1-yard line. ... "

Charlie is listening.

"The quarterback took the ball (Linus goes on), faded back behind his own goal posts and threw a perfect pass to the left end, who whirled away from four guys and ran all the way for a touchdown! The fans went wild! You should have seen them!"

Charlie stands there, his football at his side.

Linus goes on. "People were jumping up and down, and when they kicked the extra point, thousands of people ran onto the field laughing and screaming! The fans and the players were so happy they were rolling on the ground and hugging each other and everything!"

Linus clasps his hands together in warm contentment and says, "It was fantastic!"

At which point, Charlie Brown looks blank.

Finally he turns to Linus and says, "How did the other team feel?"

Anyone who paid attention to Charlie Brown's gang for even a little while surely came away smiling at the great good sense. I cut out, pasted down and enlarged a strip that begins with Snoopy at a typewriter atop his doghouse. The first panel shows Snoopy typing one word, "It ... "

Then comes a panel showing the world-famous writer in deep thought. Finally, he types "was ..." followed by more panels in which Snoopy furrows his delicate brow before finishing the first sentence of his novel

" ... a dark and stormy night."

Snoopy then looks at us and says, "Good writing is hard work."

At that work, I've long followed the advice of Lucy Van Pelt. On a shelf in my office, I have propped up a cardboard figure of the know-it-all grouchy center fielder. A word balloon carries her philosophy of life: "If you can't be right, be wrong at the top of your voice!"

My, my, the trouble that girl's gotten me into. But today, for once, I'll be right, and I'll say it softly. We'll miss you, Charlie Brown.

CHAPTER 2

Glove Letters

Glove

APRIL 6, 1992

Any excuse to write about baseball gloves is a good excuse. Unbeknownst to them, several readers have given me a great excuse to wax rhapsodic about an old friend, the Wilson A2000.

Those readers have written to the Voice of the Fan suggesting that Ye Editor set fire to my hair. Many of these letters used language normally reserved for toe-stubbings in dark bedrooms. "Short Anglo-Saxon words," as Churchill described his favorite expletives, "beginning with the earlier letters of the alphabet."

Nineteen pen pals weighed in from 15 states, the mail running 17-2 against my Indian column of two weeks ago. The majority opinion was expressed by Ralph May of Stuart, Fla., who believes I wore my baseball cap two sizes too small too long. Only this, he said, could explain "the hare-brained admonishments that changes should be made to placate a relative few misguided nabobs, none of whom are sports fans."

Mr. May suggested that if sports teams yield to Indian demands that offensive nicknames be changed, where would it end? Would the Greenpeace people want to sink the Whalers, Oilers and Lakers? Would the bird-watching folks object to Cardinals, Blue Jays, Seahawks? Would animal rights advo-

41

cates object to ... and so on. The mailman trudging toward 1212 N. Lindbergh Boulevard in St. Louis must have felt the heat radiating from these letters. "Nonsense," cried a man from Ohio. "Racist," Utah said. Idaho demanded, "Get real." Missouri felt "literally sick to my stomach." "Ludicrous and inane," said North Carolina while California nearly had reached "the point of no return."

Indiana weighed in with the warning that if we keep going, we'll wind up with no nicknames at all and find ourselves cheering "for the St. Louis 9's or the Chicago 12's."

A disinterested observer might think that Kindred, the fool, had demanded a worldwide, superpower-ratified, U.N.-inspected, death-to-offenders ban on Indian nicknames. The fact is, my manner was milquetoasty. I resolved, in my little part of the world, in this space, to suggest that some words are offensive to human dignity.

Anyway, dear readers, while your pens, pencils, and computers are in a corresponding mode, let's change to a kinder, gentler subject. Write me another letter but make it about your favorite baseball glove. Tell me a story in which the glove is the star.

Opening Day is near, and I want to hear about baseball gloves, old and new, yours and your father's and your grandfather's. Tell me about the plays you made. Tell me who took you to the sporting goods store. Tell me what the glove means to you. Is it, as Roger Kahn once wrote, the first object a boy really cares for in the sense that he not only begged for it as a gift but then tends to its needs?

I, for one, slept with my Rip Repulski model.

Within arm's reach of this infernal typing machine that keeps me on double-secret probation with the Voice and Ye Editor, I have the best baseball glove ever made, the Wilson A2000. It's the last glove I ever bought, $35 if memory serves, which in those days, 1962, was a week's pay.

The A2000 is golden in the light through the window and is distinguished by a thin cover of darkness, which is the residue of infield dirt gathered all over central Illinois. Every now and then the typist stops at his hard labor and slides a hand inside the glove and slaps a fist against the leather. It reminds him of a dear, departed time when he could go to his right and throw out a fast runner from the hole. A very dear, very departed time.

The whole truth here, painful even now: Sliding his hand into the A2000, the typist yet can feel a baseball thudding against the heel of the glove and falling into fair territory. It had been a high pop-up, into the sun, with two men out, a 3-and-2 count, bases loaded, everybody moving on the pitch. They all scored. O, diary.

Tell me about your baseball gloves. I've had it with .226 infielders getting 10 times Babe Ruth's money. Charles Barkley, about when he had earned forgiveness for his last stupidity, blinks out again with trashtalk about how proud he is to be a " '90s nigger." There's Magic's virus and the Mets' alleged rape. There's handcuffed Mike Tyson smirking into the TV cameras. There's Michael Jordan admitting he's a high-stakes gambler while declaring, "I'm no Pete Rose."

This week I'd rather talk baseball gloves.

Babe Ruth's first glove in reform school was a catcher's mitt that he wore backward on his right hand. When Ty Cobb left Royston, Ga., going off to play pro ball, he carried three bats and his Spalding fielder's glove. Joe Morgan played forever with a glove barely larger than his hand because Nellie Fox told him a second baseman couldn't afford to get the ball lost in there.

As Roger Kahn did the legwork for his classic book, "The Boys of Summer," he had the old Dodgers heroes autograph his A2000.

One of the first great fielders using the newfangled gloves in the 1870s was Bob Ferguson, whose nickname was "Death to Flying Things."

Roger Hornsby folded his glove and stuck it in his rear pocket while hitting.

Pete Rose said that when he stood on first base after breaking Cobb's record, he felt naked without a bat or glove, the totems that marked his life's progress.

Because the Cincinnati outfielder Bobby Tolan didn't catch everything hit his way in the early 1970s, a merciless teammate slid a large glass ashtray across the clubhouse floor and said, "Tolan, here's your glove."

Ozzie Smith, the greatest glove man ever, began without one. He used a brown paper bag.

At shortstop for the Cardinals, Smith once leaped over a diving left fielder to catch a fly ball for what he called his second-best play ever. The best play came on a ground ball in 1978 when Jeff Burroughs hit a ball up the middle.

Smith said, "I took four or five steps in that direction. That tells me I have to dive." As he left his feet, flying toward right field, Smith saw the Burroughs ground ball take a bad hop. It bounced to the left, headed behind him.

"My glove is gone now," Smith said, meaning it was useless in this circumstance. But he had another hand. So Smith threw his bare hand up and back, toward the sport where the bad-hop grounder surely would bounce over him and into left field. "All I can do now is hope the ball sticks in my hand ..." Here Smith smiled. "... which it did."

Amos Rusie's catcher, Dick Buckley, padded his mitt with a sheet of lead. Rodgers and Hammerstein, writing "South Pacific," portrayed Bloody Mary with "skin as tender as DiMaggio's glove." Dick Stuart was so much "Dr. Strangeglove" that the mayor of Pittsburgh wanted first base declared a disaster area. The Brooklyn outfielder Babe Herman, sensitive to accusations of incompetence, declared he would quit if a fly ball ever hit him in the head. Someone said, "How about the shoulder?" To which Babe said, "On the shoulder don't count."

Now they're making gloves, like sneakers, which you can pump up with air to improve the fit. The Japanese have experimented with a catcher's mitt that emits an electronic beam that turns on a light in the pitcher's glove as signal for the next pitch. Which reminds me. The Wilson A2000, once made in the United States, is now made in Japan. Sigh.

Glove Letters

The novelist Annie Dillard once made the mistake of looking out a window of the Hollins College library. She saw a kids' softball game. So she gave up the day's work. "Since I happened to have my fielder's glove with me in my study," she wrote, "I thought it would be the generous thing to join the game."

In 1989, Tim Flannery quit baseball, or it quit him, and the old San Diego Padres utilityman wanted nothing more to do with it. But last year his son started T-ball. Father Flannery came back, using the glove he had borrowed (stolen) from Garry Templeton a decade earlier. Flannery, a TV reporter, now carries the glove in his truck, just in case.

When the kid Bobby Cox thought his glove had been stolen in the Alabama-Florida League 25 years ago, he put his fist through a bus window.

When Bobby Cox, a Yankees coach, became manager of the Atlanta Braves in 1978, he showed up for spring training to find his old, tattered glove on his desk with a note of good luck from Yankees clubhouse man Pete Sheehy.

Glove stories—everyone has one. Kathy Blumenstock of Charlotte, N.C., had a childhood friend named Donna who took her glove to Yankee

45

Stadium on her first date and caught a foul ball. Blumenstock writes, "I doubt she ever saw the boy again. But I'm sure she kept the glove."

I asked our readers to write glove letters and they did, 32 letters (and two poems) from 18 states, one from a boy 9 years old and one from a grandmother, letters from Maine and Montana, Idaho and Hawaii. Thank you all. Here's a sampling ...

Bill McGlathery of Jackson, Miss., who paid $40 in 1962 for a Rawlings Stan Musial TG, Trap-Eze Model: "The glove will be placed in my coffin when the time comes."

Bo Kirk of St. Clair Shores, Mich., saw a big league pitcher drive up to his Uncle Ed's in 1958. "Out jumped Ned Garver with a brown grocery bag. He tossed me the bag and said, 'Try it on and don't forget to get in front of the ball when fielding grounders.' You can imagine a 10-year-old looking inside the bag and finding a brand new Wilson Nellie Fox-autographed model infielder's glove."

Jesse Seegmiller of Freedom, Me., paid $15 in 1965 for a Rawlings Ken Boyer MVP Model. "Whenever I went on an air or bus trip that required my glove to accompany me—I can't think of any that didn't—I carried the glove with me in case my luggage was lost. Traveling by car, I kept the glove inside rather than in the trunk—in case the car caught on fire."

As a boy, Ray Stinger of Winchester, Va., couldn't afford $50 gloves at the Honus Wagner store in downtown Pittsburgh. His grandmother got him a used glove from the Salvation Army. "I kept oiling it, re-stringing it and trusting it as my best friend. It never failed me, never fell apart, never caused an error. I have never felt closer to any object than to that glove. During Army basic training, when I got homesick, I'd flip a ball into the air and catch it a couple times and everything seemed OK."

Steven Rice of Boise, Idaho: "In 1959 my dad would miss my Little League all-star game because he was leaving Hannibal, Mo., for California to find a job before sending for the family. I knew I'd have to petition long and hard for the new glove I wanted before he left—and I did.

"The day before his departure, he took me with him to the bank while he withdrew traveling money. As we walked side by side, I stared straight ahead and concentrated on giving him my best reasons for that new glove. After some time and no response from him, I turned to find myself walking and talking alone.

"I looked back and found him leaning against a storefront with a sign overhead reading 'Sporting Goods.' He yelled, 'So, do you want that new glove or not?' I ran to him grinning ear to ear with a heart beating like a drum. I slept with my new glove that night. I can still smell the leather.

"Dad left the following morning. As I hugged him goodbye, my left hand was engulfed by my new glove. That afternoon he died in a car accident. I used that glove up to my high school years but, sadly, I lost it at a family reunion. That glove was more than just a glove. It was my last and only tangible link to my dad. To this day, when I think of my dad, I think of that glove and I think of my dad when I put on any glove."

Jean Anderson of Bloomington, Ill., "a baseball lover and grandmother of four," wrote about her glove, a Little Yankee. "It's a leather beauty that helped me field my position in our backyard games—center field—in front of the septic outlet. The Little Yankee also helped me receive pitches from my dad who had been a fastballer for Moline in the old Three-I League. I can still feel the sting!" Mrs. Anderson sent along a picture of the Little Yankee with an arrow drawn toward a nipped-out irregularity along the glove's thumb. She explained, "The arrow points to the tragedy that happened when our beagle Bingo and I reached for a ball at the same instant."

I wish I had room for every letter. Mark Stewart of Pottersville, Mich., says his glove is alive and does heroic acts of its own accord. Keeler Crawford of Hayden Lake, Idaho, is a softball catcher who has missed one season the last 20 years (to give birth to her son) and says her Rawlings Reggie Jackson XFG-12 has a certain "feel, smell and companionship aura."

Robyn Quinn of Bridgeton, N.J., and her father broke in a Wilson A2000 XLO this way: "We oiled it, played catch, wrapped a couple balls in it overnight, slept with it under the mattress, ran over it with the car and repeated the steps. When I look at my glove, I don't see a worn piece of leather with dirt stains and tire stitching. I see many fond memories of my life and the game I adore."

Box score

MAY 28, 2001

On Saturday, May 18, 1912, an 18-year-old Philadelphian named William Charles Leinhauser played center field for the Tigers against the world champion A's. The young man's only major league performance gained him two forms of immortality. First, he stood in for Ty Cobb. Second, Arthur (Bugs) Baer did a piece of fiction mentioning the game's box score. "The fellow who got the toughest break was the semipro picked to play Ty Cobb's spot," Baer wrote. "His monicker was too wide for the printers and it came out in the Sunday papers this way, 'L'n'h's'r.' Today nobody knows whether his name was Loopenhouser or Lagenhassinger and I bet his wife still calls him a liar when he says he once played on the Detroits."

That's because Baer believed a baseball box score to be God's honest truth.

Was then, still is.

The Tigers-A's box score of that May 18 game tells us about a dozen scrubs who worked in Detroit uniforms after Cobb was suspended for attacking a fan. We learn the first baseman was 41 years old, the catcher 46, the pitcher a seminary student, the game a 24-2 farce.

Eighty-nine years later, on May 18, 2001, box scores have evolved so brilliantly as truth-tellers that USA Today's little masterpieces rise to Hemingway's standard of good writing; they give us drama even as they tell "how the weather was." Check the last agate lines of the box from a Diamondbacks-Reds game: "Weather: 83 degrees, cloudy. Wind: 5 mph, left to right." (Hmmm, and that day the lefthanded hitting Luis Gonzalez hammered home runs No. 19 and 20.)

So let us pause to praise baseball's box scores. They are literary miniatures. They deliver biography, adventure, history. They are written in a language of their own, a code of sorts that, once mastered, certifies the reader as a Great American.

But now comes word that the code—with its abbreviations, acronyms, symbols and numbers—has caused harrumphing among academics.

Writing in a recent Editor & Publisher magazine, journalism professors Charlie Tuggle and Don Sneed contend that box scores are so arcane as to be opaque. They quote Sports Illustrated writer Steve Lopez arguing that the "box score is nearly as detailed as a Melville novel."

The professors say the box score problem is most serious for readers whose native language is not English. "Chinese immigrants, whom the New York Daily News tries to attract as readers," Tuggle and Sneed write, "call baseball box scores the most mystifying thing about American culture."

Whoa. American culture has produced Tammy Faye Bakker, Richard Simmons and lizards shilling for beer. We're to believe that baseball box scores are the devil's work? But the professors sail past any such quibble to suggest that box scores also lose people who "shy away from numbers of any kind."

Whoa, again. A person who shies away from numbers is a person three months behind in mortgage payments; that person is not likely to be in step with life let alone the enriching subtleties of wind direction during Luis Gonzalez ab's. Sorry, but that person can go fish. Numbers do matter, as authors John Thorn and Pete Palmer affirm in The Hidden Game of Baseball.

They say "statistics elevated baseball from other boys' field games of the 1840s and '50s to make it somehow 'serious,' like business or the stock market." By 1863, New York newspaper reporter Henry Chadwick had transmuted cricket statistical forms into the recognizable precursor of today's baseball box scores.

And all right-thinking people are grateful, including Jacques Barzun, the

French-born historian famous in ballparks for having written, "Whoever wants to know the heart and mind of America had better learn baseball …" He also wrote, "And the next day in the paper: learned comment, statistical summaries, and the verbal imagery of meta-euphoric experts." All this Barzun called "so much joy."

At the same time, Barzun conceded that the language of baseball "comes easy only after philosophy has taught you to judge practice." The professors Tuggle and Sneed are on that scent as well. They don't want box scores taken out of newspapers; they just want the code explained.

For instance, in one newspaper's box score, there appears the abbreviation "RMU." The question was put to a newspaper reporter who has written baseball for 25 years: "What's 'RMU'?"

"Umm," he said. " 'Runner …'?"

Yes. Go on.

"Ummmm. 'Runner.' Ummm. 'RMU'?"

Yes.

"I don't know."

Because a runner moved up is a big deal in baseball dugouts, RMUs now are reported in some box scores, along with other seamhead esoterica such as grounded into double plays (GIDP), runners left in scoring position (RLISP) and inherited runners scoring (IRS). USA Today's boxes reveal even the nature of errors ("throw," "bobble") and which umpire threw which man out of the game (though not yet revealing the nature of the miscreant's language).

"Maybe only 5,000 of our 250,000 subscribers read the box scores," says Van McKenzie, who is in charge of the Orlando Sentinel sports section. "But those 5,000 readers care passionately. If we took box scores out of the paper, there'd be an incredible backlash. And I'd be looking for a job."

The writer Thom Ross once put the form to passionate storytelling use in his "Box Score for the Little Bighorn, June 25, 1876." The familiar codes and numbers tell us the Native Americans left the 7th Cavalry for dead, 16-1. Sitting Bull and Crazy Horse combined on a six-hitter, walking one man, striking out 12. Losing pitcher G. Custer was touched for 19 hits, nine for extra bases.

Bless this hide

FEBRUARY 26, 2001

A baseball. Coming apart at the seams. We wrapped its wounds with black friction tape. Like the old ballplayers, we used one ball all day. Never white. Leathery brown, smudged with black farmland dirt. We knocked it all over the yard until the tape no longer held and the ball's cover flapped like a dog's ear. "But never mind," Roger Angell wrote, "any baseball is beautiful."

Official Baseball Rules, Code 1.09: "The ball shall be a sphere formed by yarn wound around a small core of cork, rubber or similar material, covered with two stripes of white horsehide or cowhide, tightly stitched together. It shall weigh not less than 5 nor more than $5\frac{1}{4}$ ounces avoirdupois and measure not less than 9 nor more than $9\frac{1}{4}$ inches in circumference."

A baseball. "Drop it in my hand," Sparky Anderson told pitchers being hooked, "like it was an egg."

"That glossy little planet," poet Jonathan Holden called it.

We called it a hardball.

Look around the house. You'll find a baseball. You'll pick it up, it's irresistible. You then should go play catch, an act of connection so simple and so lasting that if Congress had Yogi Berra's wisdom it would enact a law declaring: "On sunny days in February when pitchers and catchers have reported, you will go outdoors with a loved one and play catch until the ol' soup bone goes limp."

The Yale University professor of physics Robert K. Adair further defined a baseball's ingredients: "The cork nucleus, enclosed in rubber, is wound with 121 yards of blue-gray wool yarn, 45 yards of white wool yarn, and 150 yards of fine cotton yarn. Core and winding are enclosed by rubber cement and a two-piece cowhide cover hand-stitched together with just 216 raised red cotton stitches."

The stitchings are done with two threads, each 44 inches long.

About a baseball. The Atlanta baseball writer Patty Rasmussen: "When I was first falling in love with baseball, in 1988 in the Hall of Fame at Cooperstown, I went to the wall that held all the no-hitter balls. All these baseballs, none of them yielding a hit. I was struck by the number of them— and then I thought about how many other baseballs had been put in play. Hit over walls, into the stands, grabbed for by fans. Cherished by children, who fell asleep still hanging onto them."

Look around the house. Five steps away, a baseball. In ink, a boy's square-lettered printing: "No-hitter." With a place, a date, walks, strikeouts, the name of the teammate who drove in the game's only run. And another baseball, smudged with red clay, stamped with the logo of the Colorado Silver Bullets, a women's baseball team with a pitcher named Ann Williams, who had played only softball, and when she first picked up a baseball, she asked manager Phil Niekro, "Phil, what's the best way to hold this?"

In a Hall of Fame baseball life, Niekro had been asked a lot of questions. But never that one. He finally said, "Whatever's comfortable," and Ann Williams discovered she didn't need to wrap three fingers around the ball, as she had done with a softball. A baseball, this glossy little planet, fit under her index and middle finger as if designed to go there, one of the game's little miracles of geometry.

Official Baseball Rules, General Instructions to Umpires: "Keep your eye everlastingly on the ball while it is in play."

Mark Fidrych talked to the ball. One summer, one happy summer for the Tigers, he backed off the mound between certain pitches and we could see him holding the ball and talking to it, encouraging it: "Come on, ball. Stay low, stay low. Hit the corner."

Bill Lee considered trust the most important factor in a pitcher-ball relationship. In his autobiography, the Red Sox eccentric wrote, "You are the ball and the ball is you. It can do you no harm. A common bond forms between you and this white sphere, a bond based on mutual trust. The ball promises not to fly over too many walls after you have politely served it up to enemy hitters, and you assure it that you will not allow those same batters to treat the ball in a harsh or violent manner."

The ball, not a clock, controls a baseball game. Author Gilbert Sorrentino: "The ball is pitched: something happens. The ball is hit: something happens. ... The ball must be dealt with scrupulously: it must be played, not interfered with, nor blocked, nor intercepted, nor stolen, nor recovered, nor rebounded. The offensive or defensive player who addresses his skills to the ball in motion may not be tampered with by a player of the opposing team. It is this inevitable quality of the interaction of player and ball that may give the game its strange and calm magic."

The magic reaches us far from great stadiums. Patty Rasmussen again: "A couple of years after my visit to Cooperstown, on a cold March day, I was taking a walk. It was a bad time for me. I was so low, so sad. I was walking around the perimeter of a high school ballfield. In the tall grass just beyond the outfield, I found a ball.

"It looked like it had gone through the mower once or twice; the leather was deeply scuffed, but the seams were still holding. I picked it up, tossed it in the air and caught it. Instantly, my heart felt lighter, and I thought of spring. Baseballs are wonderful things."

CHAPTER 3

They Wanted Baseball

Jordan

In the late 1960s, during one of Wilt Chamberlain's threats to quit basketball unless the Philadelphia 76ers paid him a whole lot, he went off to the Catskill Mountains. The Kansas City Chiefs had invited him to training camp to try football. And it was no far-fetched idea. Even at 7 feet 1 and 275 pounds, Chamberlain may be the best athlete who ever played any game.

Wearing slacks and sandals, Chamberlain outran Kansas City's best running back at 40 yards. So the Chiefs' coach, Hank Stram, thought of putting the big man at wide receiver and turning him loose on the NFL's midget defenders. Everything Stram's quarterbacks threw, Chamberlain caught. He even went up and came down with balls thrown over the crossbar. About when Stram thought he had the ultimate weapon, here came Chamberlain saying, "Quarterback."

Stram didn't understand.

"The only thing I want to play," Wilt said, "is quarterback."

The great ones become great because they believe they can do anything, whether it's Wilt Chamberlain as the world's tallest quarterback or Michael Jordan believing he can play baseball. Chamberlain never did it, and chances are Jordan never will play major league baseball. But here in the winter of

1994, as we huddle around the ol' hot stove for baseball talk, what better topic than Jordan's recent musings about baseball?

Media reports had Jordan "thinking about" spring training with the White Sox, whose owner, Jerry Reinsdorf, also owns Jordan's old basketball team, the Bulls. USA Today quoted Jordan on why he is taking batting practice three or four times a week at Comiskey Park and in a private batting cage: "I'm trying to see how good I can get. I haven't seen live pitching yet, but I'm driving the ball against the machine."

No official with the White Sox or Bulls reports hearing anything from Jordan himself. Reinsdorf has said of Jordan the baseball player, "If he was 18 and you were scouting him, you'd say he has great tools. But he's 30." Still, the owner said, Jordan loves being around the ballpark and the cage and he is welcome at spring training if that's what he wants. "I know Michael well enough to know he would not do anything to make a fool of himself. And he would not ask us to let him come to spring training unless he's proved himself."

The Bulls' general manager, Jerry Krause, once a top baseball scout, mostly dismissed the Jordan baseball talk as a media rehash of a Jordan/batting-practice story reported weeks ago. Yet, Krause also said, "You can never say Michael can't do anything. But the hardest thing in the world to do is hit a baseball—harder than anything in basketball. Let me put it this way: If Willie Mays had played only basketball from the time he was 8 years old, he'd have been Michael Jordan. And if Michael Jordan had played only baseball, he'd have been Willie Mays."

Danny Ainge, a guard with the Phoenix Suns and a .220 hitter in parts of three seasons for the Blue Jays, said Jordan's work against a pitching machine is worthless: "That's not even as good as high school pitching. There's no movement on the ball. There's no pitching machine that could lose control and come inside and up at his head."

A good amateur golfer himself, Ainge has disparaged Jordan's ambition to play on the PGA Tour, saying he would bet "my house and firstborn" that Jordan will never make it in pro golf. "I have a hard time believing Michael Jordan could ever be a consistent hitter at the major league level," Ainge said. "But he has a better chance of making it in baseball than in golf."

Jordan's baseball background is slight. Four years ago, asked to compare himself to Bo Jackson, Jordan said, "If I put my mind to it, I've always believed I could do anything I want, and I've heard him say the same thing.

Seriously, I might have played baseball, too—I was scouted as a pitcher."

Jordan once told a sportswriter, "My favorite childhood memory, my greatest accomplishment was when I got the Most Valuable Player Award when my (Babe Ruth League) team won the state baseball championship. ... I remember I batted over .500, hit five home runs in seven games and pitched a one-hitter to get us into the championship game."

While attending the University of North Carolina, Jordan played only basketball. "No one here, not even our baseball coach, ever saw Michael play baseball," said Rick Brewer, the school's sports information director.

So we're left with a mystery that may be solved only when baseball players head south:

Will Michael Jordan show up wearing a White Sox uniform?

Jordan said he quit basketball partly because fame burned him too often; why would he put himself in fame's flames again? Has he discovered that he needs a daily fix of risk to live the life he wants?

All this ol' hot stove talk reminded Jerry Krause of a story. Krause built the Bulls into a three-time NBA champion after a decade as a baseball executive. Whenever Jordan went off on one of his I-can-do-anything speeches—Jerry Reinsdorf says that Jordan once bowled two strikes by throwing the ball backward between his legs—Krause would be there to challenge Jordan's claims.

"Michael was always talking about himself as a baseball hitter," Krause said. "So I said, 'Let's go to Comiskey, and you get in there against the batting practice pitcher. You won't hit one out of the infield.' "

So, Jerry, what happened?

"Michael hit a couple in the seats."

Jordan II

MARCH 20, 1995

No .202 banjo-hitting outfielder ever made it to the major leagues at 32, not even Roy Hobbs. So Michael Jordan didn't so much retire from baseball as face up to reality now instead of later. Starting 20 years too late, he couldn't play the hardest game at the highest levels. The only shame is in not trying, and Jordan certainly tried.

The shame belongs to baseball because if the game needs anything these days it needs players who will stand up in public and say they love the game. Give that to Jordan. Whatever he did in his one baseball season, he did it sincerely. No athlete of such distinction ever submitted so completely to public embarrassment. We rise in applause.

Early in Jordan's season at Double-A Birmingham, Rangers pitching instructor Tom House said: "He is attempting to compete with hitters who have seen 350,000 fastballs in their pro baseball lives and 204,000 breaking balls. Baseball is a function of repetition. If Michael had pursued baseball out of high school, I don't doubt he would have wound up making as much money in baseball as basketball. But he's not exactly tearing up Double-A, and that's light years from the big leagues. At Double-A, pitchers can't spot the fastball and breaking ball. It will take him several years to learn the chess

60

game played by big league pitchers with exceptional control."

So, yes, Jordan's weaknesses were obvious and likely irreparable. Even so, Phil Jackson had it right. The Bulls' coach said Jordan did not fail baseball, baseball failed him.

Of the game's thousand and one self-inflicted wounds in this savage winter of 1994-95, Jordan's leaving is no big deal in a baseball sense. The woods are full of banjo hitters. But something larger is at work. Jordan's leaving is important for what it says about baseball. It says the owners' war against players has made it impossible to think of the game as a dream.

The man came to have fun. No longer fun, no longer a dream, the game now is a prisoner of war held by owners waging a revolutionary war that makes little sense to anyone and no sense to minor leaguers paid $2 an hour.

Jordan had become a minor leaguer in spirit as well as fact, just another eager kid humiliated by sliders on the fists and curveballs on the black.

He said he would always remember his minor league experience: "I met thousands of new fans, and I learned that minor league players are really the foundation of baseball. They often play in obscurity and with little recognition, but they deserve the respect of the fans and everyone associated with the game."

As much as he liked it, there comes a time to cut your losses. Because Jordan wouldn't work as a scab taking a striker's job, he had to move out of the White Sox major league camp. And then rather than hit .250 against more Double-A pitchers, just marking time instead of finally being tested against big leaguers, Jordan packed it in. Good for him.

Good for him because now he can do what he was born to do. The greatest basketball player ever has been away from his game for almost two seasons.

His return always seemed inevitable because his reasons for leaving seemed insincere. He said he wanted to get away from the media (only to walk back into it in baseball). He said he wanted to spend more time with his family (only to be gone more than ever). He said he wanted to play baseball to satisfy his murdered father's dream (that he did, if only for a year).

Even the summer Jordan quit basketball, he never really said it was over. He had won seven consecutive scoring championships; the Bulls had won three consecutive NBA titles; he had "reached the pinnacle" and saw no way to go but down, a burnt-out case weary of being Michael Jordan. Still he said, "Five years down the road, if that urge comes back, if the Bulls have me, if

(NBA Commissioner) David Stern lets me back in the league, I may come back."

A curious phrase, that about Stern, for Jordan's leaving had prompted rumors of a negotiated end to an NBA investigation into his gambling habit.

Jordan had evaded the truth about losing $157,000 to felons and hustlers on the golf course and at the card table; only under oath at a cocaine dealer's trial did Jordan admit gambling losses. When a golf hustler wrote a book claiming Jordan once was down $1 million to him, Jordan denied it at first but finally said, well, it wasn't a million but maybe it was a few hundred thousand. And he never paid it, anyway.

Few people believe the NBA had much interest in finding character flaws in its greatest star. Even fewer believe David Stern would not be delighted to see Jordan in his league again. Assuming Jordan is a harmless gambler who has learned his lesson, the league needs him.

For basketball without Jordan has been basketball without incandescence. Those of us who are moved by thunder stand in awe of Shaquille O'Neal. He's a man-slammer so ferocious that his every footfall frightens all the animals of the forest. But those of us who prefer lightning's dance across darkness have hoped for the day when Jordan would tell his shoe people, "Send 40 pairs to Chicago. I'm back."

Well, someone at the shoe company is talking. ESPN last week reported that its commercial traffic department was told by the shoe people to hold the baseball spot in which Jordan talks hitting with Stan Musial. Later, sifting entrails for portents, ESPN reckoned Jordan would return to the Bulls soon because the shoe source said the great man had indeed asked for 40 pairs of basketball shoes.

Jerry Krause is the Bulls' general manager, the dynasty builder. The other day, imagining, he could see Tony Kukoc with the ball on the run. He saw Scottie Pippen on one wing and Michael Jordan on the other. He saw Kukoc, almost 7 feet tall and a fabulous passer, coming to the top of the key with Pippen and Jordan on the fly against startled earthlings. As to exactly how thrilling it is to imagine the wonders possible from such an arrangement of the stars, Krause almost whispered: "It gives me the shivers."

Ike

On the Kansas prairie at the turn of the century, a boy hopped freight trains to get to the next ballgame. He learned to hunt and cook his kill from an illiterate woodsman who also taught him to paddle a flatboat, to find north on a rainy day and to never draw to an inside straight. When a doctor wanted to amputate his infected leg, the boy, then 13, stopped him by saying, "I'd rather be dead than crippled and not able to play ball."

He grew up in Abilene, once a dusty cow town that hired Wild Bill Hickok as its marshal. The boy, blond and blue-eyed, handsome as a sunrise and quick with a smile already irresistible, made a striking appearance when he left Abilene, 20 years old, headed east for school.

"He had filled out in the past two years, putting on 20 pounds, none of which was fat," a biographer wrote. "At nearly 6 feet tall, and weighing 170 pounds, with strong, broad shoulders and rock-hard muscles, he was the embodiment of an athlete. He was rawboned, with big hands. He walked on the balls of his feet and carried himself gracefully, as good athletes do."

His daydreams had been a boy's of his time and place. Maybe, he said, he could be a railroad engineer "racing across the land, arriving in Abilene, steam engine hissing, bell ringing, once again breaking the record from St.

Louis or some other distant, mythical place."

Or a baseball pitcher: "… to set down the next three batters on nine pitches in the last half of the ninth, with the bases loaded (of course) to the thunderous applause of five hundred spectators."

And this: "When I was a small boy in Kansas, a friend of mine and I went fishing, and as we sat there in the warmth of a summer afternoon on a river bank, we talked about what we wanted to do when we grew up. I told him that I wanted to be a real major league baseball player, a genuine professional like Honus Wagner. My friend said that he'd like to be President of the United States. Neither of us got our wish."

The Abilene of Dwight David Eisenhower's youth was a conservative, God-fearing, hard-working place where you made your life yourself. One of six brothers of a father who used the rod and a mother who gave them a sense of peace, Eisenhower worked constantly. His money went for shotgun shells, ice cream sodas and, most of all, for bats, balls, gloves and uniforms.

Historian Stephen F. Ambrose wrote, "Sports, especially football and baseball, were the center of his life. He put more time into the games than into anything else, save work, and expended far more energy on sports than he put into his studies. He was a good, but not outstanding, athlete. He was well coordinated, but slow of foot. He weighed only 150 pounds. His chief asset was his will to win."

Ambrose saw in Eisenhower humility and fair play: "One Saturday afternoon, the Abilene players discovered that the opposition had a Negro on the team. Each Abilene player refused to play across the line from the Negro, who was a center. Dwight stepped forward to say that he would play center that day, although his usual position was end and he had never played center. Both before and after the game, Dwight shook hands with the Negro. 'Rest of the team was a bit ashamed (of themselves),' he reported years later."

Military history fascinated the ballplayer. His senior yearbook predicted Eisenhower would become a professor of history at Yale. Though his appointment to the U.S. Military Academy in 1911 was a surprise to a young boy up from nothing, a generation later it must have seemed ordained.

At West Point as at Abilene, sports was so much his passion that even Eisenhower admitted "it would be difficult to overemphasize" the importance he attached to games. His first year, he played baseball and J.V. football.

Whatever happened later, and much would happen, Eisenhower never forgot 1912. That second year as an Army cadet, he became a football star described by The New York Times as "one of the most promising backs in Eastern football." For years he told friends, with delight, of tackling Jim Thorpe and believing he had hurt the Carlisle Indian School star only to see him rise up and on the next play run through Army again.

Then, in a mid-November game against Tufts, Eisenhower twisted a knee. During a horsemanship exercise a week later, he crumpled in agony. Cartilages and tendons were torn. He never played again.

Instead, even as he rose in rank to major, he worked as a football coach at Army camps. Through the 1920s and into the '30s, Eisenhower coached at San Antonio, Fort Sam Houston, St. Louis College, Camp Meade and Fort Benning. His work attracted such attention that he once turned down a job as head coach at "a northwestern university."

The biographer Ambrose: "... coaching brought out his best traits—his organizational ability, his energy and competitiveness, his enthusiasm and optimism, his willingness to work hard at a task that intrigued him, his powers of concentration, his talent for working with the material he had ... and his gift for drawing the best out of his players."

In memoirs done after his years of triumph, Eisenhower said football "tends to instill in men the feeling that victory comes through hard—almost slavish—work, team play, self-confidence, and an enthusiasm that amounts to dedication." He could reel off names of generals and admirals who had the game in common. They were men who understood sacrifice for a goal greater than themselves. They also understood their debt and obligation to men whose sacrifices made their lives worth living.

Fifty years ago this week, the old ballplayer from Kansas stood in the mess room at Southwick House, an estate near the southern coast of England. As Supreme Commander of the Allied forces in World War II, he had a decision to make. The only sounds in the room were rain against the windows and French doors rattling in the storm winds. Sometime after 4 in the morning, Eisenhower said quietly but clearly, "OK, let's go."

Then began the greatest invasion in the history of warfare.

Croteau

Why we want what we want is often a mystery created by forces not so much known as felt. Why would a girl 8 years old walk into Fenway Park and on seeing the field say to her mother and father, "I want to be a professional baseball player"? She carried a glove that day in 1979. And on a summery day in 1994, another time, she talked about walking to Fenway's right-field bleachers where she sat behind the bullpen, maybe 10 rows up.

Julie Croteau isn't sure why she said what she said. But she remembers the words and remembers this: Her parents didn't tell her that girls can't be baseball players, and it would be a while before she learned, with some pain, that what she wanted was something she couldn't have. Throughout her childhood she had played in leagues that accommodated boys and girls. Then one day she noticed an odd thing. "The girls started disappearing," she says. In time, Croteau was the only girl who wanted to play for her high school team in Manassas, Va.

Each spring she went to tryouts and each spring, when the cut list was posted, she found her name there. "Each year I really, truly, in my heart believed they would see I could play," she says. Her senior year she was a 5-foot-8, 130-pound first baseman who knew the game. That spring she found it "unbelievable" that she had been cut again.

She then decided she hadn't been cut because she wasn't good enough; she'd been cut because she was a girl. Julie Croteau called her parents that day and said, "I don't want them to get away with it."

So the family filed a discrimination suit—in vain. "The judge said a woman had no constitutional right to play baseball," Julie Croteau says.

Well, time passes. Things happen. That was 1988. This is 1994. If only that judge could see Julie Croteau now.

She is a professional baseball player, one of 20 women who are the Colorado Silver Bullets, the first women's team to compete only against men.

This summer the Silver Bullets played 44 games in $3^1/_2$ months on a 25,000-mile trip through 27 states and Canada. They played against low-classification pros and recreational league amateurs. Mostly they lost. When their record was 1-22, they had been shut out 13 times and outscored, 162-24.

The Silver Bullets won five of their next 20 games, but the numbers mean little. What's important is the team's existence as a symbol of possibilities. Even more important, the Silver Bullets moved beyond symbolism to real athleticism. These women can play the game.

They don't have the size and strength to produce the leverage necessary for explosive power. But the Silver Bullets are strong enough and quick enough with good enough hands and arms to make every infield play that needs to be made. What they feared would be their greatest liability, pitching, became their greatest asset. As for hitting, they still have miles and miles to go, much as Michael Jordan has miles to go if he wants to rise above Birmingham.

"I wasn't going to have anything to do with a circus," says Phil Niekro, the should-be Hall of Fame pitcher who won 318 major league games in 24 seasons and this spring became the Silver Bullets' manager. "Everything was going to be professional—and it has been."

Few pitchers worked with a greater competitive ferocity than Niekro. With the Silver Bullets, he has been a teacher of surpassing patience and kindness. In the spring a pitcher asked, "Phil, what's the best way to hold this?" She had played softball, jamming the ball against her palm and wrapping four fingers around it; the little baseball didn't feel right. Niekro said, "Whatever's comfortable," and then he moved the ball from her palm out onto her fingers.

Five weeks into the season, Rickey Henderson of the Oakland A's picked up a Bullets bat and declared it too heavy, even for him. "Here's a guy with muscles up to his ears," says outfielder Keri Kropke, "and he uses a bat lighter than mine. We never knew ours were too heavy. We just thought we weren't strong enough."

The Henderson lesson was one of many. Only Croteau, who went on to play college baseball without controversy, and pitcher Gina Satriano, the daughter of a major league player, Tom Satriano, came to the team from exclusively baseball backgrounds; everyone else came from softball. So they had to learn baseball's mechanics on a playing field 50 percent larger than softball's.

Because their frenetic travel left no time for practice, the Bullets learned mechanics during games in front of paying customers against players who knew how to hold a baseball from the time their daddies dropped one into the crib. And some players came spiced with resentment; one said to Kropke, "I can't believe you're getting paid more than us. That's (barnyard expletive)."

To which Kropke, making $20,000 instead of the Double-A's $10,000, said, "Now you know how it feels to be a woman making 65 cents to a man's dollar." After that, she says, the fellow became a gentleman.

So much happened that Niekro called it "the most unforgettable summer of my life." At Oakland, fans outside the clubhouse chanted, "We want the Bullets." Nearly 34,000 at Denver's Mile High Stadium gave the Bullets a standing ovation. A little boy sought out Kim Braatz and said, "I've seen Michael Jordan play right field—and you're much better than he is."

What more could a baseball player want than to play her game for people who cared? "We were treated with respect everywhere we went because we earned it," Croteau says. "We were 20 professional, focused women."

On July 21, these baseball players making a little bit of history walked into a stadium full of history. And when Julie Croteau walked onto the field at Fenway Park, carrying a baseball glove, she took a look at the right-field bleachers where she sat with her mother and father on another day in another time.

CHAPTER 4

Field of Dreams

Field of dreams: Part II

In the movie "Field of Dreams," an Iowa farmer hears the whispered words, "If you build it, he will come." So the farmer plows under his corn and builds a baseball field. Soon, Shoeless Joe Jackson materializes with ghosts in White Sox uniforms. But the field is built for a grander thing than Joe Jackson's return. It's there as a meeting place for the farmer and his father, long dead. The movie ends as they come together one more time.

Anyone who loved the movie first made a willing suspension of disbelief. For as much as we would like for such a thing to be possible, we know it could never happen. Or could it?

Judge for yourself from our story this week. It begins with a curious letter that arrived just before Joe Jackson's 107th birthday on July 16.

The letter said: "Is Shoeless Joe Jackson there? We have reports of a fashionable lady walking back and forth outside the Ed Sullivan Theatre in New York. Witnesses have reported this lady is carrying a black baseball bat in a cotton cloth. They also reported she kept saying, 'Is Joe here yet? He should have been here by now.' Could this be his wife, Katie Jackson?

"We wouldn't think any more of it, except Shoeless Joe was invited to attend Ed Sullivan's 'Toast of the Town' show on December 16, 1951. This would have been his greatest opportunity to clear his name. … But as we know, Joe had a heart attack 10 days before the show.

"These reports add to indications that Shoeless Joe Jackson may show up at Comiskey Park between August 11 and 20."

Three days later, another letter: "Is Shoeless Joe Jackson there? We have reports of a gentleman visiting Petland Pet Shops in Cincinnati. Workers have stated that this gentleman wanted a multicolored parrot that would bellow, 'You're out!' He also wanted to know if the bird could walk on a baseball.

"We wouldn't think any more of it, except Shoeless Joe sometimes carried a pesky bird whose vocabulary was limited to a screeching, 'Y-o-u'r-e out!' These reports suggest Joe may visit Comiskey Park between August 11 and 20."

The great hitter Joe Jackson took $5,000 of gamblers' money to fix the 1919 World Series in which the White Sox played Cincinnati. Though acquitted—evidence disappeared—eight players were banned from baseball.

Over the years, crusaders defended Jackson's honor by saying he took the money but played his best. He had the Series' only home run, the most hits (12), a .375 batting average and a .563 slugging average. He made no errors.

Jackson's defenders say he was an illiterate country boy duped by teammates who threatened to kill him. They say that after 76 years it's time to pardon Jackson and allow him in the Hall of Fame.

These letters were among a dozen this summer. Each came with a filip of fact about Joe Jackson's life, that filip wrapped in a piece of fantasy.

Sometimes the letter writer would cite bizarre events involving the White Sox—a no-hitter lost, 12 home runs in a game, a 459-minute doubleheader—as proof that "primal forces are at work" to bring Joe Jackson back to Chicago.

The letters were stacked on a desk, forgotten, until this summer's All-Star Game. That night in a TV shoe commercial, Don Mattingly said, "If Shoeless Joe Jackson were playing today, he'd have a shoe contract."

Well. Was it coincidence that Joe Jackson's name came up so soon after these letters arrived? Maybe coincidence is just another way of saying primal forces are at work. Whatever, we called the letter writer.

Mark Babiarz has been a White Sox fan since growing up in the northern Illinois town of Amboy. He is 36, a financial consultant in New Port Richey, Fla. One day his softball coach, Tom Malone, said it had been "my dream since long before 'Field of Dreams' to get Jackson into the

Hall of Fame."

Malone says: "Whatever damage Joe did, and we think he was innocent, there are 30 to 50 future Hall of Famers playing today who did more damage to baseball in 1994 by canceling a World Series."

So Malone and Babiarz became crusaders who built a database, mailed letters around the country (no answer from acting commissioner Bud Selig) and placed this classified ad in the Chicago Tribune: "Lost. Pair of shoes. Old Comiskey Park area. Pick 'em up August—Joe Jackson."

An intriguing touch, that. But the story seemed to end there, only one more quixotic attempt to rehabilitate poor Joe Jackson.

Then Babiarz said he also would drive to Iowa to see the ballfield made for the movie and left in place as a baseball shrine of sorts, the real Field of Dreams. Babiarz said, "Something big is going to happen there." Something with Shoeless Joe? "No," he said.

If not Joe, what? A silence and then: "I'm going to meet my son for the first time."

Babiarz was 17, his girlfriend 17. Neither was ready to be married. She raised their son. Only once did Babiarz see the boy; that was at a distance in a grocery store when the boy was 1. They had never spoken until July 5 when Babiarz heard Christopher Albrecht's voice on the phone.

"Christopher said, 'Let's let bygones be bygones. I want to know the other side of my family.' And, 'I wish you could've been there for my games.' I told him, 'You don't know how many times I wished the same thing.' "

The son is 18 now, in the Air Force just as his father had been in the Air Force. He plays baseball and basketball, as his father had. They attended the same high school. Last winter, doing a school term paper, Christopher wrote about Shoeless Joe Jackson.

When the boy said, "I just want to meet my dad," Babiarz told him about the trip to Chicago in August. And then he had an idea. What better place to meet than in Iowa? The son said, sure, he could get there.

So one day in August, on a field of dreams, a father and son will play catch.

A pure baseball heart

AUGUST 14, 2000

Every old sportswriter is 82 going on 15. Bob Broeg is one such boy. The man born before the end of World War I sits at dinner, his signature bow-tie askew, and before dessert he has spoken of Babe Ruth, Branch Rickey and Grover Cleveland Alexander, Eddie Gaedel, Frankie Frisch, Casey Stengel and "the three Cardinals with the most impact ever, Stan Musial, Rogers Hornsby and Mark McGwire."

To hear Broeg talk about Memorial Day, 1928, is to believe the sun set on that glorious day an hour ago. Listen …

"The impact of the Golden Age heightens my memory of that day. Charles Lindbergh had flown the Atlantic, Babe Ruth hit 60, St. Louis had the second-worst tornado in its history, Jack Dempsey and Gene Tunney had fought their 'long count fight.'

"It was Memorial Day and with my uncle I rushed up the steps of the right field pavilion at Sportsman's Park. I'd just turned 10 and qualified to get in free as a member of the Knothole Gang. I'm not a poet, but I believe I've never seen a bluer sky than the sky that day, nor greener grass, nor anything more beautiful than the creamy whites of the home uniforms.

"Knotholers often began chants, 'We want a homer … We want a homer,' directed at Jim Bottomley and Chick Hafey. That day, just to be silly, we chanted, 'We want Alex.' "

Though they knew the ancient warrior, Grover Cleveland Alexander, rarely pitched in relief, "still we chanted, 'We want Alex.' I looked it up years later, and he relieved only three times that season. But all of a sudden, in a lower wing of the grandstand, there with that small glove and the white ball shining, looking so big, he loosened up, throwing maybe five balls. Then he walked to the mound. We were so thrilled."

Beats there a heart more pure than that of a baseball fan thrilled? No. The beauty of Bob Broeg is, that pure heart beats still.

He first wrote for the St. Louis Post-Dispatch in 1936; from 1945 on, he worked for that newspaper as a baseball writer, sports editor and columnist. Even now, after heart surgery and a small stroke or two, 15 years into retirement, Broeg writes a Sunday column, wise and encyclopedic.

The Sporting News, as you may have noticed, scoured high and low for The Best Sports City in America and found it just outside the lobby. The editors threw every sort of St. Louis justification into the stew: football, basketball, soccer, auto racing, track and field, even hockey.

Memo to Boss: Baseball's enough.

Memo, Part II: Listen to Bob Broeg. Such a story, his baseball story.

Robert William Patrick Broeg, the son of a St. Louis bread truck driver, was born on his family's kitchen table. The difficult birth was all but botched by a doctor who wielded "her forceps like ice tongs, grabbing me fore and aft, rather than left and right," Broeg wrote in his autobiography. "The doctor said if I lived, I'd be crazy. Now, that's a helluva sendoff, isn't it?"

The forceps scarred Broeg's left eye, rendering him damaged goods when it came time to play baseball. So he lived the game …

The Knotholer saw Ruth for 15 innings against the Browns in '28. As a journalist, he came to admire Rickey's organizational genius even as he distrusted the Mahatma's word. After Eddie Gaedel walked on four pitches in '51, the Browns' midget came to the press box where Broeg told him, "You're what we've all dreamed of being, an ex-major leaguer." In July of '46, each time Stan Musial came to bat, Dodger fans chanted, "Here comes the man," so Broeg's Post-Dispatch stories created the game's grandest nickname, Stan The Man.

And a Casey Stengel story …

"I was making $32.50 a week for the Associated Press in Boston in 1943 when Casey managed the Braves. Casey being Casey, he pronounced my name 'Brogue,' not 'Braig.' One night at dinner, he was feeling so low, I told him, 'Casey, someday you'll prove you're more than a clown. Someday your ship will come in.'

"Fast-forward to 1949, and I'm covering the Cardinals in the pennant race while the Yankees with Casey are in their own race. The Cardinals blew the pennant, and the Yankees won on the last day. I made the death trip home with the Cardinals on the train before returning to New York for the World Series.

"Now we're at Yankee Stadium and Jim Dawson, the big, domineering New York Times writer, pushes me to the front of the pack in Casey's office. Dawson says, 'Casey, this is Bob Broeg of St. Louis.' Casey looks up and says, 'No, it isn't, it's Bob Brogue of Boston, and my ship has come in.'"

Oddly, it's a surprise to Broeg—and no surprise—to hear St. Louis called a great baseball town.

"There was a time when the Cardinals were so successful that the fans, like Atlanta's today, became surfeited with victory. In the 21 seasons from '26 to '46, the Cardinals won nine pennants and six world championships. And during that time, the owner, Sam Breadon, once told me, 'I sure would like to move my ballclub to Detroit.'

"What has happened in St. Louis since, I'm in awe. The very thing that caused everyone to be spoiled in the '30s now works for the Cardinals—that tradition of excellence created by Branch Rickey and sustained by Sam Breadon. Tradition is a great link between the past and today."

Tradition needs storytellers. St. Louis has Bob Broeg. Lucky St. Louis.

Mining for gold among corn fields

AUGUST 6, 2001

Ellsworth Brown is a baseball scout, among the last of his kind.

Raising dust across the Midwest, he figures he has worn out 30 cars since 1946. The latest is a Dodge Intrepid that he says handles well in traffic.

Not that there's much traffic where Brownie goes. He mostly drives through towns hidden between corn fields. "My address? Beason, Illinois, Poverty Row." As to what he's doing: "Got off the road at midnight last night, been out to Iowa, going to Peoria tonight for a Midwest League game."

Such has been the sweet music of a baseball life lived by a man who played with Grover Cleveland Alexander, discovered Bill Madlock, signed Kirby Puckett, and now, 87 years old, beats the bushes for the Twins.

Listen, if you will, to Brownie's music ...

"When I started as a player, you couldn't make any money. Class D ball might promise you $150 a month. But it was 1931 and sometimes they'd pay you and sometimes they'd say, 'Get you next month.'

"I was a 5-foot-11, 181-pound first baseman. Good fielder, not much of a hitter. Thing was, I was 17 1/2 years old, and when they told me to report to the Kansas City Triple-A team the next spring, I just went home. I was homesick. Probably a mistake. Should've stayed with it.

77

"I found some work. Made some money playing summer ball, too. And a few years later, that's how I came to play for Grover Cleveland Alexander's barnstorming team. Somebody said, 'Pete Alexander wants you to join his club for the summer.'

"I loved that old man. Everybody said he was a drinker, which he probably was, but some of it was his epilepsy. He was good to me. I played one inning with him pitching. He was 52 years old then, 1939—and he'd gone into the Hall of Fame the year before. Such control he had. Every pitch was right where he wanted it. Four pitches, and I got all three putouts at first base."

Some people get lucky and make a living doing what they love.

Sportswriters do it, bless 'em all. And in 1946 Ellsworth Brown became a baseball scout. Asked to describe his work, he says, "Have fun." Watching games from March to October, driving two-lane roads, floorboards covered with notebooks, Brownie did the job the way it was done by scouts building the major leagues.

Kevin Kerrane's book, "Dollar Sign on the Muscle: The World of Baseball Scouting," quotes the late catcher/manager/scout Birdie Tebbetts on pre-World War II scouts: "They drove all over hell to find ballplayers, and they made final decisions on their own about how valuable the players were, and they competed to sign them. They weren't just leg men; they built ball clubs. ... I've been in every seat in baseball, and I'd have to say that the old-time scouts were the most important people I ever came in contact with."

Just last year, Ellsworth Brown signed a player he'd watched from high school through college, Josh Rabe, an 11th-round draft pick now hitting .285 for the Twins' Class-A Quad City team. Says Rabe: "Brownie would sit and talk with my parents at all my games. He's such an all-around nice guy."

It was 20 years ago when the scout, old even then, stopped by an Illinois community college to take a look at a short-coupled kid named Kirby Puckett.

"A guy in the Twins' office had seen Puck the year before and liked him but couldn't sign him," Brown says. "When I saw him, Puck was playing third base. To be honest, I thought his arm was going to need work." But he liked the young man's strength and quickness at bat. The Twins chose Puckett third in the first round of the 1982 winter draft.

As to how Brown signed Puckett, the old scout laughs. "Might have been the little extra cash. About $20,000 I gave him."

And on Sunday, Kirby Puckett goes into the Hall of Fame.

"I haven't talked to Puck in years," Brown says. "I'd love to be at Cooperstown for the ceremony. But I don't suppose I could afford it. Too long a drive, anyway, the way I'm feeling. Fell on ice last winter and busted up ribs. Got some Legion tournaments the same time, too, with two, three kids to look at."

Puckett is a scout's good story. Bill Madlock is a better one. In 15 major league seasons, Madlock hit .305 and won four batting championships; only nine hitters have won more. Listen to Ellsworth Brown's song …

"I'd been down in Southern Illinois, and I was driving home to Beason. Usually I go to Lincoln and back down the highway. This time I took a back road from Decatur through Chestnut, and I saw a ballgame going on right there in Beason.

"Lincoln's Legion club was there against Decatur. It was the last inning. I saw this kid by the name of Bill Madlock swing one time, and I said, 'Boy, he's got that quick bat.' I went to Lincoln's coach, John West, and said, 'How'd that kid do the last time up?' West said, 'He reached that fence out there.'

"So I got on Madlock from the start. Signed him for the Senators in 1970."

Fifty-five years on the road, wearing out cars, and our hero finds a batting champion five blocks from his house in the middle of corn fields.

Such sweet music.

Deep affection

SEPTEMBER 20, 1999

Two weeks before he was to get married, minor league baseball player Chuck Antczak heard from his girl that she'd changed her mind. She had her reasons. He'd be gone on all those road trips, riding buses to scruffy places, and for what? If you put a pencil to the hours and the money, it came out to maybe $5 an hour to play baseball.

"So she gave me the ol' boot," the poor guy said.

The way these things happen, when it rains, it pours. He lost the girl and lost the job, too. That was in 1997. He was out of baseball for the first time since he was 6. Never a phenom, a good college pitcher/outfielder, he hung on in pro ball as a backup catcher. There's no glory in that dust, except for this: It kept the dream alive.

"And when I got back in the game in '98," Antczak said, "I promised myself I was going to have fun."

Which brings us to Chuck Antczak's 77 home runs this summer. He hit them for the Clearwater Phillies of the Class-A Florida State League. Unless you're a reader of the little stories in newspaper sports sections, you may not know about the 77 homers. That's because he hit them all in batting practice. In real games, he hit none.

"If the single hardest thing in sports is hitting a baseball, the single hardest thing to do when you hit a baseball is to hit it out of the ballpark," Antczak said. And who would know that better than a guy who hits 77 dingers at 5 o'clock but can't go yard even once when real pitchers start throwing curves?

We introduce Chuck Antczak as preamble to one more examination of the mighty work being done by Sammy Sosa and Mark McGwire. In this summer of Taters Tremendous, they again have made this hard thing look easy.

Baseball purists, traditionalists and other grouches, go ahead, say what you will. Say the ball is juiced. Say it must be juiced if two men hit more than 60 home runs in successive years when not even one man did that in a century and more. Say the players are juiced. Say ballparks are smaller and that second-class pitchers are squeezed into a postal-slot strike zone. Say all that, and, yes, you may be on to something.

Baseballs are winding up in the next time zone. Cal Ripken Jr.'s 400th home run broke a fan's nose. Greg Vaughn sent Waveland Avenue residents into the basement seeking shelter. The Reds became Murderers Row reborn. Steve Finley hit three in a day. STEVE FINLEY!

Still, if major league baseball created a ticket-selling conspiracy to make everyone a power hitter, wouldn't there be a stampede to 60 home runs? There isn't. Only two men are on this march. In fact, Sosa and McGwire are so good at what they do that they have separated themselves not only from today's pack but from history.

If they were to hit 60 apiece this year, they'd have 256 in successive seasons. That's 47 more than the next-best ever by two men in the same league, the 209 of Ken Griffey Jr. and Juan Gonzalez ('97-98). It's also 62 more than Mickey Mantle-Roger Maris ('60-61), and 68 ahead of Babe Ruth-Lou Gehrig ('27-28).

Midway through this summer, our hero Chuck Antczak realized he could put up what he calls "McGwire-ish numbers." In his first minor league season (1995), he hit a home run off Jose Jimenez, who pitched one of the big-league's three no-hitters this season. "He had a nasty, just nasty, slider, and when I hit it, guys were saying, 'Man, you're gonna rake.'"

Antczak sighs. "Five years later, that's still my only professional home run."

But a boy can have baseball fun a hundred ways. Every time Antczak hit one out in batting practice this summer, he marked a line on his helmet. When the lines added up to 25, he had an idea. Why not go for the record?

Why not hit 71?

Clearwater manager Bill Dancy and coaches Darold Knowles and Tony Scott "did their best to hit my bat," Antczak says. "Finally, we got past 61. Who hit 61, Gehrig?" Roger Maris. "Oh, past Maris, past Sosa's 66. But we were running late in the season to get to McGwire, and it got kinda anxious."

To celebrate his 71st BP home run on the last weekend of his team's regular season, Chuck Antczak circled the bases, slapping high-fives with his teammates and coaches. Then he fashioned a trophy to give to the coach, Knowles, who threw the historic pitch. The trophy was a little cardboard box with a ball of adhesive tape perched atop it.

From 71 he flew to 77, which sounds like a good number until you hear Antczak say, "Hey, McGwire's probably got 7,000 BP home runs. What he and Sosa do is unbelievable. Every at-bat they see 90 mph fastballs, nasty sliders, the ball cutting and diving, and they stand there like nothing's going on. They're so special."

At 25, Chuck Antczak has only 200 pro at-bats; he went 3-for-4 in Clearwater's season-ending game, raising his average 73 points to .258 with two doubles and, of course, zero/nada/zilch dingers. Though he no longer thinks of playing in the big leagues, he'd like to make it as a coach. Thus, the grunt work in bush league bullpens.

He's also avoiding marriage for the moment. "My last girlfriend threw me a curveball," he said, "and, Lord knows, I can't hit a curve."

A Cubs fan needs heroes, too

JULY 3, 2000

To understand why Sammy Sosa is on his way out of Chicago, we first must understand the awesome incompetence of "those ultimate empty suits" who run the Cubs. These men, general manager Ed Lynch and team president Andy MacPhail, have mounted "a cynical campaign to destroy the image of a hustling, beloved, hard-working superstar." This Gang of Two has "employed the media power of its employer, the Tribune Co., to condition Cubs fans for the payroll-liquidating giveaway that will be billed as 'an investment in the future' when, in fact, the company will never spend the dollars necessary to provide Cubs fans with a new hero."

The quotes come not from a baseball insider.

They come from a better source.

They come from a Cubs fan.

"The ice-water types who inhabit the Michigan Avenue tower of the Tribune Co. feel they can depend on the magnetic love we all have for Wrigley Field to keep the turnstiles humming despite their pathetic product," says my friend, Bill Stone, as passionate a Cubs fan as the law allows.

He's 63 years old. For 58 years, he has attended Cubs games at Wrigley Field. He calls the old ballpark "heaven on earth." He's a member of the Emil

Verban Memorial Society, named for the sweetheart Cubs infielder who in 2,911 major league at-bats hit one home run. (Incidentally, Stone would vote for the expulsion of a fellow member, Hillary Clinton, on grounds she has been seen wearing a Yankees cap.)

Ask Bill Stone the age of his father, Harold, and the answer is, "Born the year the Cubs last won a World Series, 1908."

As an elementary school patrol boy, little Billy Stone worked an intersection near Wrigley Field's right field bleachers. Maybe the first 50 Cubs games he saw, he saw for free. He clambered up an ironwork grill to a box-office roof, leaped over a small fence and took a seat in the bleachers.

Later, he wangled a ballpark job picking up seat cushions. Given his choice of 65 cents in pay or a free admission to a game, he chose baseball over money.

In 1946, at age 9, the boy tore from *SPORT* magazine a photograph of Cubs slugger Bill "Swish" Nicholson. The headline: "Old Swish Can Still Swat." He got his hero's autograph on the photo, mounted it on cardboard and encased the prize in plastic before storing it, carefully and for all time, along with a complete set of 1948 Bowman baseball cards, in a cigar box.

Stone was at Wrigley Field on June 15, 1949. That day's news: a 19-year-old Chicago girl, Ruth Ann Steinhagen, had gone to Eddie Waitkus' hotel room the night before and shot the Phillies' first baseman. Stone remembers "commiserating with players" over the injuring of Waitkus, a former Cub for whom the girl had a twisted infatuation.

He was there as well on the bittersweet day his hero, Swish Nicholson, also traded to the Phillies, returned to Chicago. This time, Billy Stone came prepared with more than words of commiseration. He stopped at Fishman's Market, near the ballpark, and spent his own money to buy Swish a welcome-back present: a pouch of Beech-Nut chewing tobacco. Stone's snapshot of memory: "Swish was really pleased."

We all grow up. William A. Stone, a graduate of the University of Michigan, now is the owner/CEO of the Louisville Plate Glass company in Louisville, Ky.

We all grow up, sort of. Stone installed, in his business conference room, the wiring necessary for cable television. The television is used for one purpose: Cubs games.

From Swish to Hank Sauer and Ernie Banks to Andre Dawson and Ryne Sandberg and Sammy Sosa, from day games to night lights, from radio to cable-TV, the Cubs have been a constant in my friend Bill Stone's life—and now he boils with indignation born of the idea that "those ultimate empty suits," Lynch and MacPhail, would trade away Sammy Sosa.

"There's truth to it when people say it doesn't matter if the Cubs win or lose, the ballpark will always be sold out," Stone says. "But the fans do care, and they certainly care about heroes. We've always had a hero to adore, whether it's Swish Nicholson or Ernie or Ryno. Mark Grace is wonderful, but he doesn't quite have it to be 'the reason.' Sammy is today's 'reason.'"

Stone understands the money issues involved. Sosa soon will want $15 million to $20 million a year, and the Cubs evidently think that money could be better spent on prospects. But Stone also understands that the Tribune Co. has more money than God and nearly as much as Bill Gates. Because he also despairs of Lynch's ability to judge talent, he reckons any Sosa trade is a gamble not worth the risk.

"If Ernie Banks were playing for the Cubs now with a contract year coming up, Ed Lynch would trade him for nobodies rather than put his job on the line by demanding that his corporate bosses pay the going rate," Stone says.

Whether we're whacking computer keys or running a baseball team, those of us in the sports business need listen to the passionate folks who make the games necessary. We need to listen to the Bill Stones who remember ballpark days a half-century old.

We need to hear Bill Stone sing of Sammy Sosa even as he remembers taking a pouch of chaw to Swish Nicholson, whose autographed picture he stored carefully in that cigar box and kept for …

For how many years now, Bill?

"When I went to college, my mother heaved it," he says.

Yikes. And the Bowman bubble-gum cards …

"Gone," he says. "Worth $5,000 a set today."

Mothers. They have much to answer for.

CHAPTER 5

To 70
and Beyond

A man among children

DECEMBER 15, 1997

Here's Mark McGwire in his little castle on a California island. It's an impossibly gorgeous December day. The big man is at ease on a couch, wearing a T-shirt, blue jeans and sneakers. Behind him, a harbor channel sparkles diamond blue. Docked at the pier a few steps away is his boat; its name is Four Bases.

For Mark McGwire, there's one question. So, 61?

"People talk about 61 like, 'It's your goal, isn't it?' It's never been a goal. Can it be accomplished? I've never talked to Ken Griffey Jr. about it. But I'm going to speak for him. If we sat down, we'd say, 'Yeah, you know what? I think it can be done.'

"We were close to it. We had bad Julys. If we did halfway decent in July, home run-wise, we're at 61 or over 61. Will it be done? It has to be one of those years when somebody walks away from the game and goes, 'I did everything I could possibly do.'"

But that kind of season, everything working perfectly—has it ever happened?

"I guarantee you, ask any hitter, if you'd asked Ted Williams, he'd have said, 'You know that .406? I could've hit .420.' Roger Maris might've said,

'Hey, I could've hit 65.' That's how baseball is. That's what drives guys to work harder."

Here Mark McGwire allows himself a little smile, almost a smile of mischievous anticipation. He's morphing into Huck Finn hefting a $34^{1}/_{2}$-inch, 33-ounce stick. Somehow, with the red hair and green eyes, the big man has a little-boy look to him.

And he says of that hitter's dream season, "It's never happened. But, you know what? It could happen."

Amazing, what 58 home runs will do for you the year after you hit 52. You become a person. Not that Mark McGwire hasn't been a person.

But he's no media hound confirming his ego on an hourly basis. He prefers the work to the celebration. So we hardly knew him beyond the extravagant numbers he put up.

We saw the man only when we saw him cry.

Amazing. He calls hitting a home run the most difficult act in all of sports. "Or more people would do it more often," he says. And then in two seasons he hits 40,000 feet of home runs. Hits them so hard that Sandy Alomar is glad one clanged off Cleveland's scoreboard. "Or else it goes around the world and hits me in the back of the head," the catcher says.

A Babe Ruth for the new millennium, McGwire hits rising line drives of such distance that outfielder Steve Finley of the Padres says, "I don't chase Mark McGwire's shots—I admire them."

After he turned around Randy Johnson's heat and sent it 481 feet, McGwire circled the bases head down rather than admire the missile's flight. "I respect pitchers too much to show them up," he says. From the mound, the Mariners ace caught McGwire's eye in the dugout and touched his cap bill, power saluting power.

"Mark hits it farther with less effort than anyone ever," says Tony La Russa, who has managed McGwire in Oakland and St. Louis. "The arc of Ken Griffey Jr.'s swing has gotten bigger than when he hit line drives. Juan Gonzalez is a terrific power hitter, too. But you look at Juan's arc and look at Mark's—Mark's is more compact, simpler.

"It's timing, and it's a gift not everybody has. He reaches the ball at the exact moment when he can max it out."

Amazing, he gives the Cardinals a bargain deal. The city loves him, he loves the city, and in 10 hours he does a three-year, $30 million deal. Instead of auctioning himself on the free-agent market and busting the bank somewhere, he takes $7 million a year. He defers $2 million so the team can use it for other players. And gives away $3 million the next three years to his Mark McGwire Foundation for Children to help youngsters who can't help themselves.

For that singular act of faith, hope and charity, as well as for a singular season of excellence, The Sporting News honors McGwire as the 1997 Sportsman of the Year.

"The quantity and sheer power of Mark's home runs have put him in a class of his own, but his moving example of selflessness and loyalty have made him equally unique," TSN president James H. Nuckols says. "For both of these reasons he has helped us see the game differently and made it an exceptionally easy choice for us to name him as Sportsman of the Year."

Amazing, the athletic feats, the scoreboards dented. Amazing, as well, to witness on a daily basis a larger evolution at work: "More impressive than anything he's done on the field," La Russa says, "has been Mark's development personally. So much attention is given to the ball leaving the park that we don't see his completeness, the player, not just the hitter. And he's become a team leader by example and by voice. He's what a major leaguer is supposed to be."

He does all that hero's work with grace and modesty. Then at a news conference announcing his new contract, someone asks about his interest in abused children. He hesitates. How to answer? He doesn't know how to turn a life's experience into a sound bite.

How to talk about Polly Klaas, the 12-year-old girl whose 1993 abduction and murder chilled the Bay Area during McGwire's years with the A's. How to talk about the "missing children" sweatbands he wore in games. What does a man say about his fears borne of divorce so soon after he became a father? How can he convey his girlfriend Ali Dickson's passionate involvement in the protection of abused children? All that inside him and no way to get it out.

He falls silent. A reporter's clock on the silence: 33 seconds. When he finally speaks, it's in generalities. Children have a special place in his heart. They are God's gifts to us. And the biggest big man in baseball cries.

"We had never seen the depth of the personal side until then," La Russa says. "He showed us, 'This is a better way to be.'"

Though McGwire had no way to know it, at that moment he made it out of the hole. He remembers the hole. It's October 1991. He's a mess. And not just in baseball, which is bad enough. Worse, it's his whole life.

Love has skipped on him. A woman he couldn't live without became a woman he couldn't live with. At work, this strongman who hit 49 home runs as a major league rookie has a nightmare year. Whisperers say he can't catch up to fastballs because he's afraid of them. They say the A's will trade him before he loses all value. Even he wonders. Is this it?

He hits .201 with 22 home runs. He is in free fall from his rookie season four years earlier when he hit .289 with the 49 home runs. It is the latest evidence of a melancholy pattern that threatens to break him before he breaks it.

He throws his gear in his car. He drives south. He drives $5^1/_2$ hours to Los Angeles. He drives alone.

No radio.

No phone.

Driving, thinking. He asks himself questions he has asked during the season. "Do I know who I am? Do I like what I see in the mirror?"

One word answers both questions.

No.

It's December 1997, and Mark McGwire has new answers now. "I was in a deep hole, and I didn't think I could climb out," he says of the darkness of 1991. "A live-in relationship problem affected me off the field. And you can say you're going to go out and play the game and not let it affect you professionally. But ... well, everything accumulated and accumulated and just came crashing in on me.

"I was walking on air—in a bad sense, not a good sense. I wasn't grounded in any firm beliefs about how to live my life. I allowed no positive energy in my life.

"It was horrible, and yet it was the biggest learning experience of my life, both in baseball and in life. I learned that I had to be who I am, not somebody somebody else wants me to be."

McGwire now sees the elements of failure invisible to him then. Married a year out of college, a father soon painfully divorced, he wasn't ready for love again. Complicating the complexities, some Einstein figure in an A's uniform had a brainstorm about changing the way McGwire hit.

Quit pulling everything, the genius told the dead-pull hitter. Use the whole field, go to right more.

Which is like telling Michael Jordan, "Quit the jumpin', son."

Problem was, McGwire followed the fool advice. He tinkered with his hitting mechanics so much as to build a swing that incorporated a zillion moving parts.

"He'd gotten into a terrible, defensive position, much too complicated, allowing the ball to travel too far before initiating his swing," says Doug Rader, hired by La Russa as the A's hitting coach in the winter following the '91 debacle. "It was no character flaw. His approach was just so bad that he was getting beat by fastballs."

Or, to quote La Russa: "Mark had gotten a little funky with his stroke."

McGwire went along with the foolishness out of one of life's famous paradoxes. As some beauty queens want to play Shakespeare and 7-foot centers want to bring the ball upcourt, sluggers want to slap singles to right.

"I had the label of being a home run hitter," McGwire says, "when I wanted to be known for my defense, too, and for being a complete player. I fought against that label."

In McGwire, then, baseball had its first recorded case of a man reluctant to be known for hitting balls out of sight—until, in the winter of 1991, after that long drive down the California coast, he realized, "I needed to change my life."

So he began regular sessions with a psychiatrist. Nothing dramatic, he says. Just common-sense explanations of life.

"But you'd be amazed," McGwire says, "how many people don't want to use common sense."

Such as: If the first hit of your Little League career is a home run, if you knock down fences in college, if you get to be 6-5, 245 pounds and hit 49 home runs as a rookie, you're pretty much entitled—nay, even obligated—to think of yourself as a home run hitter.

"I decided I wouldn't fight it because that is what I am, a home run hitter, that's me, that's what God put me here to be," he says. "Now if I get a hit to right field, you can pretty much count on it being an accident."

In 1992 McGwire moved from that sickly .201 to .268, from 22 home runs to 42, from 75 runs batted in to 104.

"I started becoming who I am," he says.

For the old questions, then, came happier answers.

"Who am I? I'm Mark McGwire, the man I'm supposed to be. Do I like what I see in the mirror? Yes."

Ginger McGwire, the hitter's mother: "As a boy, he'd lay on the floor watching baseball games on television. He wouldn't take the trash out as long as there was a game on. He always had that dream of playing in the major leagues."

John McGwire, the father: "Our son Dan up in Seattle called to say he'd been asked if it was Mark himself who had been abused as a child. Well, yes, we abused him—with love."

As near to abuse as the McGwires came was the father's refusal to let Mark play Little League ball at age 7.

"I'd heard too much about arguing, meddling parents and bad coaches," the father says. "I didn't want anybody to screw up my son. When I told him he couldn't play, he cried and cried and cried."

The next year, finding a coach he liked, John McGwire allowed Mark to play. "His first at-bat, against a 12-year-old pitcher, Mark hit a home run over the right-field fence. The surprising thing was he had an innate sense of how to play. He knew where to position players, he just knew. It was spine-tingling, his understanding of the game at such an early age.

"The old-timers who sat around the railroad tracks and talked baseball would say, 'This kid, he's something. He's going to light up the world.'"

From Damien High School, an all-boys Catholic private school in Claremont, Calif., McGwire went to the University of Southern California, recruited as a pitcher.

"I had a shot at making the big leagues pitching," he says now. "But I went to Alaska for a summer league and came back as a third baseman." Someone had noticed the ball leaving the park quickly.

Two full minor league seasons (the second ending in a September call-up to the A's) preceded the '87 season, when at age 23 his 49 home runs set a major league record for rookies. Over the next four seasons, his batting average fell from .289 to .260, .231, .235 and .201.

"Did we consider trading him? Yes," La Russa says. "His problems had started before the .201 year. The game can get away from you, you lose the feel. It's a sensitive thing, playing major league baseball. He couldn't have had another couple years like those.

"And 'salvage' would not be too strong a word for what he was then able to do in '92. He was at a crossroads. But as with most good people, he never lost himself during the struggle. Being a man of great pride, he was stung by all the criticism. And you could see he was carrying a great burden. But he never did anything to embarrass himself. The way he handled the adversity, that's what you look for in a person."

Foot injuries cost him most of the '93 and '94 seasons; he played only 74 games and says of those dispiriting years, "I couldn't have gotten through them if I hadn't had '92. And I wouldn't have had '92 without the bad year of '91. I'm a firm believer that things happen for a reason, and I know that just watching the games those years made me a better hitter. I learned a lot just watching. I learned much more of the mental side. I learned how to stay positive."

Now the melancholy descent at the turn of this decade has become an ascent of an unprecedented kind.

After 39 home runs in the strike-shortened '95 season, McGwire hit 52 home runs in '96. Then came the 58, making him only the second player to hit 50 home runs in successive seasons. Babe Ruth did it 70 years ago.

So one day the telephone rang, Mark McGwire calling for Ali Dickson. They'd met at a casual dinner with friends in Boston but had neither seen nor spoken to each other for a year.

"Why'd I call her?" McGwire says. "I really don't know. Just out of the blue on a road trip to L.A., I called her."

She worked as a movie director's assistant. She'd heard of him, a baseball player somewhere. Truth is, until the phone rang, she'd pretty much forgotten the dinner a year earlier.

She had her life. After graduation from UCLA, where she'd been a varsity volleyball player, Dickson worked as a volunteer with sexually abused children. For a year now, she has done her work at Stuart House in Santa Monica, west of Los Angeles.

Her passion is palpable. The daughter of a social worker, familiar with dysfunctional families, Dickson had a college friend who'd been a victim of physical abuse as a child.

"All her trouble in life was evident in her family story," Dickson says. "She was always searching for the love she missed at home."

It's a story too often told. Dickson says abuse touches one in four girls, one in eight boys.

"I came home one day and talked to Mark about it," she says. "I said, 'God, can you believe this is happening to children?' I shared with him what I had learned and what I saw at Stuart House every day. I said, 'Something has to be done.'"

McGwire says that when he visited Stuart House with Dickson, he, too, was touched. They saw children laughing, children apparently happy. But they knew pain cowered under the laughter.

"Mark started talking about the foundation idea," Dickson says. "He asked, 'How about $1 million a year?' Then, 'Do you think $500,000?' He said, 'How about $100,000?' I had no idea what he was going to do until the day he did it."

When Ali Dickson heard that McGwire would give $1 million a year to his children's foundation, she says, "I started crying."

We know he's big. Anyone 6-5 and 245 pounds is big. His 17-inch forearms, 19-inch biceps and ham-hock hands could be Paul Bunyan's. His shoulders are so wide you expect him to turn sideways to pass through doors.

But somehow he doesn't look big. His waist is a little guy's 32 inches. His legs are trim as a basketball player's. If there's 5 percent body fat, it survives two-hour weightlifting sessions six days a week in the offseason and a half-hour three times a week in season.

Babe Ruth, buff.

So, 61? Expert testimony from Rader, the hitting coach, once a Gold Glove third baseman with power.

"Mark's a terrific guy, I love him. He doesn't act to shower himself with praise. He's very elegant in the way he accepts all this stuff. I mean, here's a guy who had 49 home runs his rookie season and he bolts the last day to see his son born. He says he'll have another chance to hit 50 but no other chance to see his son born.

"He has the purest, simplest swing this side of Paul Molitor. His plate coverage and his bat speed are second to none. Everybody thinks he's sitting on fastballs, but he's the best curveball hitter I've ever seen. Because of the short length of his swing, he has fewer variables than anybody.

"Here's the bottom line: If you're not on top of your game, he's going to hurt you. And if he's on top of his game, he'll hurt you no matter what."

So, sir, 61?

"It's impossible to size him up historically. It may not even be in his best interests to participate in this day and age. At a time when hitting 25-30 home runs was truly extraordinary, he'd have been a 40-home run man. He's been shortchanged by this era."

So, 61?

"Everybody thinks of 60 as a benchmark, but that's a bogus number. Look, if they keep adding two teams to the big leagues, Mark might hit 105."

McGwire mania and The Man

SEPTEMBER 7, 1998

Congregants at the Mark McGwire worship services this summer often meet neighbors outside the St. Louis ballpark in the shadow of baseball's neatest statue.

It's a mighty bronze raised high on a grand pedestal. It's a hitter in a stance so peculiar it was best described as "looking like a little boy peeking around a corner." The pedestal is inscribed with words delivered by baseball's commissioner the day Stan Musial retired: "... here stands baseball's perfect warrior ... here stands baseball's perfect knight."

Stan The Man is an American hero 77 years old and young as springtime. He's eager to see Mark McGwire do it and he's certain he's never seen anything like it before. Not with Ralph Kiner, Willie Mays or Hank Aaron. "With McGwire," Musial says, "it's a potential home run on every swing. Amazing. Every swing, a home run swing."

We're talking home runs with the great man because we're in St. Louis and there's a $500 municipal fine if you're caught in conversation about anything else. So Musial said, yes, he remembered that danged cheapskate chicken-wire screen strung up 36-feet, 8-inches high in front of Sportsman's Park right field pavilion to keep balls out of the customers' hands. Many a time Harry Caray fell into despair: "A Musial line drive—off the screen." Now Musial laughs out loud and says, "A few more home runs, maybe. But they'd have caught a lot of popups that fell into that screen and turned into doubles."

Only 310 feet down the right field line, Sportsman's Park ran 426 deep to center and 351 to left. "Pitchers used the ballpark to their advantage," Musial says. "And that was fine with me. They pitched me away, I hit 'em away."

Two seasons in the flower of his youth, Stanley Frank Musial, the happy, simple son of a Polish immigrant, hit 'em away so often that he wound up with 20 triples. "I could run," he says on a day a half-century later. Then that wonderful laugh again: "This bad knee I have, I just had too many triples. I should've hit more home runs, so I could take it easy."

Ted Williams believes hitting a pitched baseball is the most difficult act in sports. To hit it beyond catching is to raise the difficulty exponentially. Or, to quote Musial, a .331 hitter who in 22 seasons hit 475 home runs, "A home run, you never know when it's coming."

He remembered the day he hit five home runs with a chance for a sixth in a doubleheader (May 2, 1954. In the first game he went 4-for-4 with three homers and a walk; in the second, he went 2-for-4 with another walk). "And for the first time ever," he said. "I tried to hit a home run. You can't do that. You swing too hard, you get off-stride, you take your eye off the ball. I just popped up."

Well, Stan, there was the '55 All-Star Game won by your home run on the first pitch in the 12th inning.

"The guy threw one up in my eyes," Musial says, his old-man eyes made young by the memory.

If Musial the boy recognized Babe Ruth's 60 home runs in 1927, he doesn't remember it. Even Roger Maris' 61 in '61, near the end of Musial's career, made only a passing impression because "it was all Maris, Mickey Mantle, Babe Ruth—a New York deal. This McGwire deal, it's different. It's not just New York now. The whole country's involved."

Getting involved with McGwire, Game 131: it's a McGwireFest at the ballpark. One man (blushing here) spends $126 on McGwire souvenirs before he leaves the parking lot. Everyone wears Cardinal red. When McGwire first moves to the plate, everyone stands and applauds. It's thanks for what the big man has done and for what they hope he does that night.

Jack Buck has been the Cardinals' radio voice for 34 years. "McGwire is living the role, 'Home Run Hitter,' Buck says. "He's not 'using the ballpark.' He's hitting home runs and he's hitting .295 doing it."

One man's notes on McGwire's first time up: "Relaxed, twisting, grinds hips. Outside box, holds bat straight up in front of his face. Looking at what, trademark? Soft grip. Now scratches dirt with right foot, plants left wide. Drops bat low, twitches it to and fro, a pendulum, 5/6/7 times. Brings it back and upright late, only when pitcher starts arm back."

Lesser hitters would have been ordered to get the bat back earlier. McGwire is so strong with wrists so quick that no one needs advise him on fundamentals. The second pitch McGwire sees, the home run swing identified by Musial—a long, quick, upper-cut stroke—sends a ball on a high flight toward center field. The ball seems to separate itself from gravity, rising on a tail of fire.

Buck has seen it before. "When he hits one, I first look to where I think it's going to land. Then I watch the outfielder to see where he's going. Then I look back for the ball—but McGwire hits them so high I can't find them the second time. They're so high they don't come down the way everybody else's do. I told Mark about that and he said he has the same problem."

This one comes down three feet in front of the 402-foot sign, a tall out on what becomes an 0-for-4 night.

Oh, and one thing more from Musial—this on McGwire's use of a nutritional supplement legal in baseball but banned in football and Olympic sports: "Nothing like that in my day. I'd have a steak and a couple drinks." Which caused him to laugh out loud again. "I was a low-ball hitter and a high-ball drinker," said Stan The Man.

The class of '98

So, what's next?

"My ambition is always the same, to try to get to the World Series," Mark McGwire says. "That's what we play this game for."

The number 71, does it mean anything?

"The numbers game, what I did last year, that's not going to happen every year for Mark McGwire. People have to understand that. Between 40, 50 home runs, I'm very happy there." Those are good numbers.

"Nobody thinks hitting 50 home runs is much, and I don't understand that. I don't understand why people don't want to talk about that. The first time in history, someone, me, hit 50 home runs for three straight years. One of my goals is to extend that streak."

What'd you think about the MVP thing?

"Everybody told me before I went on vacation that Sammy was going to win. I have no problem with him winning. He deserved it. What surprised me was the voting. I thought it should have been closer than 30-2. It made me think the writers were hanging out with Cheech and Chong in a room one day."

During the whole great circus, you said you wanted to see the Maris family afterward. Have you?

"I saw them during the fourth game of the World Series, but they were too far away to speak to. Maybe in spring training I can see them because they live in Florida. I'd like that."

Nice catch of that foul ball in the Series, by the way.

"Thanks. Y'know, I felt like Ferris Bueller picking up that ground ball in Wrigley Field. That's why I held it up like that."

How's life after 70?

"I was a little bit busy to the end of October. But it's been quiet since then. The biggest thing is, I can't go anywhere without being recognized. Not that that's bad. Like in Australia. I went there on vacation. Just hung out at the beach. People recognized me. But not every single day. Anyway, it made me feel good that people around the world thought that what I did was a big thing."

Do you understand, yet, what happened in '98?

"Not really. That's why I've said I wouldn't write a book because five years from now I might feel totally different from how I feel today. I don't want to write something now and as time passes come to understand it all in a better way. When I write a book, I want to walk away from it knowing it says exactly what I've come to feel."

But something extraordinary was going on, wasn't it?

"Some kind of force. That's why I said I wished every ballplayer could feel what I was feeling. You come into a visiting ballpark ... you come to a town and see in the paper, 'Come out and watch Mark McGwire take batting practice'—that just doesn't happen. But you know what? It happened to me. It's unbelievable that people across America were appreciating what we were doing. We, Sammy and me."

You're right there.

"The great thing was, it wasn't just something that Sammy and I did on our own. The fans did it, too. They were pushing us. Hey, they'd boo us if we just got a single. So many standing ovations, so many curtain calls—and in the other teams' ballparks. Like the first one, late August in Pittsburgh, I heard the cheering and I said, 'You gotta be kidding me.' The guys in the dugout said, 'Get up there.' So I did. I hope the Pirates' players didn't mind. Then again in Miami. Like, wow."

Around the All-Star break, you got edgy, you talked about being a "caged animal." But after that, you seemed to have fun. Someone said Sammy told you to just enjoy it.

"I don't know if he ever said it that way. The big thing was knowing that somebody understood what I'd been going through since January. Sammy started getting it in July. But in January, they were already asking me if I could hit 62. Then when Sammy hit 20 in June and was on his way to 66, he started seeing what I'd been going through. All of a sudden, out of nowhere, we've got these hundreds and hundreds of media following us, one group with him, one with me. Just knowing he understood it really helped me."

Could either of you have done it without the other?

"I don't think so. Here's Sammy Sosa and Mark McGwire rooting for each other rather than badgering each other. In sports today, somebody's always badgering. Like, 'You can't keep up with me; I'm better than you.' That wasn't the case with Sammy and me. We had total respect for each other. He's just as normal a guy as I am."

How these normal guys, Mark McGwire and Sammy Sosa, came to save baseball is a story so far beyond normal as to be the stuff of myth. Black and white, Dominican and American, from poverty and privilege, from hellhole and dreamland, one scuffling in grimy streets to shine shoes for $2 a week while the other sits in college classes—these are men born into parallel universes with no likelihood of meeting, let alone becoming partners in history.

All they had in common was baseball.

But then, what more did they need?

When their passion for the game finally delivered them into the same universe, they sat, improbably and delightfully, broad shoulder to broad shoulder, for a dual press conference the day after McGwire hit his 61st home run.

Sammy Sosa, the Dominican imp, then with 58 home runs himself, said, "Baseball been berry, berry good to me." His words sparkled with such sincerity and good nature that only the seriously humor-impaired could have taken offense at the self-parody.

There at Sosa's side, McGwire tilted back in laughter, gave his buddy a high-five and said, "God bless America."

Sosa said, "What a country."

What a thing these men did. Not the 70 home runs, not the 66. Good things, yes. Mighty things. But the best thing they did was bring back baseball's smile.

For that, The Sporting News is honored to honor them.

"Mark's $1 million a year commitment to helping abused children and Sammy's commitment to Dominican youth as well as his nation's relief effort after Hurricane Georges are symbolic of these men's goodwill and sportsmanship," TSN president Jim Nuckols says. "In this season when they did so much on and off the field, they were exceptionally easy choices as our Sportsmen of the Year."

Sammy Sosa's smile, soft and sweet, is an invitation to share his joy. "He comes to work every day with a smile on his face," Cubs manager Jim Riggleman says. "He has a sense of peace about him." Billy Williams, the Cubs' dugout coach, says, "This is easy for him. Shining shoes, that was the pressure."

The death of Sosa's father left his mother to raise a family of seven children. Sammy shined shoes for money to buy food. He was 14 when his older brother, Luis, saw in Sammy an athlete's body and told him to put away his shoeshine kit and go play baseball.

For young men in San Pedro de Macoris, a city of hovels made of cardboard, tin and dirt, major league baseball provides the fantasy of escape from poverty for thousands otherwise consigned to sugar cane fields and factories. Dozens of players have made the fantasy real.

In 1984, then 16, Sosa signed with the Rangers' organization for $3,500. Four seasons later, he made his big-league debut. Criticized for a lack of discipline, both at the plate and off the field, Sosa did little in the next four years with the Rangers and White Sox to suggest stardom.

That changed in 1993. In his first full season with the Cubs, Sosa hit 33 home runs and stole 36 bases, joining a small group of 30-30 players. It also was the start of a star's rise as Sosa averaged 34 homers a year from 1993 through '97, once reaching 40.

Still, as a power hitter, he was no Mark McGwire and he knew it, even in July of '98 when a 20-homer June moved him into the conversation about Roger Maris' record 61.

"Mark is my idol, and I always say Mark is the man," Sosa said then. "I've got my money on him."

Who didn't smile when we saw the big man pick up his little boy? That September night in St. Louis, diamonds of light dancing around the ballpark every time Mark McGwire stood in, we saw the 62nd scream outta there, over the left field fence, its tail on fire, gone so quick that Sammy Sosa, working right field, saw only a white blur and murmured, "Mmmmmmm," enjoying a delicious thing.

Reaching home plate that night, McGwire did what every father ought to dream of doing. He hugged his son.

Matthew McGwire is 11 years old. He lives with his mother, McGwire's ex-wife with whom he has a friend's relationship. McGwire's contract with the Cardinals reserves a seat on the team plane for Matthew. For some of the '98 season, Matthew suited up as the Cardinals' batboy.

"Our feelings, his mother's and mine, have always been to protect Matthew from the publicity," McGwire says. "I don't remember how it happened that he became our batboy, whether I said it or he did it. But all of a sudden, he was there. Now, even if I'm protecting him, I'm not going to tell him he can't be a batboy. Who wouldn't want to be a batboy?"

So the boy was at home plate. When the father brought home history, his son waited. McGwire put his hands under the batboy's arms and lifted him into the night, into noise so mighty he felt it on his chest, lifted him into the celebration, his hands full of the flesh of his flesh, and from way up there, the boy still holding onto his father's bat, Matthew looked down, saw his father's joy and answered it with a smile from here to there.

That moment was born in March when McGwire walked with his son in a little park near the boy's home.

"The week before spring training," McGwire says, "I asked Matthew, 'What do you want daddy to hit this year?' He said, 'Sixty-five.'

"I said, 'OK.' "

Just like that, a father's contract with his son.

On April 14, Matthew's first day as batboy, McGwire hit three home runs. On July 11, slumping, McGwire asked Matthew to kiss his bat—bingo, home run.

"I asked him more than once to kiss my bat and then I hit home runs," McGwire says. "I wanted him to have something to remember this season by. So now, if he mentions to his kids someday that he was there, he's got something to really tell them, doesn't he?"

Baseball's smile had gone away. The media yammered about the game's problems. Club owners held up cities for taxpayer-funded stadiums. Fans groused about $6 hot dogs eaten in the presence of players who whined about $80 million contracts.

The game we loved had been washed away in a river of bitter waters. We admitted it in 1994 when baseball did to itself what world wars and an earthquake couldn't do. The lords of the game canceled the World Series.

If the 1919 Black Sox World Series is baseball's most profound episode of shame, the 1994 season is next, a witch's brew of bile and arrogance.

Yet, optimists that we are, we hoped for better times. And we hoped with reason. Somehow, baseball always has found a way to survive the fools who run it.

We needed an antidote to 1994's poison. We needed a hero in an unheroic time. We needed someone who cared about baseball first and fame last. We needed a star who understood humility, respect, dignity. And this star should do what every great baseball hero has done: Stand in there and whale the bejeezus out of it.

In St. Louis and Chicago, there were two such men.

Mark McGwire, asked to explain the wonders of 1998, says, "Some things are unexplainable. Let's leave it unexplained."

Sammy Sosa explains, "Thank you, God."

And when it came time to light the national Christmas tree at the White House, whose smile did Hillary Clinton want to see?

Sammy Sosa's.

The First Lady is a Cubs fan of long standing. During her Central American and Caribbean tour to deliver hurricane relief, she met Sosa in the Dominican where he, too, was distributing aid. Together, they rededicated a hospital in San Pedro de Macoris, after which Mrs. Clinton invited Sosa to Washington for the tree lighting.

So last week, on the White House grounds, Sammy Sosa stood with the Clintons and said, "On behalf of my country, my people, thank you very much."

When someone in the crowd asked Sosa if he was ready for next season, he said, "I can't wait for spring training."

Might he hit 80 home runs?

One more sweet smile and he said, "I'll let you know next year."

We can't wait.

Romancing the Stone

July 30, 2001

How the writer would know is anyone's guess. But an ink-stained wretch passing through the Giants' clubhouse says Barry Bonds' black leather recliner is a $3,000 piece of furniture. It sits in front of Bonds' three lockers, a living space three times that of players whose talents, if stretched, might amount to one-third of Bonds'. In this year when all things Bonds are up for analysis, that cushy recliner has come to be symbolic of … what? Careful what we say here, for the temptation is to extrapolate from the evidence of his interior decoration that Bonds is an elitist and that the clubhouse throne represents a nature at once imperious and self-indulgent.

That temptation should be resisted. There's precedent for exalted recliner status, and it comes from a player who was admired, respected, even beloved. After his second straight Most Valuable Player season in 1983, Dale Murphy carried into the Braves' clubhouse a lordly recliner and lolled in it as his playmates plopped their lesser glutei onto wooden stools. Full of aw-shucks and golly-gee, Murphy said, "They made me bring it in here."

Well, Barry Bonds has won three MVPs, as many as any player ever, and he well might have won two or three more had he leavened his pound of crabbiness with an ounce of charm. He has won eight Gold Gloves and is the game's only player with more than 400 home runs and 400 stolen bases (nearing 500-500). With Willie Mays and Hank Aaron as his primary competition, Bonds may be the game's greatest living player.

So the question is: If two MVP seasons earned the sainted Murphy a reclining view of sweaty jockstraps, what's our problem with Barry Bonds?

Bonds says fans "think I'm arrogant. Not nice. Not fan-friendly."

In a New York Times piece last week, he despaired of "these people in the stands (who) think they can pay money and insult you all day." As for Bill Cosby's long-ago advice that Bonds should smile more: "He said just because someone's mean to you doesn't mean you have to be mean back. (But when) Bill does a rerun show, they can't yell in his face, 'This is a rerun show!' or 'I hate Jell-O!' The public has so much access to us."

There's something about Barry Bonds. There's a tightness about him, a gathering of strength and mass that is different from that in other great baseball players. He moves swiftly and surely, and yet at 6-2 and 210 pounds reminds us more of a tight end than of an outfielder fleet and graceful. The bat held 2 inches from the knob, the big man taking a little man's compact swing, Bonds hits more home runs by accident than most players hit by intent.

The tightness is psychological, as well. Bonds wears a silver cross in his left earlobe, even when playing, combative and defiant of convention. And while Bonds well knows the $3,000 recliner is a sitting-duck metaphor for journalists parachuting in to do another gifted-jerk piece, the easy chair still sits in front of his private TV, the furniture practically shouting, "I'm Barry Bonds and you're not."

We're all insecure, even (particularly?) those of us with thrones.

"I'm saying, 'God, why now? Why not in October, God?' " Bonds said last month on television. It was Bonds' admission that for all the wonders he has done, he has not done them when the air is electric with suspense. In 27 division series and NLCS games, he is hitting .196 with one home run and six runs batted in. Folks in Pittsburgh still ache to think that the Braves' lead-footed Sid Bream scored on a single to left—to Bonds, whose throw was a foot wide, a heartbeat late—and kept the Pirates out of the 1992 World Series.

Bonds admits to feeling pressure. This season he has said: "I'd really like to stop talking about homers. That would take a lot of pressure off me, ease my mind a little bit." … "The next thing you find out, you're knocking on the door and you're a little bit nervous. You find you're on center stage. You're out there by yourself alone." … "I don't like a crowd of people around. I just don't feel comfortable. I don't know if I get nervous, or if I feel choked or whatnot. It's scary."

Though he all but promises not to hit 71 home runs—"I'm not Mark McGwire"—some witnesses these days see an uppercut plane to his swing.

Some have even seen boyish and endearing joy in his demeanor, as on the night of his 500th home run when he leaped at home plate and stomped the dish with both feet.

And some believe that night was revelatory for words Bonds used in a ceremony after the home run. He thanked his parents, and he thanked Willie Mays and Willie McCovey. Then this fellow famous for surliness said to the fans at Pac Bell Park, "Most of all, thanks to all of you. I love you, and I'm proud to be in a San Francisco Giant uniform."

Ah, sweet love in the summertime.

Romantics hope it lasts into the winter.

Bonds gets the record but not the credit

NOVEMBER 12, 2001

Somehow, and it's odd, it didn't much matter if Barry Bonds did it or not. It was like the Rickey Henderson thing. Suddenly, Henderson was lionized for having scored the most runs ever. Doesn't that just mean a lot of guys got hits behind him? Granted, he long has been an offensive force in every way, but scoring runs is an orchestra's work, not a soloist's.

So as Henderson slid across home plate into the embrace of teammates with the run that put him ahead of Ty Cobb, here's what I thought: I'm historied out.

One question: Who do you want, Rickey Henderson or Ty Cobb?

Next case.

In sports today—in life today, for that matter—there's an excess of excess. Or am I the only person in America who has seen too many choreographed celebrations? We have lost the true joy of Yogi-in-Larsen's-arms spontaneity.

Even Cal Ripken Jr., who has made real history, called it "embarrassing" to hear ovations each time he came to bat on his goodbye tour. He's a baseball lifer who respects the game, and all the huzzahs, sincere though they are, have nothing to do with baseball (as a man going 2-for-48 knows).

Another question: What happened in Yankee Stadium in 1927 when Babe Ruth yanked a home run to right, his 60th, breaking his record of 59 set six years earlier?

Did Lou Gehrig fall into a love-ya-man embrace of the big galoot? Did Ty Cobb telegraph his congratulations? Did eBay auction the ball?

Crossing home plate, Ruth perfunctorily shook hands with Gehrig. Back in the dugout, out of sight, Ruth, who had been challenged by Gehrig as the game's preeminent slugger, shouted, "Sixty, count 'em, 60! Let some other (profanity deleted) match that!"

That's good ol' country hardball.

Today, we have baseball as show business.

After Barry Bonds' 70th and 71st homers, we had communal festivities with everybody out of the dugout—there to be seen in the historic gathering, there as proof of camaraderie, there with batboys, sons and daughters, wives and mothers, maybe even an Amway sales rep in the scrum.

It seemed not contrived exactly, but contrived sort of. It had been 34 years between Ruth and Roger Maris, 37 between Maris and Mark McGwire.

But it was only three years between McGwire and Bonds—too brief an interlude to create national tension about another pursuit of the home run record.

It didn't help the story, either, that Bonds is a natural loner with a sneer for those he considers his inferiors—which, to judge by the frequency of his surly behavior, seems to be most of us. Somehow this husband, father and professional athlete has reached 37 years old without learning to play with others.

The shame is, Bonds has been robbed of full credit. This year, long before the celebrations began, Bonds had proven he is one of baseball's best ever. Hitting a baseball thrown 90 mph from 60 feet, 6 inches away remains an athletic feat all but incomprehensible even to people who have done it; home runs are the ultimate wonders.

OK, you say everybody hits home runs nowadays. OK, maybe the balls are juiced, maybe players are juiced, maybe Barry Bonds' bat is cut from magic wood.

Or maybe not. Maybe baseball's world has changed in the last decade the way it changed 80 years ago. If there are three times more home runs today, maybe there are 300 times more home run swings. Maybe those swings are taken by better athletes. From a population base of 500 million-plus people of all races—in the United States, Japan and other countries—even a one-eyed scout could find more home run hitters than baseball found in the 1920s pool of fewer than 100 million American white folks.

One thing is for sure: When Mark McGwire said he had it much harder in 1998 than Bonds did this season—he was the first to chase 61, he had to endure months of pesky media scrutiny—the whining revealed McGwire to be small-minded and wrong-headed.

With Sammy Sosa as his sweetheart sidekick, endearing them both to fans everywhere, McGwire rode a wave of shared good feeling past Maris. Bonds, in contrast, was on his own. He was portrayed darkly in the news media, cast as the prima donna disliked even by teammates. He worked in a pennant race with pitchers refusing to throw him strikes. Maybe most important in any discussion of Bonds' mettle, he did the last of his great work after September 11.

Under those circumstances, a man reaching 73 home runs though he never before had hit 50 has left McGwire in the shade.

And where, you may ask, does it leave Ruth? In 1927, Ruth hit more home runs than 12 of baseball's 15 other teams. To match that mathematically, to hit more homers than 80 percent of baseball's other teams, Bonds would have needed more than 73 homers this season, more than 100, more than 150. He would have needed 208.

Could be done. But only by a real Ruthian (profanity deleted).

CHAPTER 6

One Man, Alone

Alone

He played first base and batted second against Boston righthander Johnny Sain. He went 0-for-3 against the Braves, grounding out, flying out, laying down a sacrifice and hitting into a double play.

On the cloudy and chilly Opening Day of April 15, 1947, he changed baseball forever.

Brooklyn outfielder Carl Furillo asked four decades later, "Where the hell would the big leagues be today without Jackie Robinson?"

Another question could be asked, as well. Where the hell would America be? For the first time in the 20th century, a black man had walked into a white man's world. One black man, alone, and he did a thing mightier than play baseball. He put his name in history books.

"You'll find Robinson there," broadcast journalist Howard Cosell said, "because of the bloodless social revolution he created."

Only Jackie Robinson, who did the work, could measure its pain against the joy. Only he knew the price paid and the rewards gained. Only he knew how deeply the slurs cut, for on that day in 1947, on the 16 big-league teams, Jack Roosevelt Robinson was the only black man.

One man, alone.

"If it had been me, a white man, trying to be the only one in the black leagues, I couldn't have done it," said Pee Wee Reese, the Dodgers' shortstop in 1947, now 78 years old, a Hall of Famer who put a hand on Robinson's shoulder when it helped the most. "What he had to endure, the criticism, the catcalls—I wouldn't have had the courage."

Robinson was black in a white baseball world infamous for common meanness and racial bigotry. During a 1921-44 tenure as baseball's high holy commissioner, Kenesaw Mountain Landis ordered teams to leave black players in the black leagues. In the spring of 1947, some Dodgers petitioned to have Robinson removed from the roster.

Alone, this black man heard cries of nigger, nigger, nigger. He was 28 years old in 1947, bright and handsome, a veteran of World War II, a college graduate, a powerfully built athlete who starred at UCLA in football, basketball, track and baseball. Alone, he heard nigger and coon, jungle bunny and spearchucker. He heard about white women and ropes strung over high limbs. He heard the Klan wanted him dead.

Through it all, he remembered how it started. In August 1945, Branch Rickey read to him. The Dodgers' president and general manager, as much a 19th-century preacher as a baseball man, read a passage from Giovanni Papini's book, "The Life of Christ."

Rickey began, "Ye have heard that it hath been said, 'An eye for an eye and a tooth for a tooth: But I say unto you that ye resist not evil. But whosoever shall smite thee on the right cheek, turn to him the other.'" As Rickey read, Robinson listened. For three hours, he listened. He heard Rickey go on with Papini's thought: "The results of nonresistance, even if they are not always perfect, are certainly superior to resistance or flight. To answer blows with blows, evil deeds with evil deeds, is to meet the attacker on his own ground, to proclaim oneself as low as he. Only he who has conquered himself can conquer his enemies."

Then the preacher in Rickey asked the ballplayer in Robinson, "Now, can you do it? I know you are naturally combative. But for three years—three years—you will have to do it the only way it can be done. Three years—can you do it?

"What will you do," Rickey shouted, now pacing the room, then sitting only to stand, his fists clenched, "what will you do when they call you a black son of a bitch? When they not only turn you down for a hotel room, but also curse you out?"

And Rickey put a fist in Robinson's face and screamed, "What do you do?"

Robinson's answer came in a whisper. "Mr. Rickey, I've got two cheeks. If you want to take this gamble, I'll promise you there will be no incidents."

America in the 1940s and '50s was inhospitable to blacks. South Carolina's legislature passed a World War II resolution declaring that American troops were "fighting for white supremacy." A U.S. senator from Mississippi, Theodore Bilbo, said from the Senate well, "We will tell our nigger-loving Yankee friends to go straight to hell."

The Baltimore Sun reported a scandal. It discovered that in a federal relief work camp, "colored women live in screened-in cabins." A sign on a fence in Mississippi: "Easter egg hunt, White children 9:30 a.m.—colored children 3:30 p.m." A Southern black man could expect to earn $634 a year. Throughout World War II, even as black heavyweight champion Joe Louis fought to raise money for the war effort, the Red Cross kept "white blood" and "Negro blood" in segregated containers.

After signing Robinson in 1945, Rickey sent him to the Dodgers' top minor league team in Montreal, where the manager, Clay Hopper, a Mississippian, asked, "Do you really think that a nigger is a human being?"

Before the '47 season, baseball's owners met so Rickey could ask their support for Robinson's promotion to Brooklyn. "It is the right thing to do," he said. But the 16 teams voted against the move, 15-1.

Furious, Rickey brought Robinson to spring training anyway—only to find his team in rebellion. Veteran star Dixie Walker started a petition asking that Robinson be left off the roster.

Walker and his friends are vividly portrayed by Maury Allen in the biography, "Jackie Robinson: A Life Remembered." Allen wrote, "(They) believed that taking a shower in the same large shower room with a black ballplayer would infect and contaminate them. They lived by the racial cliches of the time. They thought of blacks as slaves, a generation removed: maids, porters, local laborers, shiftless, dirty, unintelligent. Dixie Walker was a kind, decent and gentle man (who) saw no question of hatred. ... He was a God-fearing man who saw the separation of the races as part of the divine order."

When it came to God, Rickey took second to few men. He was a son of devoutly religious parents, Methodists, social liberals whose core belief was that all men are indeed created equal. So Rickey rained fire and brimstone upon the mutineers—and the Walker petition died aborning.

On April 11, 1947, the Dodgers' clubhouse man assigned Jackie

Robinson uniform number 42, gave him a locker and showed him where to put his valuables.

Because he came to the big leagues so late, Robinson played only 10 seasons. He was Rookie of the Year in '47; batting champion, stolen-base leader and MVP in '49; a record-setting fielder at second base; and a .311 hitter who played on six pennant winners and one World Series champion, stole home 19 times, scored more than 100 runs six times and in 1962 was elected to the Hall of Fame.

Roger Kahn in "The Boys of Summer" wrote: "In two seasons, 1962 and 1965, Maury Wills stole more bases than Robinson did in all of a 10-year career. Ted Williams' lifetime batting average of .344 is two points higher than Robinson's best for any season. Robinson never hit 20 home runs in a year, never batted in 125 runs. Stan Musial consistently scored more often. Having said all those things, one has not said much because troops of people who were there believe that in his prime Jackie Robinson was a better ballplayer than any of the others."

How Robinson played the game is what mattered then and matters now. He did the work as if doing the work gave him more than money and more than fame. It gave him life.

"Mr. Rickey always said Ty Cobb was the fiercest competitor he'd known," Dodgers radio broadcaster Red Barber said. "And next was Jackie."

"He was like an alley fighter, he wanted to win so bad," pitcher Preacher Roe said. "He also had the most confidence of any ballplayer I ever saw. He made an error one time in a close game I was pitching. A guy does that, he usually stays away from you on the bench the next inning. Not Jackie. He says, 'Don't worry, I'll win it for you.' Then he gets up the next inning, hits the ball out of the park, and we win it, 3-2. That was Jackie Robinson."

Joe Garagiola, a catcher with the Cardinals in the '40s, said, "Jackie was simply the most exciting player I have ever seen on the bases. ... When he got in a rundown, he would have everybody involved, including the vendors. The park would be in an uproar.

"Jackie had an inner conceit. He drove pitchers and catchers crazy. He would actually yell at the pitchers, 'I'm going, I'm going. Do anything you want, pal, you can't stop me.' Then he would go and steal the base. When he got on, it was like 'Jackie Robinson Hour.' "

Robinson's first manager in Brooklyn, Leo Durocher, said, "If I go to war, I want Jackie Robinson on my side. What a fighter."

They had called him nigger so often that Howard Cosell would say, "Baseball tortured him, tormented him. What he had to live with was the greatest debasement of a proud human being in my lifetime."

But in time they came to learn other words. They would call him righteous and fearless, intimidating and thrilling. They would call him friend. Pee Wee Reese, who proclaims no courage, was the first Dodger brave enough to treat Robinson as his equal. During games in Cincinnati and Boston, when venomous fans screamed at the black man, the white man walked across the infield and put a hand on Robinson's shoulder, teammates talking, not white and black, but a shortstop and a second baseman.

"In Atlanta for an exhibition game, Jackie got a letter saying the Klan would kill him," Reese said. "So before the game, we're warming up and I'm there by Jackie and I say, 'Damn, Jackie, get the hell away from me, will you? The guy might be a bad shot.' Jackie laughed, and we went on warming up."

Old enemies came to understand. "In 1965, I went to Mr. Rickey's funeral," said Bobby Bragan, who had signed the Walker petition, "and I sat next to Jackie. We shook hands warmly. I don't think either of us thought anything of it, or of the past. It was a new time. I changed. Jackie changed. The world changed."

Bragan changed, the world changed. Jackie Robinson remained Jackie Robinson. Columnist Red Smith wrote that Robinson "established the black man's right to play second base. He fought for the black man's right to a place in the white community, and he never lost sight of that goal."

After leaving baseball, Robinson sought black empowerment through politics and economics. At the 1972 World Series, baseball honored his work against drug addiction; in his response, Robinson said he hoped, someday, to see a black manager. (Frank Robinson would be the first, in 1975.)

That was October 15, 1972. Robinson was sick. Only 53 years old, heavy and weak, his hair white, blind in one eye, losing the sight of the other, he had survived a heart attack and lived with the ravages of diabetes and high blood pressure. Robinson said, "I've got nothing to complain about."

On October 24, he died.

It is September 30, 1951, late on a gloomy afternoon, the 12th inning of a game the Dodgers must win or give the pennant to the Giants. With two outs and the bases loaded, Philadelphia's Eddie Waitkus lines a shot up the middle.

Red Smith wrote of that moment, "The ball is a blur passing second base, difficult to follow in the half-light, impossible to catch. Jackie Robinson catches it. He flings himself headlong at right angles to the flight of the ball; for an instant his body is suspended in midair, then somehow the outstretched glove intercepts the ball inches off the ground."

And two innings later, Robinson wins the game with a home run to set up baseball's most memorable playoff.

"Of all the pictures Jackie Robinson left upon memory," Smith wrote at the great man's death, "the one that will always flash back first shows him stretched at full length in the insubstantial twilight, the unconquerable doing the impossible."

Playing ball for the fun of it

SEPTEMBER 5, 1994

All he ever wanted to do was play ball and he got to do plenty of that, even if it paid him nothing for a long time before he worked up to $700 a month in the Negro American League.

So Buck O'Neil was a happy man in the 1930s, and he is a happy man all these years later. This fall he will become a star when the Ken Burns documentary on baseball gives him room to tell us what the game was like, for black players and black fans, in a time when Americans lived in separate worlds under separate laws.

John Jordan (Buck) O'Neil is 82 years old. Ask him why baseball means so much to so many people and he say, "Baseball is the American sport. Really, everybody knows baseball. There's just something there that belongs to us.

"You can tell because, I don't care how good a player is, there are people up in the bleachers watching him and saying, 'I could do that.' They're not saying that about 7-foot basketball players dunking balls, and they're not saying that about 300-pound football players. But baseball, they say, 'That sucker do that, I can do that.'"

Buck O'Neil was laughing out loud, his laughter a wonderful sound in these miserable days for major league baseball. These days are this miserable: What Hitler couldn't do, the men and women who own today's teams are about to do—stop the World Series. If the owners do that, they prove beyond doubt they are fools beyond repair.

Yes, what a joy in this dead summer of 1994 to hear Buck O'Neil remember a glorious summer day in 1946 when he came to bat needing a triple to do something he had never seen anyone do.

"First time up, I had the single," he says. "Then the home run over the left-field fence. We were playing in Memphis, the Memphis Red Sox. After that, the double.

"The last time up, I wanted that triple. I hit the ball with a good swing and it was headed toward left-center field where the power alley was 375 feet. I was running saying, 'Don't go out, don't go out, don't go out.'"

A half-century later, Buck O'Neil still sees that ball flying to left center. He laughed again as he spoke across time to the distant baseball. Don't go out, don't go …

"It hit off the top of that fence and bounced back between the center fielder and left fielder. I wanted that triple, so I was running to third no matter what happened.

"Got to third easy. Got there standing up, if you want to know. I could have probably gone on around to home. But I stopped there. I wanted to hit for the cycle because I had never even known anybody who did it."

Because he was black, Buck O'Neil never played in what white America knows as baseball's major leagues. He worked in the Negro American League for 17 seasons as a first baseman and later as manager for the Kansas City Monarchs, the league's royalty. By the time the white folks of America decided to allow African Americans in their baseball leagues, Buck O'Neil was too old.

He would have liked to have been there with Jackie Robinson and Larry Doby and Monte Irvin. But his time as a player had come and gone. Even leading the Negro A.L. in hitting in 1946 did him no good; he hit .353 at age 34. His only regret, all these years later, is that integration of major league baseball killed the Negro Leagues.

"First, what's important for people to know is that Negro League baseball wasn't 'The Bingo Long Traveling All-Star and Motor Kings,'" says O'Neil, naming a 1976 movie about barnstormers in broken-down buses. "Negro League baseball wasn't anything like that. It was like the white major leagues, serious baseball, well organized.

"There were 16 Negro League ballclubs, each with at least 15 players—the Monarchs had 18 players. There were all those people putting on the games, booking agents, traveling secretaries, trainers. Baseball was black entertainment and was important to black communities.

"We were very happy that integration happened, but it killed our business. Thing is, it could have been done a different way. Clubs like the Monarchs could have been used as farm clubs for the major leagues. But our businesses were taken away from us and there was nothing we could do about it. Nothing we could do against corporate America. So integration was a bittersweet thing."

Though he said it again, slowly, "Bitter … sweet," Buck O'Neil asks to be understood: He enjoyed every day of his baseball life. He left Sarasota, Fla., to play in the Negro minor leagues at Shreveport, La., where, on some nights, if any tickets were sold, he was paid 50 cents a game.

"The happiest day of my life was coming to play with the Kansas City Monarchs," he says. "It would be like a white boy going to play for the New York Yankees."

He dreamed of becoming a manager because, in his boyhood around Florida spring training camps, Buck O'Neil had seen John McGraw managing the Giants and Connie Mack waving his scorecard from the Athletics' dugout.

"The idea of managing fascinated me," says O'Neil, who in time won five Negro league championships and two World Series managing players named Ernie Banks, Elston Howard and Hank Thompson. In 1962, O'Neil was hired by the Cubs, the first black coach in the big leagues. He now is active in building a Negro Leagues museum in Kansas City.

A baseball life 82 years in the making, and one night not long ago, all these years after Sarasota, after Jim Crow, after lives in parallel universes, John Jordan (Buck) O'Neil came to stand on a stage with Ted Williams and Mickey Mantle, heroes talking baseball. O'Neil stood there proudly and told anyone who would listen that the old days weren't hurtful. He said, "It was the time of our lives. All we wanted to do was play. We loved baseball."

From miner to majors

Of the segregation that kept baseball white, the grand old man Piper Davis said, "Wasn't the game's fault." Of his years in the Negro Leagues, trapped in a parallel universe, he said, "Wasn't no crusading." Asked how he could have placed no blame and felt no need to right obvious wrongs, Piper Davis said, "We looked to play ball, is all. We knew what we could do."

There it is, truth stronger than fact.

If white folks didn't want to let Piper Davis play baseball with them, their actions said more about them than about him. Their loss. "Fun, is what we had," he said.

Piper Davis' death last month at 79 is reason to ask: Did anybody ever enjoy baseball more?

The last time I saw him, eight years ago, memories of base hits a half-century old moved him to glorious laughter. "Praise the Lord," he said, "baseball got me out of the mines and into the sunlight."

His father was a miner for the Piper Coal Company. They lived in the company town, Piper, south of Birmingham. The town is not on Alabama's map today because it disappeared when there was no more blessed/cursed coal to be scratched out by men lowered into the earth at the end of a rope.

124

A lucky man could make a dollar a day in the mines during the Depression of the 1930s. So, as his father had done, Lorenzo Davis became a miner because he had to. An unlucky man could be killed by a cave-in or by fire or by gases.

In three months, Davis quit. "I was afraid," he said. Besides, there was baseball to play.

An infielder with speed and power, he left home at 19 to play in Nebraska and soon became a Negro American League star alongside Satchel Paige, Josh Gibson and Cool Papa Bell. "Hit everywhere from .275 up," Davis said. "Be a million-dollar ballplayer today."

Instead, he made $350 a month as one of the hundreds of Negro Leaguers who loved the same game white folks did and played it in an America divided into black and white by law and custom.

Jim Crow laws said black people couldn't eat in some places, couldn't drink water from some public fountains, couldn't sleep in some buildings.

Baseball's segregation, not a matter of law, may have been made of the sterner stuff of hide-bound custom. Davis fought no civil-rights fights. He only wanted to play for the Birmingham Black Barons, identified by the adjective to separate them from the city's Barons in that other universe.

"Wasn't nothing the white Barons did, we couldn't do," Davis said. "We outdrew 'em playing in the same ballpark. We'd have a few whites come to see us, couple hundred a night. They appreciated good ball."

During World War II, Davis even played basketball for the Harlem Globetrotters, two games a day for $300 a month with $2 a day meal money and another dollar if you would ride the bus all night rather than sleep in a hotel. "The business manager of the Black Barons was also the manager of the Globetrotters, Abe Saperstein," he said. "I was in the biggest black cafe in Birmingham, Bob's Savoy Cafe. The owner, Bob Williams, told Saperstein, 'This boy Davis can play basketball, too.' "

In 1950, three years after Jackie Robinson joined the Dodgers, Davis entered the white man's leagues, signing with the Red Sox organization. Then 32, Davis reported to a Class-A team where for a month he led the team in hitting, home runs, runs batted in and stolen bases. "The deal was, if I was with the organization after May 15, certain things would happen," Davis said, meaning a pay raise and promotion. "On May 15, they handed me my paycheck for $500 and said the general manager wanted to see me. I figured I'd be moving up to Triple-A. But he said, 'We got to let you go.' I said, 'For what, man?' 'Economical conditions,' is all he said."

Maybe it was money, maybe race. The Red Sox were infamous for making decisions based on both. Piper Davis said only, "Too old, I guess."

But he was not too old to play another seven years, six in Class-AAA ball. One of his managers along the way, the Hall of Fame hitter Mel Ott, once used Davis at all nine positions in a game and afterward said, "Piper Davis is the best all-around player I ever saw."

Nice words, but Davis knew better. "I'd seen Willie Mays," he said.

As player/manager of the Black Barons in 1948, Davis had heard of the teenager Willie Mays, whose father, so quick he was known as Kitty Cat, had been an industrial-league star in Birmingham.

"Willie was 17, thereabouts, 11th grade in school," Davis said. "I had the Black Barons up to Chattanooga. I had a fella pick up ballplayers and bring 'em to the game. So I see this li'l ol' boy out of high school and I say to him, 'Don't you know if they catch you out here playing ball for money, they won't let you play high school ball no more?' And Willie says, 'I don't care.' So I called Cat, and Cat says if Willie wants to play, let him play. I let him play the second game of a doubleheader out in left field. My center fielder could out-run Willie, but he couldn't out-throw him.

"Next day, I put the lineup up in the dugout, and I got Willie in center field. I'm out on the field, and I can see the fellas in the dugout saying, 'What's wrong with Piper, putting that li'l ol' boy out in center field?'

"Well, Willie was pretty good right off. I had to do some corrections with his throwing, coming in on balls, hit the cutoff man, like that. I didn't bother with his hitting.

"Yes, sir. Willie's my man. Came into home plate one day in Memphis and the catcher was blocking the plate. So Willie went into him with his spikes. Ripped the catcher's pants from under his crotch down to his knees. After that, nobody tried to block the plate on Willie Mays."

A face to remember

JUNE 14, 1999

We're sitting with Hank Aaron in his office, which seems not so much anchored to the glass and steel of the Braves' executive suite as it seems to float over left field, the better for the great man to survey the world he helped make. It's lunchtime, and a friend delivers Chinese, which Aaron offers to share.

"Just had a cheeseburger," a visitor says.

"Gotta stay away from those things," Aaron says. "That, and all this running around, isn't good for the waistline."

In the 25th year after Aaron's 715th home run, major league baseball folks have done a good and overdue thing. They've said thanks to Aaron. They've asked him to come to their ballparks so they can honor him for the work he did. They have Hammerin' Hank running around America.

"Hard to believe," he says, "that it was 25 years ago when we were across the street." Across the street, now gone, dynamited to make room for a parking lot, stood Atlanta-Fulton County Stadium. The baseball ground is outlined in white on the asphalt with a plaque marking the flight of the 715th.

"I see that and I think, 'Was I really standing there? Were there really 54,000 people there?' It's like it might have been a dream. So you're happy

127

and pleased that so many people remember it really happened."

In Kansas City, there is an extraordinary photograph that ought to be seen by everyone who knows, or wants to know, what Hank Aaron made happen in baseball and America.

The picture is on a wall in the Negro Leagues Baseball Museum, a beautiful building at 18th and Vine streets in a Kansas City neighborhood once the Midwest's answer to jazzy Harlem.

Because the museum is so full of fascinating stuff, the picture could be overlooked. It's one of those grainy black-and-white photos that suggests a forgotten time. But there's an arresting quality to the image of a young man standing alone outside a railroad station. His eyes are narrowed, as if against a harsh sun or gritty dust from the railbed.

Although there's no one else in the picture, the feeling it conveys is not so much loneliness as solitariness. Then you read the caption. It identifies the young man as Hank Aaron at age 15.

"A rare photo," says Bob Kendrick, the museum's director of marketing. "I don't think Hank knows we have it."

You stand there a long time. You see how thin Aaron was and you see the strength in his forearms. You see that face. An amazing thing, that face. The longer you look, the more extraordinary that face is. Even then it is the face of the man we all would come to know, a man of uncommon grace and dignity.

What a picture. At first, it's just a young man facing the camera. You figure he's about to catch a train to somewhere, alone, about to begin the adventure of his life, maybe frightened, maybe homesick before the train even arrives at the station, let alone leaves.

Then you look into the young Aaron's eyes, and you see him looking back at you, and you know he didn't so much as blink once when the photographer pointed the camera at him.

There's an assurance there. Not a cockiness, not any suggestion of false bravado. Aaron is simply there, looking into the camera, steady and calm, sure of who he is, as if on that day at the railroad station, he already knows how it's going to turn out.

"I haven't seen that picture," Hank Aaron says at age 64. "But I'd say it was taken when I was leaving home for the first time."

He thinks he must have been 18, not 15. A skinny shortstop who hit cross-handed, he'd been signed to a $200-a-month contract by the

Indianapolis Clowns of the Negro American League. He was headed to the Clowns' spring training camp in Winston-Salem, N.C.

"I might have been scared," Aaron says. "But I felt all right because I had in my mind what I wanted to do. At that time, there hadn't been many other black players make it out of Mobile (Ala.) to pro ball. I was determined to give it everything I had to be successful."

He was 20, a rookie with the Braves in 1954, when the Dodgers played Milwaukee in a spring training game. Heaven. His ambition had been to play alongside his hero, Jackie Robinson. Now Robinson saw Aaron play and told a reporter, "You're going to be watching him hit for a long time."

Only an amazing man could live through 17 at-bats against the fearsome Don Drysdale, let alone hit 17 home runs. Henry Aaron did that. By the time he quit in 1976, he had 722 more total bases than anyone who ever played. Another 265 home runs and Babe Ruth would still be three bases behind Aaron.

We're in Hank Aaron's office, talking baseball, when the talk turns to Willie Mays. One of Aaron's teammates, Hall of Fame third baseman Eddie Mathews, always said Hank could outrun Willie; he just didn't lose his cap doing it.

"I don't think there was anything Willie could do that I couldn't do," Hank Aaron says. "He didn't run the bases any better than me. It's just that I'd do it with no flair. And I was always a better hitter than Willie. That's a given."

CHAPTER 7

Progress of the Seasons

April

Ah, April and baseball's back.

All seven batters struck out by San Francisco pitcher John Burkett were caught looking. As to whether this is a record for righthanders in turtleneck shirts on 52-degree nights near a body of water, we'll know next spring when Seymour Siwoff and Bill James bury us with decimal points. Right now, we know only that seven caught-lookings is unusual. As Atlanta rookie Greg McMichael says, "In all my two weeks in the big leagues, I've never seen anything like it."

Two Atlanta gentlemen were kicked out of the game for suggesting to umpire Mark Hirschbeck that the caught-lookings were more his mistakes than theirs. These gentlemen believed Hirschbeck had called strikes on pitches so far outside they could be reached only by hitters willing to leap across the plate, Roberto Clemente-like, and then throw their bats, Yogi Berra-like, at the speeding baseball. A ninth-inning dispute brought the Atlanta team out of the dugout. Players stood behind manager Bobby Cox. The skipper took off his cap. He took off his glasses. Then he took off after Hirschbeck, who did a Mr. Umpire thing. He took off his mask and put on an attitude. The attitude was approximately this: Out of my face or I'll slap the cuffs on

133

you and you'll spend a month of Sundays in the Crossbar Hotel.

Ah, April. Sweet spring. Blue mornings and starry evenings. The ball-parks are alive with folks wanting to murderize umpires.

Forget hockey. Forget basketball. Forget Reggie White waiting for heavenly advice about where he should bash heads. Forget 'em because it's April, and baseball stuff is happening. Wonderful stuff, inexplicable and fabulous stuff, is happening in America's ballparks.

The biggest crowd in history sees the Colorado Rockies. Sparky Anderson wins his 2,000th game and his Tigers score 20 runs twice in five days. Carlos Baerga switch-hits home runs in the same inning. Nobody had done that, just as no one with a plastic hip had hit a home run in his first at-bat after surgery until Bo Jackson.

And Burkett racked up seven called strikeouts. He is a nice pitcher with good control. But numbers show he strikes out four men every nine innings. What he did to Atlanta, then, was unusual on several levels.

It was as if Burkett had been transformed into Walter Johnson, only better. Or maybe he discovered, seeping through the San Andreas fault, an ointment from the middle of Earth that made baseballs invisible to everyone except the all-seeing, all-knowing Hirschbeck.

There are other possibilities. Perhaps the Atlanta hitters had come down with Lou Novikoff disease. "The Mad Russian," as Novikoff was called when he came up to the Chicago Cubs in the early 1940s, developed the distressing habit of watching third strikes. To encourage Novikoff to be aggressive, Cubs owner Philip K. Wrigley paid Novikoff $5 if he struck out swinging. After hacking at a pitch over his head, Novikoff trudged to the dugout only to hear coach Charlie Grimm call out, "You must be awful short of dough."

Perhaps, in this curious Atlanta case, the shape of home plate kept changing, as if it were part of a Salvador Dali painting in which reality melts sideways. Yes. Perhaps a corner of the plate melted and flowed an extra foot away from the hitters. Then Burkett's pitches would be so far from reach that not even a big league hitter would consider swinging. But Hirschbeck, infallible by his decree, would see the plate melting sideways and declare the pitches strikes.

Ah, April. Wonderful things happen. Things that happen in a context 100 years in the making. Things we understand when they happen, but things we can't know will happen.

Look. The other night Cincinnati led St. Louis, 4-1. St. Louis had the bases loaded. Two outs. Last of the ninth. Then pinch-hitter Luis Alicea's single, bounced between first and second, scored two runs.

Cincinnati right fielder Reggie Sanders should have thrown to third base to keep the tying run at second. Instead he threw home. Pitcher Rob Dibble cut off the throw. Dibble shouldn't have been there. He should have backed up third.

Dibble threw to third trying to get Ray Lankford. The throw went wild, bouncing into the bullpen. So Lankford headed home with the tying run— when a wonderful thing happened.

Left fielder Cesar Hernandez, in the game as a late-inning defensive substitute, alert enough to back up third base, picked up Dibble's wild throw and threw out Lankford. The Reds won, 4-3.

So: 11 players were involved. Four St. Louis runners sprinted around the bases; four Cincinnati fielders touched the ball (Dibble twice, with three other Reds lunging at it); two runs scored; Lankford slid both at third and home; the Reds made three fundamental fielding mistakes, and they made one brilliant defensive play that brought the game to a mad, crashing, grand conclusion the likes of which has been seen only by folks who remember the last time they saw a 9-1-7-2 putout.

April in the ballpark, even with Mr. Umpire, is better than almost anytime anywhere else. In Baltimore's Camden Yards the other day, Mike Devereaux's apparent game-tying, eighth-inning single became a bases-loaded, rally-killing double play. Somehow three Orioles wanted to be on third base at the same time.

Here we are, baseball in April of 1993, and we can connect Camden Yards to Ebbets Field, where in 1926 the Dodgers hero Babe Herman smote a long one with the bases loaded. Before everyone was done running, Babe wound up on third base. So, alas, did two other runners, a highly illegal circumstance which gave John Lardner reason to write of Babe, "He never tripled into a triple play, but he once doubled into a double play, which is the next best thing."

Baseball's corny, but . . .

It's corny, but irresistible. Kids at the ballpark. Painted-face kids with intertwined NYs on their rosy cheeks. Kids carrying baseball gloves big enough to use as pillows later (much later, in the car, going home).

At Yankee Stadium, a boy had taken a Yankees jersey and a Mets jersey, cut them in two and sewn them together to make—what, a Metsees jersey? When the going got tough, a girl with pigtails popping from under her Mets cap crossed all four fingers on both hands, four pairs of good-luck talismans, and laid her chin on them to wait. Wonder if she had her toes crossed, too. Kids at the ballpark. Kids of all ages. Do you remember July 30, 1949? Bud Selig does. It was his 15th birthday. All these years later, he can stand behind home plate at Yankee Stadium and point to where he sat that day. "Up there," the baseball commissioner said, lifting high his left arm toward the right field upper-deck seats, halfway out. "The Cleveland Indians played the Yankees. I think Bobby Avila may have hit a couple home runs." (Or may not have; in only 14 at-bats that year, Avila had no home runs.)

The boy Bud Selig had come to New York in '49 with his mother, Marie, a teacher, who preferred art museums but indulged her son's passion for baseball. "She brought me for my birthday, but she said, 'I'm not doing this anymore. If you go, you go by yourself.' So I went all by myself—on the subway—even though my mother grumbled."

The boy's subway series of adventures included that '49 birthday when he sat in the upper deck and saw, being wheeled onto the field, a giant birthday cake. Among his thoughts just then: "How'd they know? For me?" Only to discover the cake was for another eternally young boy, the Yankees' manager, Casey Stengel.

It's corny, and delicious, to consider hot dogs. What's a World Series without kids and without hot dogs?

Try this: Walk through Yankee Stadium and don't stop for a hot dog. Even if you've eaten in the previous hour, even if you're on a mission to buy a cap for a niece, even if the hot dog lines are so long they curl sideways in the ancient corridors at Yankee Stadium—you cannot not buy a hot dog at the World Series, especially in "The House Where Ruth Ate a Thousand Hot Dogs."

With mustard, please.

And gimme one of those pretzels the size of Idaho.

More mustard, please.

It's corny, all this, and we love it because it speaks to a moment's pleasure in ways we may not fully understand other than to know that somehow there is something here that feels just right. Somehow, a good shortstop fielding a hard-hit ball in the hole will throw out a good runner at first by a half step. As it was so on Bud Selig's 15th birthday, it's so today when Derek Jeter rights himself on the left field grass and guns out Edgardo Alfonzo.

Mrs. Selig can have her art museums, which are useful to unfortunate souls whose isolated lives have deprived them of the beauty of a double play completed under pressure. Game 1, last of the 10th inning (free baseball!), bases loaded, one out, the Yankees with victory for the taking—only Paul O'Neill's two-hopper becomes a 4-6-3 double play, the second baseman Alfonzo and shortstop Kurt Abbott moving so swiftly, gracefully and surely with such economy of motion that the complexity of their performance goes all but unnoticed.

Mrs. Selig's son, rightly preferring Yankee Stadium to the Guggenheim, this time rode by chauffeured car to the ballpark. And he sat not in high right field but near enough the catcher to hear baseballs clanging off Todd Pratt's mask when they weren't clanging off his elbow. By then the commissioner had done his own good work—by deciding to honor the sailors of the USS Cole in a pregame ceremony.

"We'd thought about it," Selig said, "but we didn't want to, well ..." He searched for a word. "We didn't want to be insensitive." Selig had been concerned that a World Series ceremony dedicated to the Cole might be seen as exploitive of the tragedy in Yemen, where 17 U.S. Navy service men and women were killed by a terrorist bomb on October 12.

But after William Rhoden of The New York Times spoke to Navy officials at the Cole's home port in Norfolk, Va.—home of the Mets' Class-AAA farm team—the commanders there told Selig they'd be flattered to be honored at the Series.

"They're 'flattered'?" Selig said. "We're the ones flattered."

Vance Wilson, the Mets' third-string catcher, spent most of this season at Norfolk. Injured and not on the Series roster but in uniform, he sat in the dugout before Game 1. He looked toward center field and saw the American flag at half-staff.

"My best friend is a Marine who served in the Mediterranean," he said. "I know how bad I'd feel if he'd been one of those 17 people. So it's great we're honoring the Cole. Just seeing the sailors around Norfolk was inspiring, their discipline and all. Those are America's sons, daughters, fathers, husbands—we need to honor them all the time, not just when its tragic. What they do, to give us freedom, is something we'll never be able to repay them for."

That night, corny as it sounds, wonderful as it sounds, Wilson paid particular attention to the words of our national anthem. He said, "When you hear 'perilous fight' and 'bombs bursting' and 'home of the brave,' I mean, whoa."

Talkin' baseball

OCTOBER 25, 1993

We're talking baseball. We're standing by the cage, talking country hard ball with the old banger from Binger, Johnny Bench who once said his Oklahoma hometown is so small they saved money by putting CITY LIMITS on both sides of the same sign. We're standing by the cage at the World Series talking catching with the best there ever was, Johnny Bench saying there are two ways to catch: "Either you do it by the Spalding Guide ABCs," he said, "or you do it the way my father told me: 'Just go back there and catch every ball,' " which for 20 years the obedient son did with such efficiency and flair that the silver-haired orator, Mr. Sparky Anderson, once admonished a reporter. "Don't compare nobody to Johnny Bench. You just embarrass that guy."

We're talking baseball at the World Series. We're talking Robby Alomar. A scout saw him at age 13 and said, "He played with the ball; the ball didn't play with him." Tony Gwynn saw Alomar at 20 and said, "A real natural swing, real fluid, real to the point." Now 24, Alomar has done so many wonders at second base and at bat that Toronto's manager, Cito Gaston, said the Hall of Fame words and this: "He knows the play he wants to make before it happens." We're talking Robby Alomar, who caught a line drive that passed

139

over his first baseman's head and said, "I don't know how I did it, but I did it and when I did it I began laughing. How'd I do that?"

We're talking the future. The future is now. The SkyDome. What a place. Play all the World Series here. Be fine with me. Restaurants in the outfield. Hotels in the upper deck. TV screen big as Utah in center field and there was Joe Carter, 55 feet tall, talking to us as Joe Carter, 6-foot-3, stood at home plate waiting for the larger Joe Carter to please shaddup. OK. The future is here: Give us interleague play. Give the N.L. the D.H. Let's get on with it.

We're talking how ugly are these Phillies? The Toronto Sun asked its readers. A Mike Batty replied, "So ugly their mothers wrap their sandwiches in road maps."

Talking baseball. Talking Robby Alomar, Hall of Famer who did a bone-head thing in Game 2. Got picked off second, carrying a big run in the eighth inning. Picked off by Mitch Williams' predictable spin move. Talking to Robby Alomar, who made no excuses: "I should have stayed at second. Shouldn't have done it. After, I knew. It's behind my back now. Can't do nothing about it. Big mistake on my part."

We're talking hardball with Lenny Dykstra, who said it was about time he made two good catches in Game 2. "I proved I could play center field with them two plays," he said. While at it, Dykstra also told us he certainly could hit, hit with power, run, run with speed and do just about anything that Hall of Famer Rickey Henderson ever thought of doing. Amazingly, Dykstra said all that without once sprayin' foul liquids on innocent passers-by.

We're asking Johnny Bench the toughest pitcher he ever caught. Not a knuckleballer. "Sparky one time told me they were thinking about trading for Phil Niekro. I told him, 'Trade for his catcher, too, because I'm not going back there.' Toughest one for me was Wayne Simpson. Threw 95 miles per hour and he never knew which way the ball would move. It might move four ways at once. I'd be about to catch it and it'd dart down. After Wayne's games, my palm was swollen twice its normal size."

So a Toronto newspaper columnist, a friendly, goes to John Olerud, the squeaky-clean, low-key, batting champion/first baseman of the Blue Jays. She says to the choir boy, "The Phillies come in with the reputation of bad guys. What's the baddest thing you've every done, John?"

Olerud is mystified. He wants to help the friendly reporter. You can see him trying. His delicate brow becomes furrowed. He is riffling through the file of crimes he has committed. He begins to speak.

He says, "Gee, what a question."

"Really, the baddest thing," the reporter says before giving up and moving to an alternate line of questioning: "How about superstitions? You do any really odd things?"

Olerud raises an eyebrow. It's in his upbringing to help those who ask for help. He really wants to help. You wonder what he'll come up with. Will he confess to pulling Peggy Sue's pigtails that day in second grade? Will he say he sometimes wears socks of different thicknesses? Does he leave his bubble gum on the bedpost overnight before big games?

He finally smiles. Here it comes. And he says, "I've just got no good answer."

So the phone rings. This is when Philadelphia eliminates Atlanta in the N.L. playoffs. You remember Atlanta. I remember Atlanta. I called Atlanta the best team since the Yankees of Mantle, Berra & Ford. Then Philadelphia beats this team for the ages in six games. And no sooner is the foul deed completed than the phone rings.

A voice on the phone says, "This is Ernestine, the telephone operator. I have a collect call from Mr. Sparky Anderson, Mr. Anderson says he is calling on behalf of the Big Red Machine. Mr. Anderson says, no, he is not a tractor salesman. He says we're talking baseball. Says the Big Red Machine would have Atlanta for breakfast, lunch and dinner. He wants to speak to Mr. Kindred. Are you the gentleman to whom I am speaking? Are you Mr. Kindred?"

I say, "Never heard of him."

Baseball's best moment is now

OCTOBER 4, 1993

September becomes October and baseball's long season grows desperately wonderfully breathtakingly short.

Spring becomes summer becomes the World Series and anxiety runs so high that one year, still an hour before the Fall Classic would begin, Baltimore outfielder Curt Blefary said, "If this damned thing doesn't start soon, I'm going to fly straight up in the air."

Author Jonathan Yardley, an Orioles fan, recognizes only two seasons in sports. He says there is baseball season after which comes The Void. Only fools would argue with such a wise man. And in the epic war that baseball's thousand little battles become, there is no better moment than September becoming October, every scene a drama from which we dare not move our eyes. It's September 25, 1993, in Philadelphia, eighth inning, nobody out, Atlanta with a man on third, leading by a run, when shortstop Jeff Blauser pops up.

Just another pop-up, one of hundreds a team hits. Chances are Blauser did it in April and no one, except perhaps an infielder, watched the ball fall out of the sky.

But Blauser's pop-up is in the September air and it's different now. The second baseman backpedals into short right, calling. It's a one-run game and Atlanta sprinter Otis Nixon is on third. With the heat of the order coming up, would Nixon dare try to score? A sacrifice fly to the second baseman?

Little truths add up in baseball. The little thing you learn in April, when there is no drama in a pop-up, can become big in September. You learn that Otis Nixon can fly. And now the Phillies make a mistake. The second baseman shouldn't catch this pop-up. It's the right fielder's ball because his momentum moves him forward; Nixon wouldn't run on an outfielder 150 feet away.

But when Atlanta's third-base coach, Jimy Williams, sees the second baseman calling, the coach shouts at Nixon, a few steps down the line.

Tag up, the coach says.

It's September.

We're daring 'em now.

Because the second baseman's throw can be no more than a lob, Nixon scores. And somehow, in a way athletes understand instinctively, victory is decided on Nixon's dare. How can a team lose when it scores a pennant-race run on pop-up to second baseman? Next pitch, Ron Gant's home run makes it 9-6 and Atlanta wins, 9-7.

"To be in a pennant race," Otis Nixon says, "this is what baseball is all about."

September becoming October, pennant races becoming a World Series, men becoming boys chasing dreams.

Gabby Hartnett said, "Blood rushes out of your head and you get dizzy." Mickey Mantle wept all the way home on the Yankees' plane after the 1960 World Series. Trying to catch the Dodgers in 1966, Willie Mays scored from first on a September 12th-inning single and the great man said he ran all that way for one reason, running ahead of throws, running on a bad leg, daring lesser men to beat him—Mays did it for one reason: "We had a plane to catch," he said, "and it was time to get it over with."

Always the hero of his own stories, Reggie Jackson remembers his first September in New York, a night when Yankee Stadium seemed "part Broadway opening, part Fourth of July fireworks in Central Park, part heavyweight championship fight." Ninth inning against Boston, scoreless, and Thurman Munson tells Reggie, "I'm going to single between first and third, and then you get me home." So Reggie hits a 430-foot home run and says he circled the bases thinking, "I wanted to have a microphone in my hands to say to the people, 'This is why I came here. This is why they pay me the money.' "

Spring becomes summer becomes the end for Nolan Ryan. In 27 seasons, he threw 100,000 pitches. They flew 1,145 miles. At 90 miles per hour, they stayed in the air 13 hours. Alas, George Brett told us good-bye, too, a catch in his voice. What a piece of work, George Brett: an absolutely beautiful hitter. And an imp, a perpetual boy. Only George could have told us about his hemorrhoids this way: "My troubles," he said, "are behind me."

September becomes October becomes a beginning for Tom Glavine. The Atlanta lefthander, born in 1966, Ryan's second pro season, now has won 20 games three straight seasons. That's good work never done by Ryan, never done by Steve Carlton, never done by 18 pitchers in the Hall of Fame (among them Sandy Koufax, Don Drysdale, Tom Seaver and Whitey Ford).

"All I'm thinking about now," Glavine said, turning away talk of a Cy Young Award, "is winning the pennant."

Earl Weaver, the Baltimore manager, had thoughts of a pennant in mind one night in 1974. He closed a hotel bar at 1:45 a.m. and stepped onto an escalator. There he saw his catcher, Earl Williams, an exasperating character who could, Weaver never forgot, hit you a three-run homer.

"Hey, Earl," the manager said.

"Hi, skip," the catcher said.

"Where are you going?"

"I'm going out."

"It's 1:45."

"I've got plenty of time," the catcher said. "I don't have to be anywhere until 2."

Weaver was at the top of the escalator and Williams at the bottom when the manager thought to say one more thing. He told the catcher to remember there was a game that afternoon.

CHAPTER 8

The Craft

Home runs

Against an everyday major league pitch thrown 85 mph, a bat must move 76 mph to hit a baseball 400 feet. To send that same pitch 450 feet, the bat must reach 86 mph. That's an increase in bat speed of 13 percent with a resulting 28 percent jump in energy. "This is a very large difference," says Robert K. Adair, a Yale University professor who wrote a book on baseball's physics, "and we estimate that 450 feet is the human limit under such standard conditions."

So far, then, eight men this season have proven themselves more than human. They have hit home runs ranging from 464 to 538 feet. The A's big man, Mark McGwire, has home runs of 464, 485, 514 and 538 feet.

The professor gives his theory some wiggle room. If a pitch arrives at 95 mph and the hitter has a 10-mph following wind on a 100-degree day in a city high above sea level, then maybe a ball could fly 545 feet.

"And if the foreman in the ball-manufacturing factory had set the tension on the winding machine too high one afternoon so as to generate a gross of rabbit balls," Adair says, "who is to say how far one of those balls might go off a strong hitter's bat?"

With a chuckle, the professor says, "In Denver, under the right conditions, Andres Galarraga might reach Kansas."

We're talking home runs because McGwire has Babe Ruth and Roger Maris in mind. And three weeks ago McGwire hit his 538-footer with no following wind, at room temperature, at sea level—albeit off a 97 mph laser leaving Randy Johnson's ray gun.

Have you, dear reader, ever hit one out? Felt good, didn't it?

The temptation, by a banjo-hitting infielder, is to say there is no reason a home run is better than a defensive play that keeps a run from scoring. The result is the same: You helped your team by one run. But cold logic is useless in a world of passion. There the home run is the ultimate symbol of domination. One swing for one run quickly establishes who's the best. As the passionate Earl Weaver, himself a banjo-hitting infielder, has said, "The best play in baseball is the three-run homer."

When Hollywood created the mythic baseball player Roy Hobbs, it didn't fool around. Hobbs was no clever shortstop going deep into the hole to save a run. He was a hitter—with a magic bat, Wonderboy—who once drove a ball so far, so high and with such velocity that it not only reached an outfield light tower, it crashed into the steel with such force as to twist the tower off its moorings and light the night sky with electrical explosions.

How mighty it must feel to drive a baseball beyond catching.

Asked by Steve Marantz of The Sporting News to articulate the feeling, even McGwire ran out of words: "When a round ball meets a round bat perfectly, there's just a feel of …"

Maybe here McGwire groped for a thought expressed by Reggie Jackson, who once explained, "It's better than sex."

McGwire again: "I don't know if anybody but a baseball player could relate to it. It would be like a golfer hitting a 300-yard drive, a tennis player hitting a 100-mph serve, a bowler throwing a perfect strike."

One begs to differ with McGwire because in his analogies there is a common fact that makes each of those feats less significant than a home run. In golf, tennis and bowling, the ball waits to be used by the player at the moment of his choice. In baseball, the ball belongs to a pitcher whose ambition is to throw a deceitful and/or frightening pitch that will reduce the batter to a banjo-hitting bum.

Professor Adair, in his book "The Physics of Baseball," talks about a hitter facing a 95 mph fastball: "Since the batter takes about one-fifth of a second to swing his bat, he must start the swing when the ball is about halfway to the plate. He still has a little time to change his mind and re-orient his swing—but not much. After his swing is underway for one-tenth of a second (and the ball is now about 15 feet from the plate), he won't be able to check it and he has little if any ability to change his point of aim. And about 50 percent of the deviation from curve, hop, or drop occurs in that last 15 feet."

Yikes. No wonder Yogi Berra said nobody can think and hit at the same time.

If hitting a major league pitch is the single most difficult act in all sports, hitting that pitch into the seats will make you a millionaire. And if you're Mark McGwire with 31 home runs by the All-Star break, you will find your name in the public prints alongside Ruth and Maris.

Numerologists point out it was 34 years from Ruth's 60 home runs to Maris' 61 and now it has been 36 years since Maris. The suggestion is it's time for this generation to step up.

Right now, McGwire, Ken Griffey Jr. and Tino Martinez are about halfway there. But history has taught us that the last half of the season is the most difficult, now more than ever because the ubiquitous media creates burdensome attention. Maybe, if these men are lucky, they will find a moment to themselves such as Maris did late in his chase of Ruth.

It happened when the reluctant Yankees star came to bat in Tiger Stadium, that glorious opera house of a ballpark. The stadium's two levels rise high to embrace the diamond's stage. From home plate the world is out of sight if not out of mind. As Maris stood in against the Ruthian myth, an odd and wondrous event occurred. A flock of geese flew across the open space above the ballpark's center.

All a man could see of the outside world were the geese gliding to a destination unknown. Maris backed out of the batter's box to watch. Umpire Nestor Chylak, though he might have done otherwise, called time. He wanted Maris to enjoy his moment's peace.

No one did it like Mike

JANUARY 23, 1995

One day late in the greatness of his career, Mike Schmidt came out of the Phillies' dugout wearing a woman's curly wig and sunglasses.

There fell upon the gathered multitude at Veterans Stadium a silence of stupendous proportions, for surely their eyes betrayed them. They saw the tall and lithe frame of the athlete they'd known for a decade and more. They even saw the familiar No. 20.

But Mike Schmidt? The brooding Mike Schmidt whose face so often was a leave-me-alone scowl? That Mike Schmidt was throwing out grounders to his infielders while wearing a goofy disguise? Sooner would the Philly fans have expected Ben Franklin to drop from a kite in the sky.

Then the silence was transformed into laughter and applause, some of it delivered by people who stood in recognition of Schmidt's jest-in-truth.

Truly he had reason to work incognito in 1985. He had called Philadelphia fans "a mob scene" and accused them of being spoiled by his excellence even as they were jealous of his money. The bad feelings were mutual: fans long considered Schmidt an arrogant pretender who, after all, hadn't taken the Phillies to a World Series since going 1 for 20 when they lost to Baltimore in '83.

Never a good idea in any town, picking a fight with Philadelphia fans is always a bad idea. Philadelphia has wonderful museums, universities and institutions of business and society that are models of sophistication. It's also a place where the Liberty Bell isn't the only thing that's cracked.

The schizophrenics there celebrated Schmidt when he helped win the 1980 World Series (8 for 21 with two homers and seven RBIs against Kansas City) and denigrated him after the '83 defeat that reaffirmed the city's tradition of failure. Three times the N.L. MVP, the elegant and graceful Schmidt couldn't please folks who adored athletes called "Concrete Chuck," "Hammer" and "Nails."

"This isn't so much a sports town as a hardware store," Philadelphia writer Glen Macnow once declared. "When it comes to sports, we are strictly row homes and lunch pails, clock-punchers and blue collars. ... We demand our heroes to be gritty and rumpled, perhaps with a broken nose and a little dried blood caked under the fingernails."

So the Eagles linebacker Chuck Bednarik became a god who clotheslined Frank Gifford. The Flyers won with acts of criminality forgiven because they were committed on ice. Joe Frazier was Rocky Balboa, only with talent and real blood. As for the Phillies, Tug McGraw once said the trouble with losing a big game on the road was getting past the machine-gun nest at the airport.

Pete Rose understood the place: "It's not hard to become a fan favorite in Philly. Play hard, get dirty. Cuss and spit and never let them see you loafing. One more thing: Never lose a game."

Schmidt's best years came alongside Rose, who could make the brooder laugh and whose lust for notice relieved Schmidt of attention he never wanted. In Rose's years with the Phillies, 1979 through 1983, Schmidt reached career highs: .316, 48 home runs, 121 runs batted, .644 slugging average.

In those seasons, the Phillies won two N.L. championships and a World Series. "Rose made the difference," Schmidt said last week when he was elected to the Hall of Fame (the heartfelt start of a campaign to persuade baseball to pardon Rose, who as a young player in Cincinnati had been a hero to a teenager up the road in Dayton named Michael Jack Schmidt).

Rose on Schmidt: "Mike was the best player in the league three or four days a week when I got there. By the time I left, he had learned to be the best seven days a week."

Still, the wonder of Schmidt's career is that he did it all in Philadelphia, where fans who wear their hearts on their sleeves were never sure Schmidt had a heart. He was stoic, cool and studious, a college graduate, of all things, an artist sipping wine in a bully's shot-and-chaser town.

Utterly unfair. The man's only crime was to come to the ballpark with a gift so large he made hard things look easy. Schmidt also came with an integrity that marked him as a man to whom family and religion mattered more than his work, which, as he showed for 18 seasons, mattered greatly.

The irony of Schmidt's alienation from Philadelphia fans was that few players were ever more intent on success.

To critics of his introspection, Schmidt said, "Someone put the pitcher's rubber 60 feet 6 inches from home plate. Six inches closer and the curveball doesn't have time to break; six inches farther back, it breaks too soon. Now you're going to tell me this game doesn't deserve a great deal of thought?"

Schmidt also said, "If effort equated with dirt, my uniform would be as black as a coal mine in night time."

The best third baseman ever, baseball's best player for the last 20 years, Mike Schmidt at bat was an efficient wonder of power, his hitting stroke beautiful in its quickness and compactness, the bat moving from a high position sharply downward to send the baseball a great distance in a hurry.

With a glove, Schmidt deserved mention in paragraphs starring Brooks Robinson, there with Graig Nettles as fielders whose acrobatics were those of jungle cats chasing down the night's dinner.

Thirteen seasons he hit over 30 home runs. Only Henry Aaron, with 15, did it more often. Eight times Schmidt led the N.L. in home runs. No one else has done that. Ten times he won Gold Gloves as his league's best fielding third baseman. Outside of Michael Jordan, no athlete more effectively combined offense and defense than Mike Schmidt.

And yet he came to work one day in 1985 certain to be the target of wrath. Instead, with his wig and sunglasses, Schmidt rendered the boo-birds silent. "I really had 'em for a minute," he said, but, alas, not much longer. On his retirement, the Phillies refused his entreaties for a front-office job, saying his baseball skills didn't necessarily translate to leadership and talent judgment. Hurt, Schmidt left Philadelphia and now lives in Florida.

One step yields what might have been

No more beautiful athlete ever moved on a baseball field than Willie Mays, whose father worked in Birmingham's steel mills and played a pretty fair brand of industrial-league ball. They called the father Cat because he moved so quickly with so little effort. Cat's boy, Willie, learned to walk by chasing a baseball his father rolled across the floor and in time would move in center field with such speed and surety that his glove became known as the place triples go to die.

Even now, all these baseball summers later, we watch in wonder the black-and-white film showing Mays going back on the Vic Wertz fly ball in the 1954 World Series. All that room in center field at the ancient Polo Grounds. Mays once said the place "seemed bent out of shape." It was 475 feet to the wall in dead center. Room enough for Willie Mays to do most anything.

In full flight so long ago, his back to the infield, the ball dropping out of the sky over his right shoulder, Mays caught the Wertz fly ball five or six steps short of that distant wall. Anyone who cares about baseball knows the catch. Some of us saw it when it happened. It is now one of the memories that we call up when we want to enjoy again the beauty of Willie Mays. I am think-

153

ing now of Bo Jackson. It might have been in Kansas City. Maybe Baltimore. It was in left field. A line drive headed for the wall. Jackson chasing it. At full speed he caught the ball a step in front of the warning track. Two steps later, Jackson put his left foot up onto the wall. Then he turned left, partly in answer to gravity, partly because the inning was over, and took one more step coming down the wall.

Three steps. Onto the wall. Up the wall and down again. Spider-Man as left fielder.

Another son of a Birmingham mill hand, another athlete with gifts denied most of us, Vincent Edward Jackson now has left baseball in the way Willie Howard Mays left it. Used up. Hurt. His gifts worth nothing.

For Mays, baseball lasted more than 20 years and time was the thief of his gifts. At the end he stumbled at bat and misjudged fly balls, no longer the Willie Mays he had been. For Jackson it was not time. It was much crueler than time's inevitability. Mays was 42 and an empty vessel. At 29 Jackson had the best years waiting for him—until he took one bad step.

It is easy to forget how fragile youth is. Especially when we're young. We think this is fun. This is wonderful. And it is. And we should enjoy every moment of it.

We should enjoy it because one bad step can change it.

The first three or four times I saw Jackson go down on videotape, I saw nothing unusual. Football in hand, Jackson had broken clear down the right side. All I saw was someone drag him down from behind.

Finally I saw it happen. Jackson is reaching out with his right leg while a tackler grabs at him. His right knee is bent, but because his momentum has been slowed by the tackler Jackson doesn't move forward onto his right foot. This is awkward. Motion has been disrupted. Jackson's foot is flat against the turf and his body should be moving forward to roll the foot up for the next step. But the tackler won't let that happen.

Nor does Jackson's knee move. Now the force of Jackson's momentum is directed toward that planted foot and ungiving knee. This force has to go somewhere. Not able to go forward, the force is transmitted from the femur, the long bone in the thigh, back to the hip socket. You can see Jackson's pelvis tilt upward. It is as if the femur is being pushed through the pelvis and toward his rib cage.

As doctors would tell us later, that trauma ruined the joint where Jackson's femur enters the pelvis. Cartilage, tissue and blood vessels were destroyed. Now it was bone on bone in there. And there wasn't enough blood flowing in to sustain the bone's life. Avascular necrosis, that's called.

One bad step.

And Bo Jackson is gone.

He came back from that injury to play the last month of the 1991 baseball season as a designated hitter for the White Sox. But he was not the Bo Jackson he had been, not by a half. And in spring training this time, he was less than that. He had been a 225-pound sprinter. This spring he ran like an old man whose legs had forgotten the routine.

Now he's gone and while Bo Jackson's absence from baseball is not the stuff of tragedy, it does provoke a sense of sorrow in that so much was lost so soon and so quickly. One bad step.

We came to know Jackson the way we come to know most celebrities in the 1990s. By their TV commercials. The Nike ads portrayed Jackson as the master of all games when, in truth, his work suggested greatness without ever proving it.

He hadn't done enough at football or baseball to be Hall of Fame material. His NFL career produced 16 touchdowns, a season's work for a Walter Payton. In 535 baseball games he hit 112 home runs but struck out three times as often, hit under .250 and was an undependable outfielder.

Baseball players held Jackson in awe not so much because of his work as his pure athleticism. They seldom see such bodies in their locker rooms, seldom see any baseball player so big, so strong, so fast. And while Jackson certainly was not your average NFL running back, he only suggested, a game or two a year, that he deserved to be in a sentence with a Jim Brown or a Barry Sanders.

Bo knows Bo. He told us so. And what he often told us was that he was motivated by critics who said he couldn't do this or that. So he'd show us. He'd play baseball, if that's what we said he couldn't do. He'd show us and he did. Couldn't play major league baseball and pro football at the same time? He's show us and he did.

What he couldn't do is what no one can do. He couldn't take the risk out of his life. One bad step is all it takes and by playing both sports Jackson increased the risk. He sowed the seeds of his sorrow, for as awesome as his body is, it could not be expected to endure the annual trauma of football without rest. Nor could anyone play a summer's worth of baseball without leaving himself weary for football and more susceptible to injury.

The one bad step became inevitable. And now? Maybe he can come back. Maybe there'll be no surgery. Maybe a year's true rest will heal the bones. Joe Montana came back from spinal surgery when not even his doctor would think of it. A. J. Foyt is driving 180 mph barely a year after doctors wanted to amputate his legs. Maybe Bo Jackson can come back.

There is even talk of hip-replacement surgery and maybe Jackson can come back running on bones connected to metal and plastic. Maybe he is what he posed to be while at Auburn University. For a publicity photograph Jackson posed coming out of a telephone booth wearing a Superman outfit.

I am reminded of Muhammad Ali, who once told a flight attendant he didn't need to fasten his seat belt. "Superman don't need no seat belt," the champ said. The flight attendant replied sweetly, "Superman don't need no airplane, either."

For me, baseball is a joy

Rex Hudler points it out. "My name is a dog's name."

Naturally, people have called him Rex the Wonder Dog.

Of those few major league baseball players who have a dog's name, fewer admit it. Only one seems proud of it. Only Rex Hudler stands in left field at Wrigley Field and laughs along with the Bleacher Bums who shout, "Hey, Rex, do you hold your head out the window when you go for a ride in the car?"

The day he heard that question, Hudler scratched his ribs on the right side; as he scratched, he stuck his right foot straight out behind him and put it to twitching, the way your dog Rex might.

"For me, baseball is a joy," Hudler says. "Every day's a laugher."

At the Ballpark in Arlington, fans gave Hudler positioning tips. "One step to your left," they called, and he took one step left. "Two steps in," and he did it. "Give us a knee," they shouted, and before the next pitch Hudler touched a knee to the grass quickly: "So what's it hurt? Nothing. And the fans love it. I gave 'em a knee, they lost it."

Rex Hudler, a utilityman for the Angels, is a red-haired, freckle-faced kid 35 years old going on 12. He's Huck Finn come to play some ball. His baseball career is a tale best told as an odyssey with a laugh track.

A sensational wide receiver who caught 22 passes in his last high school game in Fresno, Calif., Hudler in 1978 had his choice of big-time colleges, even Notre Dame. Instead, the sensational infielder signed with the Yankees for the then-fabulous sum of $125,000. He was the 18th choice in the first round of a draft distinguished in history by Baltimore's second-round selection of a gangly kid named Cal Ripken Jr.

Ripken and Hudler played in the Class A Florida State League in '79, but their career paths soon diverged. Hudler spent four full seasons and parts of two others in A ball, the baseball equivalent of repeating kindergarten five times. He played parts or all of 11 minor league seasons before sticking in the majors and now has played parts or all of 10 big-league seasons. He has played for five big-league teams (including Baltimore, where he was alongside Ripken), been released in spring training by a sixth and even left the hemisphere in 1993 to play for the Yakult Swallows. During Japanese games, he ate live worms. "Good protein," he explained.

Rex the Wonder Human Being plays baseball as if his hair were on fire. He once made a catch sliding into someone's bullpen and cried about it: "I cry two or three times a year while I'm playing because I realize how lucky I am to be in the big leagues." He has done stumbling cartwheels just past first base as a result of mad dashes on routine ground balls: "I run like I haven't eaten in three days and there's food waiting at first."

Some people call him Rex the Hotdog. "I prefer 'ferocious and intense.' Throw me back with the Gashouse Gang. All I want is for fans to say, 'He loves people and he comes to play.' Baseball's a game you play with your heart, and if having fun is a crime, they should lock me up."

To be near Rex Hudler is to feel the short hairs come up on the back of your neck. The man is alive. He is alive in the way electricity is alive, hot and dangerous and dancing in the dark.

We see him now. We see him in the California Angels' clubhouse. We see and hear Rex Hudler talking baseball, which is a wonderful thing, because he is a baseball lifer, the beating heart of the game, mostly unknown, mostly unappreciated, a veteran utility infielder who is an antidote to the venom created and spread by spoiled-brat millionaire stars.

On a December day, Hudler is one of only two players in the clubhouse. He's the one talking baseball to a young outfielder, a Yankees minor leaguer whose name is Matt Luke and whose eyes are fixed on this Rex Hudler piece of electricity because Hudler suddenly has made himself into …

"Andy Van Slyke," Hudler says, his voice a mix of evangelistic fervor and conspiratorial whisper, "always gives it this." Wearing sweats and a ball cap, he does two casual steps to his right and leans down to scoop up a rolling baseball that only he sees. Hudler then makes a little hop preceding a grand sweep of his throwing arm, the ritual performed by the casually elegant Van Slyke a thousand times—and one too many times because in 1995, when Van Slyke was briefly an Oriole …

"I hit one two steps right of Cal Ripken, and I'm running out of the box because I know it's going to Van Slyke's right. …"

Hudler interrupts himself. "Matt, it's speed. Whitey Herzog called me 'White Lightning.' I hit .300 against lefthanders. That keeps me in the league. That, and my defense. They used to call me the fastest white man in baseball. Not anymore. I gave up that title. But it's speed, and you gotta use it if you've got it because speed distorts everything.

"I know Van Slyke's going to do this"—Hudler again does his Van Slyke impression—"so I'm running out of the box, flying around first, because I know I'm going to second all the way.

"Rip's out on the grass to take the throw when, uh-oh, he sees me coming, and it's … no play! I'm in at second with no play, a double, because I had speed and I knew something, and you know what, Matt Luke?"

Luke is a four-year pro, an eighth-round draft choice in '92, a product of the Anaheim area. He, too, is working on his conditioning. The smile on Luke's face is one of great and happy wonderment. He slowly shakes his head, no, he doesn't know what, but he knows he is about to hear what.

"You ought to hear what they say in the clubhouse. They say, 'Rex Hudler, he'll do anything to win—anything.'"

There in his sweats and ball cap, there with a young, aspiring player in the clubhouse on a winter day, Rex Hudler raises his chin a click. "'Anything.' That's the best compliment there is."

When you're 35 years old and in the major leagues, you better work at being a kid.

Now we're in the Angels' workout room just off the clubhouse deep in Anaheim Stadium.

This will go on for 45 minutes. Rex Hudler will ride a stationary bicycle, run on a treadmill and be tortured while strapped into a machine that approximates the work involved in climbing a ladder with a zillion rungs, maybe more.

"Gonna puke before this is over," Hudler says.

He didn't always work so hard. The way teen phenoms often do, he figured it would last forever. There came late nights and alcohol and dabbling in drugs and girls in every town. "All that," he said, "and I put God on the shelf."

Hudler joined the St. Louis Cardinals in 1990. There he saw an amazing thing. Four hours before a game, he saw Ozzie Smith taking ground balls. Not only taking ground balls but taking them on his knees, on fire-breathing carpet, snatching them backhanded and in one motion throwing to first.

Rex Hudler saw the game's best shortstop on his knees and he thought this: "Wow." He also thought, "Rex, you better step it up; this is the big leagues."

The quintessential 24th man on any roster, Hudler can do a little of everything but not a lot of anything. He plays seven positions but none so well with his glove as to earn an everyday job. He hits lefthanders better than righthanders. In six full major league seasons and parts of four others, he has played in 607 games, gone to bat 1,302 times and hit .257 with 35 home runs—numbers that cause him to say: "I'm a top-hand, ugly hitter who 50 percent of the time grounds out. But it'll be bang-bang, and I'm falling down, and people applaud because they like the way I'm trying."

We're 20 minutes into the workout. Hudler is on the treadmill. He still is talking.

"It's not that a lot of players don't hustle. But there's a handful of guys. And it's some guys who make big money. I'll see a guy not run out a ground ball, not give a good effort, and it makes me …"

He searches for a word.

" … nauseous. And if he happens to be a player on my team, there's a good chance I'll tell him, 'Look at the people in the seats who pay your salary. And this is the message we're sending them?'"

Here Hudler cups his hands alongside his eyes.

"They're wearing blinders. They don't see the world. Where do they think the money comes from? A funnel from the bank to their office?"

We're 35 minutes in. He's still talking. The 1993 season in Japan was at once wonderful and terrible. His team won the league championship, he hit

.300, and he earned $1 million. But the manager kept asking: "The American player we signed, when's he getting here?" Hudler says: "He asked why I swung at so many bad pitches. Well, they hit me eighth and I didn't get any pitches. So I said, 'If I wanted to walk, I'd have been a mailman in America.'"

Done with the aerobics workout, Hudler disappears into another room and on his return smiles. "Peed. Didn't puke."

He and Luke do another 20 minutes of flexibility exercises, after which the gasping veteran says to the smiling kid who is broad-shouldered, raw-boned, tall and strong:

"Only been at this a week, Matt, and look at you. Your body's getting hard already. You go to camp this spring, you walk through the clubhouse in nothing but your jock strap. Let 'em see you're ready. Strut through that room. Don't make any eye contact. Just let 'em see you. Intimidate 'em."

Hudler says there are two kinds of people: fountains and drains. "Either you're a fountain to draw from, or you're a drain taking people down. I choose to be a fountain. I learned that from my mother."

His mother, Ann, a registered nurse, was divorced when he was 5. She remarried soon after, Hudler says, only so he and his brothers would have a father. She continued the marriage at the boys' request, ending it when they left high school.

"She always told me to stay positive because it's a tough world out there," Hudler says.

Six trips to Class A ball might have discouraged most phenoms. Hudler instead hand-delivered a letter telling his boss it was time he moved up to Class AAA. His boss at the time was George Steinbrenner, who liked the kid's gumption and ordered him straight to AAA.

Since then, the kid who put God on the shelf has put God back in his life. In 1988, he married Jennifer Myers and in 1994 they became parents of a daughter, Alyssa, three days after the Giants cut him from their spring-training roster. Within a week, he signed with the Angels. He is under contract through the end of this season, at $300,000 per year.

What's next for Hudler? Maybe he'll play until he's 40. Maybe there's television-radio work in his future. All we know for sure is that Cal Ripken Jr. had it right one night in 1994.

That evening, on his first trip to Baltimore's Camden Yards, Hudler hit a long home run into the left-field seats. Later, Ripken came to him laughing.

"Hey, nobody's ever hit one into those seats," he said, and then the great shortstop added words that work in more than one way: "Rex, you're in a league of your own."

Baseball's comic relief

APRIL 25, 1994

We could talk about Jimmy Johnson and Magic Johnson, the men leaving and coming back, coming back and leaving. Or we could talk about Steve Carlton proving it's better to remain silent and be thought a fool than to open your mouth and remove all doubt. There's the senator from Maine who'd rather wear a baseball cap than a judge's robe. We could talk about Cecil Fielder being too big to do what he does and Muggsy Bogues being too little.

Or we could thank Betty Ford for Pat Summerall and Mickey Mantle, the old heroes alive and, at last, glad of it. The ball is juiced, some folks say, and it's flying out of the ballpark in record numbers. We could talk about that: We could say that'll end when the umpires make the strike zone bigger than a mail slot. So much to say.

But it will have to wait. We're talking sliding this week. We have strawberries and noodles, broken cigars and mustardy hot dogs. We have Rick Dempsey as Babe Ruth. We'll tell you how to build a sliding pit. And we have Michael Jordan doing the limbo, sort of, at home plate.

We begin with Pete Rose, forever famous in sliding annals for having explained his face this way: "If you'd slid head first for 20 years, you'd look like this, too." We begin with a Rose strawberry, this in a spring long ago. Anyone who ever threw himself down on a gravelly infield knows about strawberries. They're red, ripe and tender. As Rose cleaned grit from the strawberry atop his thigh, a man made this diagnosis:

"Ouchee-wawa."

"It's from noodles," Rose said.

"Noodles?"

"Did it making a commercial for a Japanese noodle company," Rose said. "Musta slid for an hour."

We're talking sliding, a fundamental act of baseball instinct, an act given full demonstration any time the 1980s Orioles had a long rain delay. Then catcher Rick Dempsey stuffed his uniform with towels until he took on a Ruthian silhouette, after which he circled the bases and flung himself head first on the tarpaulin, sliding through the rain.

Alex Hawkins, the old football flake, once said he knew what baseball's trouble was:

"Nowadays, you don't ever see a fella sliding into second base and breaking his cigar."

Too bad he missed Gates Brown and the hot dogs. On August 7, 1968, Brown wasn't in the Detroit lineup and so, always a hungry player, he sneaked from the dugout to the clubhouse and came back with two hot dogs slathered with mustard—only to be ordered by manager Mayo Smith to pinch hit.

Brown's solution to his problem—he couldn't let the skipper see his snack—was to stuff the hot dogs in his jersey. As he would tell it: "I always wanted to get a hit every time I went to the plate. But this was one time I didn't want to get a hit. I'll be damned if I didn't smack one in the gap and I had to slide into second—head first, no less. I was safe with a double. But when I stood up, I had mustard and ketchup and smashed hot dogs and buns all over me.

"The fielders took one look at me, turned their backs and damned near busted a gut laughing at me. My teammates in the dugout went crazy." After fining Brown $100, Smith said, "What the hell were you doing eating on the bench in the first place?" Brown: "I decided to tell him the truth. I said, 'I was hungry. Besides, where else can you eat a hot dog and have the best seat in the house?'"

Anyone talking about sliding needs to track down the textbook by Al

Campanis in 1954, when he was a smart guy. A generation later Campanis became a dumb guy by trying to explain to Ted Koppel that some people didn't have the, the, the, the necessities to manage a baseball team. It was in his smart days as the Brooklyn Dodgers' director of player personnel—he found Roberto Clemente and Sandy Koufax—that Campanis wrote "The Dodgers' Way to Play Baseball."

Using 10 pages of text and illustrations, Campanis told readers everything about sliding. "Sliding is rapidly becoming a lost art," he wrote. So he spelled out the fundamentals and explained drills necessary to reinforce a player's instincts. Campanis even included instructions for the building of a sliding pit:

"A 16-foot square is excavated to a depth of three or four feet. This is filled with fine sand and some sawdust is sprinkled on top. A strap is anchored in the exact center of the pit, coming up through the sand. The base is attached to the strap so that there is some play to it. ... A rake should be on hand during sliding practice as the sand and sawdust need smoothing out after a few slides have been made."

Maybe Michael Jordan's next investment in Birmingham should be material for the construction of a sliding pit. Here's why.

Jordan reached base last week on an infield scratch, his specialty. From third, on a wild pitch, he headed for home. In this Information Age, we could see this drama unfold on ESPN. We could see the catcher's throw to the pitcher covering. We could see Jordan coming into the picture from the left side. We waited to see him slide into home. What a fabulous moment this would be.

Er, no. Not exactly. Jordan needed to slide. He wanted to slide. He tried to slide. He just couldn't slide. So he sort of stopped. And leaned backward, away from the tag, leaning backward until he lost his balance and touched the dirt with his hands.

And while he did all this, he let his feet go forward. They made little baby steps of an embarrassed nature. His embarrassed feet tippy-toed toward the plate while the rest of his body leaned backward.

"And Michael is called out," ESPN's Keith Olbermann said, " ... for TRAVELING."

CHAPTER 9

Absent Friends

An artist at life

AUGUST 30, 1999

When the world was young, the telephone rang in The Louisville Courier-Journal's sports department. An agitated woman asked to speak to Pee Wee Reese right this second.

Someone said, "Ma'am, Pee Wee doesn't work here."

"But," she said, "he wrote a story in yesterday's paper about how to catch popups."

"Oh, that. You'll want to talk to the guy who wrote those stories for Pee Wee."

So the phone went across the desk to Pee Wee's ghostwriter on a series of instructional pieces for young players. The woman said, "I want you to know that my son read what you wrote yesterday."

"Thank you," I said.

"His nose hasn't stopped bleeding yet."

"Oh?"

"Don't you remember what Pee Wee said? To catch a popup, he said to get under the ball and watch it coming down like it's going to hit you in the nose."

"Oh."

"That's exactly what my boy did," the mother said, "and the ball hit him right in the nose."

That poor mother may have been the only person ever with a legitimate beef about Pee Wee Reese.

Such a wonderful life he gave us. You've heard the story about Pee Wee touching Jackie Robinson when lesser men wanted Robinson gone. The story tells us important stuff—that a white man born and raised in a racially divided nation can treat a man of color the way he'd want to be treated.

It happened in Cincinnati, and it happened in Boston. Racists screamed slurs at the black man until the white man from Kentucky walked across the infield and put a hand on Robinson's shoulder. The act said they were in this together. They were black and white, human beings and Dodgers.

There is an even better story. It defines Reese's personality and explains why so many people came to think of him as extraordinary. It tells us about his poise, wit and courage. It tells us why he was the Dodgers' captain and why, half a century later, his friends still call him The Captain.

It happened in Atlanta in 1947. A letter had come to Robinson with a promise that the Ku Klux Klan would kill him if he showed up in that city's Ponce de Leon Park.

That night, as the Dodgers were warming up, Robinson and Reese threw from spots alongside each other. Then Reese looked at Robinson. "Damn, Jackie, get the hell away from me, will you? The guy might be a bad shot."

They laughed and went on throwing. They were Hall of Fame players, and they were better people. In the winter of 1997, preparing a magazine story on the 50th anniversary of Robinson's rookie season, a sportswriter called Reese to talk about Robinson.

"Aw, no," he said. "You know the Jackie stories better than I do by now."

"But, Pee Wee, I need your voice."

"Just don't make me out to be a hero. It took no courage to do what I did. Jackie had the courage. If it had been me, a white man, trying to be the only one in the black leagues, I couldn't have done it. What he had to endure, the criticism, the catcalls—I wouldn't have had the courage."

"Pee Wee, c'mon ... "

"Jackie could help us win, I wanted to win, I wanted him on our team. That's it."

On a pure baseball level, that was it. Norm Iler, a Louisville businessman and Reese's friend for 65 years, said, "When Robinson came in, I saw Pee Wee coming out of the service and he said, 'Of course, he's gotta be a shortstop.' (Robinson was moved to first base.) But Pee Wee accepted him. It wasn't to make a statement about race. He saw a great athlete. His interest was in making the Dodgers a better team."

We know that Robinson, coming to a closed door, would have broken it down. Reese simply opened it for him. He made Robinson's baseball life easier. He made baseball's history shinier.

Major league clubs had voted, 15 to the Dodgers' one, to keep black players off their rosters. As dozens of National League players insisted they would boycott games Robinson played, even a cadre of Dodgers demanded he be excluded. Commissioner A.B. (Happy) Chandler ignored the vote and approved the contract.

So Reese's embrace of Robinson was an act of uncommon common decency. Now, on Pee Wee's death at 81, Lexington Herald-Leader sports columnist Billy Reed proposes that a statue be raised at Louisville's new minor league ballpark. And not just any statue. "It ought to be Pee Wee with Jackie," Reed says.

We grow up with heroes. The lucky ones among us have heroes who turn out to be the real thing. I'm luckier than that. I grew up watching the Dodgers, watching the little shortstop who wore No. 1. I grew up wanting to be Pee Wee Reese, and through a newspaper job I met him, and I walked with him in ballparks and I came to know what his friend Norm Iler had always known:

"The way Pee Wee handled himself forever, so gracefully, decently, never trying to impress anybody, accepting people for who they were, he did it without working at it. He was an artist at life."

I own one piece of sports memorabilia. It's a replica of a Dodgers jersey. Its number is 1.

A legend, a Coach

DECEMBER 11, 2000

In the winter of his 18th year, the college freshman John Camardella had lost his way. His father died that summer of a stroke suffered during heart surgery. The boy had been the father's only child, a miracle baby, born after his mother had miscarried five times.

Now the young man, away at school, worried about his mother at home, alone. Nothing else mattered, not basketball, not class. A world once shiny had fallen dark, and John Camardella didn't know where his place was. "I wasn't sure I could handle it," he said.

Then, one day after practice, he sat with an old man in a grand basketball building made possible by the old man's life. They'd talked before. "Coach would keep up on your grades. He'd ask if you needed any help; he looked out for you," Camardella says. "He was into you as a person."

So Jack Horenberger recognized Camardella's malaise and came to him, and they talked for 10 minutes, a moment in time but a moment so vivid in the young man's memory that he tells you it changed his life.

"Coach told me, 'Get back on track,' " Camardella says "And he wasn't soft about it, either. I'd call it a nice scolding. He said, 'I know you've got it in you. Keep pushing. Everything'll be looking up pretty soon.' "

The semi-amazing part of Camardella's story is that Jack Horenberger could scold a young man and in the process earn his admiration. But that's only semi-amazing because the coach had done it a thousand times at Illinois Wesleyan University. The fully amazing part is that Horenberger, on that day, was 86 years old, a man born before World War I pumping up a teenager on the eve of the 21st century.

"That day had such an effect on me," Camardella says. "And everything's going incredibly now. But this—this has been a hard day."

The day we spoke, last Friday, Coach died that morning. Camardella, now a starting forward, would play a game two days later.

Jack Horenberger spent 60 years on the Illinois Wesleyan campus, first as student, later as baseball coach (37 seasons), basketball coach (21 seasons) and athletic director, finally as icon.

"He was the constant," says Dennie Bridges, a Horenberger player who succeeded him as coach and athletic director. From a shadowy old gym to today's glistening palace, from a baseball diamond laid over football ground to today's Jack Horenberger Field, from canvas shoes to Air Jordans, from four-car caravans to chartered buses, through war and peace, as everything changed, Jack Horenberger was always Coach.

Memory puts me in Coach's big, black Mercury. It's a boat of a car, and it's night, and we're floating in the darkness of a two-lane highway south. It's a baseball trip to somewhere exotic, maybe to Ole Miss (then supplying most of the Miss Americas) en route to New Orleans (where a kid first drank rum and the next day struck out four times).

"Hey, Lou," was Coach's call to signal a double steal. All these years later, remembering that, and this: a locker room before a game in Mississippi, leaving a toilet stall, buttoning up for battle, hearing Coach's high-pitched voice, "Kindred, flush it, you're in the big leagues now."

Coach had big-league players at Illinois Wesleyan, the best of them Doug Rader, a Gold Glove third baseman with power, later a coach and manager. Another big-league coach and manager, Bobby Winkles, played for Horenberger and says, "Coach taught me a baseball team is not a democracy. He was a benevolent dictator. I loved the man."

Horenberger's longtime assistant and friend Bob Keck: "The man lived an ideal life. He's led one of the great lives. Everybody loves him and respects him. What else is there?"

Dennie Bridges was on the golf course when he heard the news of

Horenberger's cancer—news delivered by the coach himself, and delivered typically. Croxton Street runs by Lakeside Country Club's 17th green, and there Horenberger stopped his car to call out to Bridges, "Winning any money?"

First mentor and protégé, Horenberger and Bridges became all but father and son. Now the old coach told the young coach he wouldn't need the kidney operation he'd been dreading.

"I got a great break," Horenberger said. "During the exams, they found out I have cancer. If I hadn't been lucky enough for them to find the cancer, I'd have had all the pain of the kidney surgery."

Bridges asked, "But, Coach, what about the cancer?"

"We'll deal with that," the great man said.

He dealt with it with dignity. He met his buddies for coffee every morning on campus, and every afternoon at the club he played rummy. As for chemotherapy, he said no.

"It wasn't that he was too weak to face chemo," Chicago Tribune columnist Bob Verdi wrote. "On the contrary, he was strong enough to recognize that quality of life entails making difficult decisions on where and when and how."

Horenberger decided to stay at home with hospice care. He'd be with his wife of 59 years, Mary Ann, his daughters, Jane and Jill, and their families.

From bed, he yet coached. "Coach filled out his own obituary form," said Ed Alsene, a morning-coffee friend, "and he told me, for the memorial service, to 'put some humor in it.'"

Near the end, Jack Horenberger comforted visitors who had come to comfort him. He was in no pain, just a funny feeling in his stomach. He told Verdi, "No complaints. … I decided long ago to smell the roses."

Then last week, flowers came to the old man's home.

One bunch came from John Camardella.

Forever we'll hear his voice

MARCH 2, 1998

Came the seventh inning one night. A foul ball went flying back to the Cubs' radio booth. Harry Caray put out his right hand, only to have the missile slap off his palm. From next door came play- by-play by the Braves' radio man, Skip Caray (an apple fallen near the tree), "That's an error. Hit Dad in a bad place. The hands." Harry's laughter rumbled across the air, out of the ballpark, to be heard forever.

I'm a child of radio who listened to Harry Caray on KMOX in St. Louis in the 1950s. Every baseball night, I went to my room with a Coke and a Velveeta sandwich, heavy on the mustard. If it got to be the 14th inning and my parents didn't need to know I was awake, I moved the radio under the blankets with my scorebook and flashlight.

Though I'd never been to a major league ballpark and I'd never seen Stan Musial, somehow it didn't matter. I'd been places and seen things with Harry because the glory of baseball's radio days was the medium's insistence that you, the listener, take part.

You joined the act of imagination that made the names come alive. Stan The Man … Duke Snider … Ernie Banks. You saw the heroes and you saw the ballparks because Harry saw them for you and shared his joy with you.

You even saw the screen-wire fencing stretched 36 feet high in front of fans sitting in the right field seats at Sportsman's Park in St. Louis.

"Musial would have a hundred more home runs if they took that wire down," Harry once said, "but the Cardinals are afraid of losing too many balls in batting practice." Implied: the cheapskates. The Cardinals paid Harry, but they didn't own Harry, who more than once suggested his personal eternal despair by biting off the words, "Musial pops up again." As if Musial's 3,630 hits would all come with the bases empty.

My radio brought home baseball games from many places. I heard Jack Brickhouse and Bob Prince, Bob Elson and Bert Wilson. All great broadcasters. And then there was Harry.

It wasn't so much he made the games fun, though surely he did. ("Here we are in the 14th inning," he once said, "and if you've gone to the refrigerator for a Budweiser every time I've told you to, you're feeling about as good as I'm feeling by now.")

Obituaries and appreciations insist Harry Caray's work for 53 years was the work of a fan, funny and cocky when his team won, angry and melancholy when it lost. We remember Harry the Bleacher Bum, taking off his shirt to broadcast from Wrigley Field's sunny and zany left field bleachers. We'll remember Harry the song leader, chewing the scenery through "Take Me Out to the Ball Game."

There was more to him than that. Orphaned as a child, scrapping to make a life, fighting for acceptance, the man born Harry Christopher Carabina built a career on a gift of talent so brilliant it was taken for granted. As Musial was a hitter, Caray was a dramatist. Along with a showman's greatest tool—an ego the size of any park, including Yellowstone—Harry brought to his work a flawless feel for story.

"Be careful," he once said to his team's pitcher, late in a game, the score tied, the count 2-and-1 to a power hitter. "Don't make it good."

Amazing. Six words. Suddenly, we had an interest in the next pitch. Might the slugger take a careless pitch deep? Six words is all. Spoken in anxious admonition, those words made listeners part of the drama, aware of possible danger. Suddenly, the next pitch—what? the 220th pitch of the season's 119th game?—became the most important pitch ever thrown.

Later, to his team's hitter: "Take a pitch. Three balls, one strike, game tied, top of the 11th, bases loaded. Do you think he can walk a man with the bases loaded?"

I dunno, Harry, but you've got me now, and I'm danged sure going to listen to find out.

"BALL FOUR. HE WALKED HIM." And here came Harry's rumbling laugh, har-de-har-har-har. "WOULD YOU BELIEVE IT?"

For 25 years he did Cardinals games, fired in 1970 amid rumors of an affair with the wife of an Anheuser-Busch executive. In his autobiography, Harry wrote, "At first, these rumors annoyed me. Then … they actually made me feel kind of good. I mean, let's face it. I wore glasses as thick as the bottoms of Bud bottles, and as much as I hate to say it, I was never confused with Robert Redford. … If you were me, would you have gone around denying rumors like that? Hell, no."

Tom Boswell once wrote of Bill Veeck, "Cause of death: life." Goes for Harry, too. Such a life, the candle burned at both ends and the middle. He probably drank too much, but what's too much if your party lasted 83 years? Ronald Reagan sat with him in the booth. Hillary Rodham Clinton dropped by. Chicago mourns. Last week, Stan Musial said, "We're going to miss old Harry. He was always the life of the party, the life of baseball."

Forever we'll hear Harry's voice. "Musial hits a drive … it's deep … way back … it might be … it could be … it IS! … HOLY COW!"

The real Washington monument

JUNE 15, 1998

The Washington Post of June 5 carried a Shirley Povich column in which the great man gently chided a colleague who suggested Mark McGwire is a better home run hitter than Babe Ruth.

"Whoa there," Povich wrote. He then quoted Walter Johnson's reply when asked to compare the Babe's shots with those of Lou Gehrig, Jimmie Foxx and Hank Greenberg: "Lemme say this, those balls Ruth hit got smaller quicker than anybody else's."

A remarkable column, as usual, because Povich brought to his work an elegance of language and a long view of history. Here's a graceful writer who sat on Johnson's porch in the Maryland countryside and asked the Senators' immortal pitcher about baseball's latest phenom, Bob Feller. "The kid throws hard," Johnson allowed. "But he's no Lefty Grove." A "comeback column," Povich called it. At 92, writing in his 75th year at the Post, he had been ill six weeks. "During my recent and enforced sabbatical, called for by the reward-ed pursuit of better health ..." So began 900 words on McGwire, David Wells and Buck Showalter's decision to walk Barry Bonds with the bases loaded.

What Povich did only he could have done. He was there when Ruth called—or didn't call, in Povich's opinion—a World Series home run in

178

1932. From Yankee Stadium in 1956, he wrote of Don Larsen's perfect game, "The million-to-one shot came in. Hell froze over. A month of Sundays hit the calendar. Don Larsen today pitched a no-hit, no-run, no-man-reaches-first game in a World Series." As for Showalter's walk of Bonds, Povich remembered a smarter play: Paul Richards ordering a 3-2, two-out pitchout so he could nail a runner whom he knew would overrun second.

Those of us who loved Shirley Povich will remember that remarkable column because it appeared the morning after our friend's death. Shirley had written it in an afternoon. A heart attack came that night. Though he'd retired in 1974, Shirley wrote occasional columns, so many, maybe 600, that he was asked when he really intended to retire. "I take it one decade at a time," he said.

Maybe 5 feet 6, Shirley Povich was the truest Washington monument. He was what sportswriters ought to be; he liked most of the games and most of the people but not all the games, not all the people. In 75 years of conversations with his readers, he spoke elegantly, delightfully and with the great good sense of a reporter who'd written war dispatches from Okinawa and Iwo Jima as well as sports columns from Notre Dame and Churchill Downs.

"The last of the fedoras," his friend and colleague Tom Callahan calls the dapper little man in the gray hat. "He was maybe 87 when we went to a fight and it must have taken 45 minutes to walk the last 200 yards to the stadium. I didn't care. He'd sit to rest and he'd tell another story. I'd have walked all night with Shirley."

Someone once asked Povich to talk about the 1920s Senator star Goose Goslin. "Dumb, but what a hitter. The Senators never could beat Red Faber until one day Goose had two triples. Afterward, Goose asked, 'Who was that feller pitchin' today?' "

He dropped that story into a round of golf during which he'd stubbed a shot 30 yards and said a sentence that one sportswriter now defines as his ambition in life. Oh, to be so lucky as to someday say, as Shirley did with a smile, "In the last year, since I've turned 89, I've lost some clubhead speed."

Even in the glad circumstances of our games, Povich saw the real world's failings. Crusading for Jackie Robinson's entry into the big leagues in 1947, he wrote a 15-part series on baseball's sorry racial history. Povich's first sentence: "Four hundred and fifty-five years after Columbus eagerly discovered America, major league baseball reluctantly discovered the American Negro."

Until the Redskins signed Bobby Mitchell in 1962, Povich for more than

20 years decried the racism of owner George Preston Marshall with sentences such as, "Jim Brown, born ineligible to play for the Redskins, integrated their end zone three times yesterday." Povich declared the Redskins colors to be "burgundy, gold and Caucasian."

Such work made him a giant in sports journalism, there with Grantland Rice and Red Smith. Presidents from Truman to Clinton read his stuff. Callahan once needed a column quote from Byron "Whizzer" White, but the Supreme Court justice came to the phone only to pass along a hello to Povich.

The billionaire tycoon Warren Buffett, on meeting Povich two years ago, said, "You're responsible for my business career." Which prompted the news-hound Povich to ask, "How so?" Buffett's first nickels came from rising before dawn to deliver the Post, now rich in all ways but then the dreary third paper in town. "The only reason anyone subscribed to the Post in those days," Buffett said, "was to read Shirley Povich. With you, I made $5 a week. Thank you."

On Red Smith's death in 1982, Pimlico Race Course dedicated its Preakness Stakes press guide to him. Povich sent it to Callahan with a note mentioning Red's wife …

"Dear Tom,

"Here 'tis. Ain't it uncommonly great that the first eight pages of a Triple Crown book be devoted to Red? Maybe Phyllis would like it. I'll check on whether the Pimlico people sent her one.

"Luv,

"Shirley."

CHAPTER 10

One, and
Only One

A century in the making

AUGUST 2, 1999

From a list of the 20th century's 100 greatest baseball players, we are asked to pick two at each infield position, nine outfielders and six pitchers. Such selection cannot be done by any rational person because differences in these players are invisible. As baseball historian Bill James has written of Roy Campanella and Mickey Cochrane, "If one of these players was worth a million dollars a year, then the other was worth $999,999.99 ... "

Can't be done? Maybe not by a rational person. But most any sportswriter can do it. Just watch. I hold an All-Century ballot provided by Major League Baseball. Either by printed form or the Internet, fans vote for a 25-player team to be announced during this fall's World Series. (The Series will take place even if William Rehnquist again must put on his famous striped impeachment robe and call balls and strikes from behind the pitcher).

I have no problem in announcing that my All-Century selections are a mixture of fact-based study, poorly substantiated opinion and outrageous personal bias. That mixture is the very foundation of All-Anything voting. That's the fun of it. It's your team, no one else's, not George Steinbrenner's, not Ted Turner's, and you can load up the roster with the heroes of your childhood.

Which explains why Stan Musial is in my outfield and Joe DiMaggio isn't. DiMaggio is New York. If they'd traded uniforms, DiMaggio in St. Louis and Musial in New York, Musial today would be regarded as the second-best player of all time, raised to Babe Ruth's side by the Yankee mythology machine.

This subjective brew of bias and fact also accounts for Jackie Robinson's place on my All-Century team. Of the major league ballot's six candidates at second base, four clearly are Robinson's superiors: Joe Morgan, Charlie Gehringer, Rogers Hornsby and Eddie Collins. But Robinson could play. He could beat you any way you wanted beaten. What he did and how he did it earned him a place in American history—not just baseball history—and any All-Century team without Jackie Robinson is not an All-Century team worth having.

I've also chosen three players whose lives and careers existed primarily in a parallel universe to the major leagues. There's no real way to measure Oscar Charleston, Josh Gibson and Satchel Paige, the best of the 1930s Negro League players, against white major leaguers of their time. Yet, if all we have are oral histories, those histories tell powerful stories.

The inimitable Dizzy Dean, a Hall of Fame pitcher, was quoted in a 1935 newspaper story about the best pitcher ever. He mentioned Lefty Grove, Lefty Gomez, Walter Johnson, Grover Cleveland Alexander and Christy Mathewson. Then Dizzy said: "But I saw all them fellows but Matty and Johnson and know who's the best pitcher I ever saw, and it's old Satchel Paige, that big lanky colored boy. Say, I was pretty fast back in 1933 and '34, and you know my fastball looks like a change of pace alongside that little pistol bullet old Satchel shoots up to the plate.

"I really know something about it because for four, five years, I toured around at the end of the season with all-star teams and I saw plenty of ol' Satch.

"He sure is a pistol. It's too bad those colored boys don't play in the big leagues because they've got some great ballplayers. Anyway, that skinny old Satchel Paige with those long arms is my idea of the pitcher with the greatest stuff I ever saw."

So here's my All-Century team:

At first base, Lou Gehrig and Mark McGwire.

At second, Joe Morgan and Jackie Robinson.

At third, Mike Schmidt and George Brett.

At shortstop, Honus Wagner and Ernie Banks.

The catchers, Johnny Bench and Josh Gibson.

In the outfield: Babe Ruth, Mickey Mantle, Stan Musial, Hank Aaron, Ty Cobb, Oscar Charleston, Ted Williams, Willie Mays and Ken Griffey Jr.

Pitchers: Sandy Koufax, Bob Gibson, Satchel Paige, Cy Young, Walter Johnson and Christy Mathewson.

To win one game to Save All Civilization, here's the batting order: Morgan, Wagner, Ruth, Mantle, Gehrig, Schmidt, Musial, Bench and Koufax.

Wait a minute, wait a New York minute, I hear a voice from my bookshelves. It's a gravely, roaring voice eager to have its say on the game's history. On page 222 of his autobiography, the author picks his own all-time all-star team. At first base, he likes Gehrig well enough but prefers slick-fielding Hal Chase:

"He was so much better than anybody I ever saw on first base that—to me—it was no contest, and I still feel that way. Chase couldn't hit as far as Gehrig or as consistently as George Sisler. But he was no punk at the plate … I'd rather have him on my team than any other first baseman in the game's history."

Talk about your outrageous personal bias. As it happens, Gehrig for years had offended the author of those words and there had grown between them a wall of jealousy, even envy. So when it came time to do his autobiography seven years after Gehrig's death, the author exacted one last piece of flesh.

This irrational judge of baseball talent was no sportswriter.

He was Babe Ruth.

Faster than the eye can see

FEBRUARY 22, 1993

Nolan, have you seen your old card? Encased
    in plastic and kept under lock and key
    marked in ink "List Price $500 Asking $400"
    you're a skinny big-eared kid in a Mets uniform
    and on the back there's a catcher whose mitt
    is on fire with flames leaping high:
    "Nolan's fast ball racked up 133 K's his rookie season"
    1968 when Joe Namath buys a mink coat LBJ quits
    Bobby and Martin die and man has not walked on the moon
    in 1968 when you're a kid with Koosman Gentry Seaver.
"That price'll be going up" the card seller declares
    "cause Nolan's retiring after this year"
    which we knew would come yet we want you
    where we can see you, Nolan,
    shining in the diamond's center
    where you won 21 and struck out 383
    in 1973 when you are an Angel
    and Nixon a crook the year O.J. goes for 2,003 yards

while we wait in line to fill 'er up
and Secretariat is beauty given wings

Rule 1.09 declares the ball to be a sphere formed
    by yarn wound around a sphere of cork or rubber
    with two stripes of white horsehide or cowhide
    stitched together weighing not less than 5 ounces
    nor more than $5^1/_4$, and the ball shall measure
    no less than 9 nor more than $9^1/_4$ inches
    in circumference and we all know, Nolan,
    the ball is smaller leaving your hand
    the thundering silent Ryan Express
    the ball reduced by velocity
    the ball smaller
    on its way
    coming
    gone.

You could throw a lamb chop past a wolf
    and the dawn past a rooster
    because you came with heat cheese gas
    fog power BBs aspirin all of it coming
    like a locomotive the Ryan Express whose
    only sound is a humming whistling whooooosh
    and men who could hear it but not see it
    called it a radio ball
    always the left knee rising to your chin
    quickly purposefully compact so very strong
    moving to the plate the long stride
    shoulders square powerful
    a portrait of power with grace
    making the ball small the ball silent
    coming whooooosh gone

When you see Reggie Jackson with the wood
    wanting what you want a gunfight a showdown
    power against power you tell

the catcher "nothing but heat"
which is your gift and like Michelangelo
who painted no garages you use your gift
the way it should be used bringing heat
your ego talking your arm your pride
and Reggie after striking out
corkscrewing into the dirt
tips his cap saying
"Thank you"

Van Lingle Mungo Rex Barney Herb Score
    Steve Dalkowski Bullet Joe Bush Sandy Koufax
    Amos Rusie the Hoosier Thunderbolt
    whose heat moved the mound back 10 feet
    and Cy Young Sudden Sam McDowell Walter Johnson
    whose "pneumonia ball" caused colds
    whose "high swift" to Ty Cobb's ear
    "hissed with danger" and Bob Feller who
    caused Lefty Gomez to take a lighted match
    to the plate not to see Feller's stuff but
    "to be sure he sees me"
    and of all these who threw it small,
    Nolan, you threw harder longer: 7 no-hitters
    5,668 K's fanning 6 sets of fathers and sons
    11 sets of brothers 17 men in the Hall of Fame
    one the young Henry Aaron who walked back
    to his seat wood in his hand saying
    "That boy can throw"

That boy now a man husband a father
    now 46 now aching now lonely for the ranch
    longer the diamond's center than anybody else
    still shining and Yaz is gone Rose is gone
    Aaron McCovey Banks Bench Schmidt
    the Beatles Elvis hot pants mood rings pet rocks
    7 presidents 5 commissioners XXVII Super Bowls
    Kareem Magic Bird Payton come and gone

while you, Nolan, brought the heat
brought it true brought it shining
and will bring it one more summer
one more summer of heat hallelujah

A you-bet-your-life season

AUGUST 28, 1995

We see Duke Snider and Willie McCovey humiliate themselves with public confessions of having cheated the tax man. We read the stories of how these proud Hall of Famers came to grief. And in these stories that are not about him but in truth tell us all about him, we see Pete Rose's name again.

We see Mike Schmidt go into the Hall of Fame. We hear him say with consuming intensity how, if he had it to do over, he would not be consumed with intensity. We smile. And there at Cooperstown for everyone to hear, Mike Schmidt brings up Pete Rose's name, a name that once made us smile.

Pete Rose belongs in the Hall of Fame, is what Schmidt says. And he's right about that because anyone with more hits than Ty Cobb should be there. But even as Schmidt says these words, even as he speaks Pete Rose's name, we think of Duke Snider and Willie McCovey and Lord knows who else, all seduced by Rose's man, Mike Bertolini, the memorabilia hustler he called "Fat Mike."

It was Bertolini acting for Rose's company, Pete Rose Hit King Marketing, who hired Snider and McCovey and paid them in cash, the better for everyone to cheat the tax man. This happened in 1989, a bad year for Rose. That year baseball kicked him out for good. That year the feds closed in with evidence that sent him to prison the next summer.

And now we learn it may not be over yet. We see Mike Bertolini's name in the papers. We see the name and we remember that Bertolini attached himself to Rose in 1985, first to trade in autographs and memorabilia; later, according to investigators, Bertolini served as a conduit between Rose, the gambler, and New York bookmakers.

Bertolini's name often came up in baseball's investigation of Rose, who in one year wrote him 21 checks of $8,000 each, always to various aliases (one was to "Herbie Lee," Rose's nickname for Schmidt, who reminded Rose of a childhood friend by that name).

Baseball's investigation produced a surreptitiously taped conversation in February 1988. On the tape, Bertolini complains that Rose owed him almost $200,000, money he had fronted to New York bookmakers to cover Rose's debts.

And now, in the paper with Rose's parasite named Bertolini, we see poor Duke Snider and Willie McCovey, seduced by the promise of easy money.

So we talk to John Dowd, who did baseball's investigation of Rose, and we hear him say, "Bertolini is singing like a canary. Aw, it's awful. All Pete had to do is write a check."

We talk to Dowd so we won't forget what Rose did. Dowd knows better than anyone because he did baseball's investigation of Rose under the direction of Bart Giamatti, the commissioner then.

Dowd had been a prosecutor in the Department of Justice given license to chase down Mafia figures. The novelist/lawyer George Higgins admired Dowd: "In the context of the Rose inquiry, to term John Dowd a lawyer formerly at Justice was equivalent to describing Alvin York in military history as an American army sergeant in World War I."

Higgins said Dowd was hired because everyone in the commissioner's office "was pretty much convinced that the attar of Rose's case was the perfume of the Mob, and that was a powerful danger to baseball."

We see Duke Snider and we hear Mike Schmidt and we talk to John Dowd so we'll remember what Pete Rose did to himself and to baseball.

The report ran 225 pages with 3,000 pages of interviews and documents. Three people swore they handled Rose's bets. An FBI handwriting analyst identified as Rose's the writing on a betting slip. Telephone records showed hundreds of calls from Rose's home, Rose's hotel rooms and the Reds' clubhouse to bookmakers and their agents.

Dowd had no "smoking gun," no videotape of Rose betting or wiretap of business with bookies. Still, his report was so painstaking in its incriminating detail that it was challenged only weakly, even laughably, by Rose's attorneys. (Their single rebuttal witness was a felon jailed for consumer fraud; he swallowed a straight pin, claimed it was in a Hostess Ding Dong cake and later explained to a judge, "I was a liar, and it was just another lie.")

Dowd's report said Rose bet on baseball, bet on his team, bet as much as $34,000 a day and may have bet $1 million in 1985, 1986 and 1987. He owed big money to bad people who could have turned on Rose. Only darkness lay ahead.

Rose wanted us to believe he cared about baseball. Near the end of June in 1989, in the Reds' clubhouse, he said, "Who has put more into baseball the last two decades than me? So why am I going to destroy baseball? Why would I destroy my reputation?"

Had he bet on the Reds? "Never." Not on baseball at all? "Never." And then he said to two reporters, "Does going to a racetrack make me a bad guy? I don't bet big. I bet more than you guys, but I make more money than you guys. My financial statement is as long as my arm. I've never had the electricity turned off because I couldn't pay the bill. I've never wanted to kill the cab driver on the way home from the track."

Even as Rose spoke, he must have known about Dowd's report. It had been completed six weeks earlier. On August 24, 1989, Rose agreed to a lifetime suspension in what amounted to a no-contest plea; baseball would not say he had bet on games if Rose would accept the punishment for having bet on games.

A lawyer for Rose said it was the best deal they could make. Dowd says Giamatti made the deal "to get the cloud off the game. He wanted to resolve it and move on. Rose's people weren't going to fight any longer. They surrendered."

In all of this sad story, a small part of the pain is that Rose couldn't admit a gambling addiction and deal with it. By now, five years later, things might have been better. John Dowd even thinks Rose by now might be in the Hall of Fame. He says, "Pete probably would have gone in with Schmidt."

A hitter first, a hitter always

NOVEMBER 14, 1994

Ted Williams is hitting. Always has been, always will be. Ted Williams is sitting by his pool on a sunny Florida day. He has an imaginary bat in his hands and his fingers are moving, as if the phantom stick of wood were a musical instrument under his touch. He twists his hands on a thin bat handle that only he feels. There comes to his old hero's handsome face a look of boyish delight, for he sees, and only he sees, a baseball coming his way. Oh, my. The joy of putting good wood on a baseball is eternal, and here is Ted Williams about to have fun.

"Hoyt Wilhelm's pitching. And Hoyt Wilhelm's all time for me. I'd get up against Hoyt Wilhelm and his first knuckleball, you could see it good but it was moving. The second one, it's moving more and you'd foul it off and you'd say, 'Geez, that's a good kunckleball. And now he throws you the three-strike knuckleball. It's all over the place, and you're lucky if you don't get hit with it because you don't know where the hell it's going. You could swing at it *AND GET HIT BY IT!*"

Ted Williams is 76 years old, and his voice is a kid's. He talks in italics and explosions of italics. The words become an actor's monologue given texture by gestures and sound effects and body language so precise that when he flutters a hand, doing a butterfly's flight, you, too, can see the Wilhelm knuckleball on its way. Oh, my. Williams bites his lower lip. He turns his hands around the bat. He narrows his eyes, and the game is on. A half-century ago they called him The Kid. Perfect.

When Williams is hitting, as he is at this moment by the pool, every nerve ending in the kid is alive to the precious possibility of a line drive off a distant fence. He calls them blue darters and scorchers. Now he is hitting against Hoyt Wilhelm, whose knuckleball confounded hitters for 20 years.

"I was always looking for Wilhelm's knuckleball because, geez, you were going to get it. I never will forget this one day. It was in Baltimore. And the ball got halfway to the plate. And I said ..."

The kid's eyes pop wide open. Astonishment.

"I said, *'Fastball!'* "

Williams all but leaps from his chair to get at it.

"BOOM! LINE DRIVE TO RIGHT FIELD!"

Then comes a smile soft with pleasure.

"I don't think I ever saw another fastball from Hoyt Wilhelm."

• • •

Ted Williams calls. Says come on down. Says he has chosen the 20 best hitters of all time. In February they'll go into the Hitters Hall of Fame adjoining the Ted Williams Museum in Hernando, Fla. He says come on down. Says he has chosen two men from each league for the Ted Williams Greatest Hitters Award, to be an annual award, the hitter's equivalent of the Cy Young.

Come on down. Let's talk.

So ...

The curving road toward Ted Williams' house stops at a wrought-iron gate. On the gate, his uniform number: 9.

Williams no longer moves with an athlete's ease. He tugs and pulls himself into position to get out of a car bringing him home from a workout.

Somewhere in the house a dog barks, and Williams calls out, "Slugger! Where are you, Slugger? Come here, boy, come here, Slugger."

And what else would you call Ted Williams' dog?

The slugger himself walks with an unsteady gait of a man on a rolling deck. He has one hand on a cane. A pair of glasses hang by a cord around his neck. He wears khaki shorts, a yellow golf shirt and brown deck shoes. There are spikes of gray in his thicket of black hair. Tall and erect, the lion in winter conjures the splendid splinter of the 1940s who for two decades and in two wars did a hero's work.

One morning in February of this year, Williams falls in his bedroom the way old men often fall. A blood vessel in the brain breaks open; the brain loses some part of its ability to govern the body. Williams had two strokes, one in December 1991, another a few months later. The latest is more serious.

It costs him strength in his legs. His left arm and left leg go numb and weak. He can see nothing, this man who had been a fighter pilot with vision once measured at 20-10. But on this sunny day nine months later, Williams no longer needs a wheelchair, no longer needs a walker, needs nothing, really. He carries a cane just in case. His sight came back, though the peripheral fields of vision remain a blur.

He counts his health as a marked improvement from February's weakness and darkness. He is even sly about it. "The only thing I'm concerned about," he says, "is my mental deficiency ..."

Someone begins to mumble something about memory loss, only to be interrupted by Williams laughing: "I'm *kidding,* I hope."

"I'm thinking pretty good. I don't see quite as well as I'd like to. If I look at you, I can see most of you but not distinctly. If I look at your head, it gets down to your chest.

"I'm exercising. My strength is pretty good. I work out three times a week, walk a mile three or four times a week. On the exercise bike four times. I do sit-ups. I take five-pound weights and work on my arms, 20 times up with each arm. I'm getting now (to) where they're giving me 35-, 40-pound barbells to lift.

"My legs are strong. Used to be, they could hold my leg down if I'm sitting in a chair. They can't do that no more. My left arm and left leg are still a little bit numb, but I'm getting better down there all the time. My appetite, geez, I can eat. I drink gallons of fluids."

Williams' eyes are watery and without sparkle. Even when he becomes animated in conversation, as he does for most of two hours, his voice an enthusiastic explosion of delight, his eyes seem to be somewhere else.

One day this summer, not long after the stroke, he told Dave Anderson of The New York Times about a dream he'd had in the hospital. He was working in he spring with Red Sox hitters, as he always did. Somehow the fearsome lefthander from Seattle, Randy Johnson, was on the mound. The Red Sox hitters say to Williams, "Why don't you get up there and take a few cuts?"

Only Ted Williams dreams this way: "I tell them, 'I haven't hit in years and I just had a stroke and I can't see too well,' but they kept teasing me and I say, 'Yeah, I'll do it.' But as I'm walking to home plate, I'm thinking, 'I'm not going to try to pull this guy because he can really throw.'

"The first pitch, he laid one right in there. I pushed at it. Line drive through the box for a base hit."

He laughs loud and long, the old man young again, made young by hitting, and you wonder if any great performer every had more fun doing his work that the kid from San Diego who in 1935 put his eye to a knothole and saw, at a great distance, a lefthanded hitter with style and, no way the kid could know this, a .349 lifetime average in the big leagues.

"Fun? The most fun in baseball is hitting the ball," Williams says. "That's all I practiced. That's all I did. That's all I could do for 20 years of my early life. If I had not become a pretty damned good hitter, there was something wrong. I had the opportunity; I had energy-plus, enthusiasm-plus, to want to do that very thing. And I certainly must have had some ability, being quick and strong."

And he put his eye to a knothole one day: "A kid copies what he sees is good. And if he's never seen it, he'll never know. I remember the first time I saw Lefty O'Doul, and he was as far away as . . . "

Ted Williams turns his head, looking across the pool, and his eyes become instruments of measure. ". . . as far away as those palms. And I saw the guy come to bat in batting practice. I was looking through a knothole, and I said, 'Geez, does that guy look good! And it was Lefty O'Doul, one of the great hitters ever."

· · ·

"Gods don't answer letters," John Updike wrote. He meant Ted Williams wouldn't tip his cap for fans. This is also true: Gods will talk all day about hitting.

Ted Williams, who dreams hitting, who lived hitting, who looked through a knothole 60 years ago and saw his future at-bat, who can see Hoyt Wilhelm's knuckler with a kids vision after an old mans stroke—Ted Williams will talk about DiMaggio with two strikes, will tell us what Hornsby taught him, will tell us he wishes he could talk to Michael Jordan.

Williams will talk about hitting and hitters. He'll tell us he could, sometimes, smell the ball. He'll say there were nights he couldn't sleep for wondering why he couldn't hit. For an hour Williams will make music that if put into one piece would sound like this . . .

"Don't swing level and don't swing down. Swing slightly up at the ball because it's coming slightly down. Get it in the air. Ground balls are a pitcher's best friend, so you gotta get it in the air with power.

"Two strikes, choke up a little Hit the ball hard through the middle. Like the great DiMaggio. Two strikes, Joe just didn't want to strike out. So hel'd hit it somewhere. Trouble with hitters today, they swing from their butt with two strikes because if you hit 34 home runs, even if you hit .260, *Whew, BIG PAYDAY!*

"Mickey Mantle was one of the greatest ever in the game. Had the almighty home-run strike. And fast, he didn't even have to hit a ball good to get a hit. The year he hit .360-something, I hit .388, everything falling in. I couldn't run a lick. I had eight or nine infield hits, and Mantle had 49. But he hit 50 home runs, too, even if he didn't know the difference between two strikes and no strikes. Had no idea, just swung from his butt. But what a player, what a guy.

"Hank Greenberg was a little on the Mantle side. Never saw Greenberg reach out and punch a ball, half-fooled, and still get a base hit with it.

"Now the great Mr. Musial would go the other way with two strikes. Every time I saw Stan Musial, he went *5 for 5!* I saw him two different days. *Five for 5 both days!* I had it once in my life, and I saw him get it twice. So, anyway, he could run like hell, and he could slap it all around, and he had a great park to hit in, and in the last 10 years of his career he bit with power.

"Power is it. I'm picking the 20 greatest hitters ever. Power. The concept of my list is that the major ingredients of the complete hitter are, No. 1, power, and No. 2, getting on base. Why is getting on base so important? Here I hit .340 and he hits .340. but I hit 40 home runs and he hits 20. Now, I've got more total bases. He walks 38 times, and I walk 138. Getting on base is how you score runs. Runs win ballgames.

"I walked a lot in high school, and in the minors I walked 100 times. It didn't just start in the big leagues. You start swinging at pitches a half-inch outside, the next one's an inch out and pretty soon you're getting nothing but bad balls to swing at. Rogers Hornsby told me, 'Get a good ball to hit.' Boy, that's it. *Get a good ball to hit.*

"I could see the spin on a pitch. If you're looking for breaking stuff, you see it's spinning 25 feet out there. Anticipation. I knew what was going to be thrown before I ever swung. I knew what the count was, what they got me out on, what the pitcher's out-pitch was, where the wind was blowing.

"And if they'd made me look bad on something, *Boy, would I lay for that son of a bitch.* I was a good guess hitter. A real good guess hitter. And when they came back with that pitch that made me look bad, *BOOM!* It would cost him then.

"Somebody asked me, if you can see the spin, you ever hear the ball? No, but I smelled it. Took a big cut at a fast ball. Didn't get but about four-sevenths of it, just nicked it back. I could smell the wood burning. I told this to Don Mattingly and Wade Boggs. Boggs looked at Mattingly; Mattingly looked at Boggs, like they're asking each other: What's he smoking? But I smelled it. And Willie Mays and Willie McCovey told me they smelled it, too.

"Good hitters today. You gotta think about Barry Bonds, Matt Williams, Jeff Bagwell. I love to watch that Frank Thomas hit. That's one big, strong guy. He can inside-out 'em like that and hit 'em outta there. Ken Griffey Jr. hits 'em in almighty clusters.

"I wish, I wish, I *wish* that I could have had a chance to talk to Michael Jordan. I am convinced that had he been a baseball player instead of a basketball player and had the baseball practice with the right surroundings he'd have been a hell of a player. He had to have the opportunity to hear all the things that can be involved in baseball, and he didn't hear any baseball.

"He's got a pretty good swing. He's got things that could be helped. I would just talk to him about the science of hitting. It's 50 percent mental. Why? Because of anticipation. Thinking who the pitcher is, knowing whether I'm strong or weak on a high ball and practicing that.

"Hitting is a correction thing. Every swing you're changing. Every thought you're correcting. Every time up you're thinking.

"My whole life was hitting. Hitting, nobody ever had more fun. I'll tell you, though, I'd like to tell you how many nights I couldn't sleep because I wasn't hitting too. I'd look up at the wall and I'd think, 'Holy, geez,' and I'd always be able to come up with some answer or some situation that started off the trouble.

"It was always more mechanical than anything else. And the biggest mechanical thing that I did was swing too hard. And when you swing hard, you're swinging big, And when you swing big, you have to start earlier. So you're fooled on more pitches. And how'd it all start? Because I went *whoosh* at a ball and, *boy, did it go!* Just a little flick and look where that ball went.

"So, I get to thinking, with a little bit longer swing, it'll got a little bit farther. Then I'd start pulling. And when you start pulling, you start bailing out a little bit early—until I'd stop that and just to back to flicking the bat at the ball, just getting the bat on the ball and then everything'd be OK again for a while."

· · ·

Ted Williams has a bat in his hand. It's a real one, a Louisville Slugger with his named burned into the barrel, the burned wood reminding him: "What a thrill, the first time you get a bat with your name on it."

That happened for him 58 years ago.

On this sunny day by the pool, a photographer has given Williams the bat and asked him to pose with it: This way, Ted, that way, hold the bat like this, lay it on your shoulder, rest your chin on it. The photographer is bending and crouching and moving, looking for a better angle, the camera shutter clicking, asking Ted for another smile.

Gods don't answer letters.

Neither do they smile seven times on requet.

Williams growling to the photographer: "That's enough. You got enough for a book."

It is the fall of 1994, just past the great man's 76th birthday, not a year since the stroke. He talks about the therapy center where he's met a girl whose name is Tricia. She's 12 or 13 and wants to be a lawyer. She, too, has had a stroke. Williams tells you about her intent little eyes watching you. He did a little something for her, he says, and she wrote him a nice little note. He says he plays checkers with little Tricia.

He wants to go fishing, Ted Williams does. For 50 years he has taken rod, reel and fly against every fish worth the fight in any water anywhere. He wants to get back to it.

He says, "No kidding about this: I didn't think I could ever use a cane by itself. Geez, now I can walk by myself. The only thing that bothers me is I don't see quite as good, and I wouldn't see something down the ground. But I'm accomodating all the time, getting better all the time. I'm never going to be able to run. I never thought I'd be able to ..."

He's about to say he never thought he'd go fishing again.

But enough.

He has heard enough of this never stuff.

Now his voice is rising. His chin comes up two clicks of defiance. He's The Kid again.

"I never though I'd be able to go fishing again, but I know *damn well I CAN SIT IN A CANOE!* And I can strip my line down here ..."

His hands are moving as if on a fishing line at his feet in a canoe on a sil-very stream somewhere. He sits straight up in his chair, tall and erect, now making a phantom cast, now whistling, "Whish, whoosh," the sounds of a reel whirring and line slicing the air.

"And I can throw it damn near as far," Ted Williams says. His face is warm with hope. "Maybe next spring. Maybe next spring I can go salmon fishing. I just feel like I'm going to be able to ..."

Lord of the flies

So one night the president of the United States goes to the Lincoln bedroom in the White House.

He wants to show his guest something. They walk to a room next door
and stop in front of two dressers with large mirrors and stacks of drawers.

There the president pulls open a drawer to reveal a cache the contents of
which are so unexpected that his guest, even years later, would say of that
moment, "Geez, I was just startled." What Ted Williams saw, that night by
Lincoln's bedroom in the White House, were hundreds of a fisherman's flies:
"Salmon flies and English flies. Flies 250, 200 years old." His voice is hushed
and dramatic, the thrilled whisper of a man afraid to speak loudly lest he end
the dream.

These flies have been the basis for tons and tons of flies. Their names are
Jock Scott, Durham Ranger, Silver Doctor and on and on. And they're all
beautifully tied. Married wings, which means duck orange, green, yellow and
red. Goose feathers, jungle cock crests, seal's fur, jungle cock eyes. "Had to be
$5,000 worth of flies in that drawer."

"It's the middle of the night in Lincoln's bedroom and we're looking at
flies, and then he took me to another place, another big drawer. Now he has

Orvis reels, Hardy reels, every big classic reel that's made. Much more than he needs to fish the way he does because he's fishing little trout, he fishes with shrimp, spinning in the Keys. But he loves to fish. Geezohboy."

What a wonderful sound, Ted Williams spinning a fish story.

He doesn't see well, and he walks with a wobble, the results of a stroke nine months ago. The good news is that at 76 he still is animated in conversation, bright and booming, sassy and passionate. He wanted to talk about the Hitters Hall of Fame and the 20 men he has chosen as charter members. He did that, and he talked about George Bush's cache of precious flies, and he answered every question fabulously …

Al Simmons? "Big guy. Gorilla with a bat in his hand."

Jimmy Foxx? "I was envious of his power."

Joe Jackson? "Everybody I talked to about Joe Jackson went into hysterics about how good he was. Eddie Collins played with the Black Sox and Joe Jackson. Eddie, when he signed me for the Red Sox, told me, 'Ted, the first time I watched you in batting practice, all I could see was Joe Jackson.'"

Lefty Grove? "Beautiful."

Tony Gwynn? "They ought to extend this season into next year, 162 games, before they say he didn't hit .400. I was rooting for him."

No World Series this year? "I'm damned disappointed and disgusted. These owners are supposed to be smart people. How can they jazz up anything that badly? And the players, they've won every situation for years and they're in such an enviable position I can't believe it. I can't fight against the players. But they gotta bend over to be reasonable."

To pick the 20 best hitters, Williams started with a statistical formula that he won't reveal. With those numbers as foundation, he then made subjective judgments based primarily on his half-century of observation. As for men he never saw play, Williams depended on history's accounts and the opinions of old-line baseball men.

No greater proof of subjectivity is needed than the absence from the list of Ted Williams. His numbers are mighty. Given weight for power and on-base percentage, as they should be, those numbers are second only to Babe Ruth's. But when questioned about his absence, the list-maker himself says, "Who cares if I'm on the list?"

End of debate.

The top 10: Babe Ruth, Lou Gehrig, Jimmy Foxx, Rogers Hornsby, Joe DiMaggio and Ty Cobb, Stan Musial, Joe Jackson, Henry Aaron and Willie

Mays.

Then: Hank Greenberg, Mickey Mantle, Tris Speaker, Al Simmons and Johnny Mize, Mel Ott, Harry Heilmann, Frank Robinson, Mike Schmidt and Ralph Kiner.

The presence of the .279-hitting Kiner may be as mysterious to some as the absence of Pete Rose, the self-proclaimed Hit King who broke Cobb's record for hits.

But Kiner in 10 years had 369 home runs; Rose in 24 had 160. And although Rose hit .303 lifetime, 3,215 of his 4,256 hits were singles. His total-base average of .469 is nearly 150 points below the list's average. Kiner's TBA is .621.

Happily, the Williams roster includes Shoeless Joe Jackson, banned from Cooperstown for having done business with gamblers. Williams: "These are the 20 greatest hitters. The Black Sox scandal's got nothing to do with it."

End of that debate.

As for that old fisherman and first baseman, George Bush, Ted Williams has plans.

"Hell of a good guy. Down to earth as can be. I was ready to go on a fishing trip with him in Labrador before I came down with this thing."

"Funny, he used to talk about his hitting at Yale. He says, 'Y'know, I was a lousy hitter.' So I kid him all the time. Anytime I get close to him and they're going to take a picture, I say, 'Two great hitters.'"

It was Whitey Ford, the sly one, who pointed out that he and Mickey Mantle combined for 539 home runs, all of them by Ford except for 536.

"That's what I'll do," Williams says, his voice a conspiratorial whisper. "I'll find out what the president did hit at Yale. Then I'll add my lifetime and his lifetime and announce: 'Lifetime between us: .326.' We'll take a great picture of two great hitters."

A wonderful sound, Ted Williams laughing.

CHAPTER 11

Yankees, Triumphant

The Boss

1999

Showboating blowhard, contemptible tyrant and stuffed-shirt bully that he is, George Steinbrenner now threatens to fire Yankee Stadium.

"Give me a stadium where I can succeed with this team," he says.

Say what?

Yankee Stadium is a hellhole?

The Yankees are about to go broke?

They last won a World Series two decades ago rather than two years ago?

This season's march into the record books happened for some other players in pinstripes with NY on their chests?

It's amazing. For George M. Steinbrenner III, baseball's most famous ballpark isn't enough. A $500 million cable-TV deal isn't enough. Three million customers a year aren't enough. The winningest Yankees team ever isn't enough. As always, George wants more.

New ballparks are driving up attendance from Atlanta to Toronto, from Baltimore to Denver, from Cleveland to Phoenix. Naturally, Steinbrenner wants one. Naturally, he wants a palace.

He wants it on the most expensive land in America, on Manhattan's West Side, where it will cause taxi-war gridlock while forcing New York's taxpayers to pony up construction costs of $1 billion so he then can sell four million tickets a year.

Although false modesty stops him short of saying it out loud, students of Steinbrenner's behavior know he would appreciate it if each and every New York taxpayer made a pilgrimage to his throne, there to bow, curtsy and thank him for extracting the Yankees from the sorry, crumbling, Babe Ruth-is-dead-anyway Yankee Stadium. Petitioners with proof of tax payments would be allowed to kiss his ring.

If he fails to achieve a new ballpark in the city, the Yankees' owner has threatened to move the team ... somewhere. He has invoked the cursed memory of Walter O'Malley moving the Dodgers out of Brooklyn 40 years ago. By also reminding everyone that the football Giants and Jets abandoned New York, he suggests the Yankees could follow them to New Jersey.

Say this for George: The man still has gall.

It has been 25 years of Steinbrenner comedy, calamity and chaos. We have seen him prancing in his underwear on Saturday Night Live. He dressed as Napoleon atop a white stallion for a Sports Illustrated cover. Asking a commissioner's mercy, he argued his own stupidity as defense for handing $40,000 to a smarmy gambler. Speaking of smarmy, he pleaded guilty to a felony crime for funneling $100,000 to Richard Nixon. Every other day, even in a beer commercial, he either hired or fired Billy Martin, who once said of Reggie Jackson and Steinbrenner, "The two of them deserve each other. One's a born liar, the other's convicted."

Steinbrenner, the icon, is so familiar that television's Jerry Seinfeld made him a character on his show (usually shouted down for trading Jay Buhner or giving $12 million to Hideki Irabu). When New York media mogul Mort Zuckerman fired his fourth editor in five years at U.S. News & World Report, a news story identified him as "the George Steinbrenner of publishing," no further explanation necessary.

Twenty-five years in baseball and what do we make of him now?

Here's a thought. Maybe he belongs in the Hall of Fame.

Yikes, let's get back to that in a minute.

On January 3, 1973, a beefy, ambitious and obscure 42-year-old Cleveland shipbuilder named George M. Steinbrenner III introduced himself to the New York media as one of two general partners leading a 12-man group that bought the woebegone, raggedy, garage-sale Yankees from CBS for $10 million.

When CBS bought the Yankees in 1964 for $13.2 million, the Yankees were proud successors to teams that had won 29 American League pennants and 20 World Series. They had had a winning record for 39 consecutive years and had drawn more than 1.3 million fans 19 consecutive years. They had three Hall of Famers in uniform: Mickey Mantle in the outfield, Whitey Ford pitching, Yogi Berra managing.

But those Yankees lords soon became paupers. Under CBS management for eight seasons, the Yankees never won a pennant, never drew 1.3 million fans and once finished 10th. Team president Michael Burke "was a charming and unfailingly cheerful man ... and even as he presided over the decline and fall of the Yankee empire, he managed to maintain his good humor and his popularity," Dick Schaap wrote in a Steinbrenner autobiography. "He was not a good loser. He was a great loser."

CBS chairman William S. Paley sought to dump the team in the winter of 1972. But he sold it only after sweetening the deal for Burke by promising him a better price if the new owners included Burke. Peddling the team, Burke spoke to Gabe Paul, president of the Indians, who passed along the name of a man who had put together a syndicate trying to buy the Indians.

That man: George Steinbrenner.

Burke had never heard of him.

George M. Steinbrenner III is the great-grandson of a woman who had taken over her father's Great Lakes shipping company in the late 19th century. A child of privilege raised on a 20-acre estate, Steinbrenner was never given money. Instead, his father demanded he start a business. He did. At age 9.

"He gave me chickens," Steinbrenner has said. "I'd get my money through them. I'd get up early, clean the roosts and then sell the eggs door to door. It was called The George Company. When I went away to school, I sold the company to my sisters."

He sold it for $50.

In 1944, near the end of World War II, the 14-year-old entrepreneur was sent to Culver Military Academy, a northern Indiana school designed to prepare wealthy young men for college work. There he played football and basketball and competed in track as a hurdler. At Williams College in Massachusetts—where he wrote the school newspaper's sports column—Steinbrenner set hurdling records and was the track team's captain his senior year.

After two years in the Air Force running the sports program at a base in

Columbus, Ohio, Steinbrenner enrolled at Ohio State intending to earn a master's degree and become a football coach. He worked the 1955 season as end coach at Northwestern and '56 as backfield coach at Purdue. His coaching career ended when his father asked him to return to the family shipping business, then struggling in competition with steel companies' own fleets.

But Steinbrenner's work as treasurer of Kinsman Marine didn't satisfy his need for athletic success. In 1960 he put together a group of investors who paid $125,000 for the Cleveland Pipers, who in 1962 won the American Basketball League championship. The ABL folded that same season. When Steinbrenner failed in a bid for an NBA franchise, he devoted all his energies to his father's shipping company.

Over the next decade, Steinbrenner, as president, built the company into a colossus. Its revenues tripled, its assets quadrupled and the company's net worth increased 300 percent. Steinbrenner had become the man baseball would know later, as the biographer Schaap described him: "the image of an owner in perpetual motion, making fierce and sometimes unreasonable demands of his employees, driving less energetic executives either into quitting or into despair, changing presidents almost as quickly as he changed Yankee managers."

That was the Steinbrenner who stood with Mike Burke on a January day in 1973 and embraced Burke as his peer in the operation of the Yankees while telling the press, "We plan absentee ownership. We're not going to pretend we're something we aren't. I'll stick to building ships."

As Burke would learn painfully, those words were an early signal that Steinbrenner regards the truth as a tool to be bent to a purpose. In fact, evidence years in the making suggests that Steinbrenner bends the truth artfully. He can be engaging, pleasant and so charming that a listener is well advised, while being seduced, to keep one hand pressed against his wallet.

Steinbrenner's brand of oratory produced a classic headline during the 1988 Winter Olympics at Calgary. The Canadian prairie often enjoys a winter phenomenon called the chinook, a sudden blast of hot air. Here came Steinbrenner to Calgary, his chest puffed up because the U.S. Olympic Committee had asked his advice. You'd have thought he was Patton storming into Ike's tent for permission to invade Russia. So that day's headline in the New York Daily News said: "The Big Chinook Arrives."

Burke felt that hot air quickly. Only four months into the deal, Steinbrenner forced Burke out of the general partner's job. He gave him "consultant" status. As best Burke could tell, Steinbrenner never consulted him.

The Burke episode put the early lie to Steinbrenner's promise of "absentee" ownership. Having found a stage to suit his ego, Steinbrenner became the very model of the ubiquitous, meddling, despotic genius of an owner. With his hands on every detail and around every throat, he has in 25 years jammed a century's worth of triumph, honor, folly and disgrace into his possession of baseball's Hope Diamond, the Yankees.

In a baseball sense, Steinbrenner himself never much mattered. All that ever really mattered was that the Yankees be the Yankees. So if Steinbrenner's mad-genius operation helped raise the Yankees from their CBS deathbed to win five A.L. pennants and three World Series, then everyone in baseball owes him a nod of thanks, however grudgingly such a nod may come.

And with that admission comes the realization that through all the Yankee turmoil of the past 25 years, Steinbrenner has been the real straw that stirred the drink. Others have come and gone. Reggie Jackson, gone. Billy Martin, gone. Thurman Munson, gone. Ron Guidry, Dave Winfield, Don Mattingly, gone. Steinbrenner, still here.

For better and for worse, it's impossible to explain baseball's tumultuous past quarter-century without mentioning Steinbrenner's name.

First, he showed how to win big with free agents. In the mid-1970s, what Atlanta's Ted Turner started with the signing of Andy Messersmith, Steinbrenner perfected by signing Catfish Hunter, Reggie Jackson and Don Gullett. The results: three consecutive A.L. pennants, 1976-78, with world championships the last two years.

Second, he negotiated a $500 million cable-TV deal that is both baseball's curse and blessing. It gave the Yankees unprecedented leverage in the free-agent market. It created a disparity in payroll structures that bedevils the game today. And it forced competitors to find new revenue streams, leading, if indirectly, to the latest round of stadium building.

Third, Steinbrenner found a new way to win. After a 1981 World Series loss to the Dodgers, the Yankees went 15 years before making it back to the Series, their longest absence in 73 seasons. During those dark years, Steinbrenner realized he no longer could win simply by writing checks; everyone had figured out that quick-fix game. So he painstakingly built a minor league organization to develop his own stars. Those players made possible the Yankees' success in 1998.

Steinbrenner did all this during tumult and warfare that might wear out a normal person but which are The Boss' very life forces. Only Steinbrenner ever was suspended from baseball by the commissioner after pleading guilty to the felony crime of corporate contributions to Nixon's presidential campaign. That 15-month suspension was ordered in Steinbrenner's first year with the Yankees. He was in the World Series three years later.

Only Steinbrenner ever asked for a "lifetime" suspension by the commissioner after admitting he gave $40,000 to a low-life gambler named Howie Spira, who insisted he was paid for damaging information about Yankees outfielder Dave Winfield. That 1990 suspension ended before the '93 season. Steinbrenner was in the World Series in '96.

Some theorists trace the Yankees' current success to Steinbrenner's most recent suspension. They say that in his absence his lieutenants were able to build stability into the farm system that has served the organization so well this decade.

Does any reasonable person buy that theory? That Steinbrenner didn't make the major decisions by remote control? It's a fact the Yankees signed Catfish Hunter during The Boss' first suspension. It's also a fact there is a pay phone on every street corner in America. And it's a fact that during Steinbrenner's second suspension, those folks who believe he is a congenital control freak gave him a new nickname. They called him "Quarters."

That was then the going rate at a pay phone.

Back to that Hall of Fame thought ... Steinbrenner never has been anything but a team owner, and only two men are in the Hall for their work solely as owners. They are Tom Yawkey and Bill Veeck, one a famously beloved sportsman, the other a showman nonpareil.

Steinbrenner is neither Yawkey nor Veeck. At the same time, it's also true that neither of those good men did the wonderful thing Steinbrenner has done. He found the Hope Diamond in a dumpster.

"Like a damn baseball machine"

AUGUST 21, 1995

An outfielder whose name escapes memory once was bold enough to suggest he might hit 50 home runs and steal 50 bases in the same season. The thought excited interest in many observers, but not in an old outfielder named Mickey Mantle. "If I'd known 50-50 was such a big deal," Mickey Mantle said, "I'da done it lots of times."

At his strongest and fastest, the best center fielder who ever played, Mickey Mantle did work Willie Mays never came near doing. He outran everyone, he hit balls farther than anyone. Righthanded, he believed he should never make an out. Lefthanded, he believed everything he hit should leave the park, and leave it now. He threw out anyone foolish enough to think he couldn't do it. And, not the least of it, no one ever looked more like a ballplayer or caused more people to stop and take in a breath at seeing a man so beautiful.

We came to see him as a symbol of power and grace, the first slugger with speed. Because we knew the costs in pain and fear, we admired him all the more. We looked in wonder at Mickey Mantle, amazed that anyone could do any of the things he did, let alone all of them—and all of them done in baseball's cathedral, Yankee Stadium, where Ruth and Gehrig and DiMaggio

213

walked before the kid named Mantle came up from nowhere.

Nowhere began in Oklahoma. At the turn of the century, lefthander Charlie Mantle pitched for a lead-and-zinc mining company team in Spavinaw. His son, Mutt, a righthander, pitched for the same miners' team. With pitchers enough, Mutt Mantle named his first-born Mickey Charles Mantle, honoring the grandfather and Philadelphia's catcher, Mickey Cochrane.

The Mantles took turns pitching to the boy, first the lefthanded grandfather and then the righthanded father. With each change in pitchers, young Mantle moved across the plate. To be a pro ballplayer, his father had decided, it would help if Mickey learned to switch-hit at an early age.

"I first heard of Mickey when he was in his third year at Commerce High in 1948," Yankees scout Tom Greenwade said in the spring of 1951. "A fellow named Kenny Jacobson, who was in the Commerce Fire Department and served as a sort of emergency umpire in local ball, told me about him.

"I went over to see him play at Alva, Mo., but I wasn't particularly impressed. The boy was only 16. They used to call him 'Little Mickey Mantle' in those days. I couldn't have signed him, anyway, because he was still in school, but Kenny kept giving me reports on the boy." The third time Greenwade saw the boy, he saw more than a boy. He saw the man. The future.

"Mickey had leg problems, so not too many scouts paid attention to him. I saw him in two games, but I didn't really see him. He looked kind of small—he hadn't filled out yet—and I just didn't recognize how coordinated he was.

"I didn't know he was a switch-hitter! In those first two games he'd only batted lefthanded … In the third game, he stepped into the batter's box from the right side, and I didn't know what to make of it.

"Mickey's father was sitting right next to me, and I asked him how long his boy had been a switch-hitter. He said, 'Since he was about 8.' Then I looked again at Mickey, and he pulled a line-shot to left for a double, and it all came together.

"Finally I could see that 17-year-old body, how it worked like a damn baseball machine, and how it was gonna fill out. I understood how he'd been blessed. And I was blessed, too."

For a bonus of $1,100 and $400 in salary for the rest of a summer in Class D, Mickey Mantle signed with the Yankees and played shortstop at Independence, Mo. The next spring, Hall of Fame catcher Bill Dickey threw batting practice to the Yankees' best prospects, one of them Mantle.

Dickey in 1951: "The boy hit the first six balls nearly 500 feet, over the lights and out of sight. He hit them over the fences righthanded and lefthanded and he hit 'em over the right-field fence righthanded and the left-field fence lefthanded.

"When he was at short, he didn't impress me as being particularly fast, but when we divided the boys up for a series of 75-yard sprints, Mickey finished first in his group, looking over his shoulder at the others. Then we had a sprint for the winners and he won that, too. Then he got sick and explained that he wasn't in shape.

"I honestly believe Mantle is the fastest man I've ever seen in a baseball uniform."

Seeing Mantle for the first time himself, baseball genius Branch Rickey passed a blank check to Yankees owner Dan Topping. "Fill in the amount for the kid Mantle," Rickey said, the gesture made for the theater of it more than for any hope Topping could be such a fool.

In 1951, at age 19, Mantle joined the big club. New York sportswriter Dan Daniel described him as a "kid in bad need of a haircut with a sport coat that barely came down to his wrists." Casey Stengel, the manager, didn't care about the kid's wardrobe. "My God," he said on seeing Mantle at work, "the boy runs faster than Cobb."

Though always a shortstop, Mantle moved to the Yankees' outfield because Stengel already had Phil Rizzuto at short and didn't want to wait three years to get Mantle into the lineup. But early that season, big league pitching was too much for the kid; the Yankees sent him to their farm team at Kansas City, where his slump continued.

Despondent, Mantle talked of quitting and going home to Oklahoma. But Mutt Mantle would hear of no such thing. His father came to Kansas City to talk to the boy. Six weeks later, in time for the pennant race and his first World Series, Mickey Mantle returned to the Yankees for good. That next spring, at 39 years old, Mutt Mantle died.

He'll always be The Mick

JUNE 19, 1995

So we think of Mickey Mantle who was every kid's 1950s idea of what a ballplayer should be, the hero Mickey with his cap bill rolled just so, the socks and pinstripes perfect where they met on his muscled calf, Mickey daring a pitcher to come with his best stuff because from either side of the plate, better than any man who ever lived, Mickey could take it deep or lay down a bunt and be at first before anyone touched the ball, a player of whom Casey Stengel said, "Mickey had it in his body to be great."

We hear the name with its wonderful rhythms speaking of power and grace. Say the name aloud, Mickey Mantle, and you hear a memory. The memory is a full-page photograph torn from SPORT magazine and taped to a bedroom wall in 1956. It's Mantle at bat lefthanded, his right knee coming toward his left. The bat is ready, its barrel tilted toward the pitcher.

Say the name aloud: Mickey Mantle. A golden boy from Oklahoma, handsome as sunrise, who once walked out of a ballpark with a blonde on his arm and told a rookie, "Stick around, kid. My legs might get tired." Strong, certain, perfect. And now, all these years later, he is in a hospital, frail and uncertain and imperfect in the ways most of us are imperfect. He is 63 and even with a new liver is in desperate trouble: The odds favor death when a

216

man under attack by hepatitis comes late to a doctor who finds a cancerous liver. How melancholy to hear his wife make a joke of Mantle's emaciation; she told him his stomach hasn't been so small since he was 20. How much it hurts to be reminded of what he used to be when he was Mickey Mantle young and strong and certain.

He came to Yankee Stadium as a kid born the year before Babe Ruth called his shot in the World Series. He came to the patch of outfield grass consecrated by Joe DiMaggio. His father, the inelegantly named Mutt, had named the boy for the great catcher Mickey Cochrane; he taught the Mick to hit from both sides and raised him to be the ballplayer Mutt never was. "All I had was natural ability," Mickey once said, meaning he almost never knew why anything happened the way it did but he was glad when it worked out so often, as on a day of a hangover when he was roused from the bench and ordered to pinch hit.

Somehow he hit a high fastball out of the park, and on returning to the bench told his buddies, "The tough part was making it around the bases," which they understood to be as true as it was funny, for even early on the kid from Oklahoma found buddies who taught him the kind of night-running that caused Stengel to speak of players as "whiskey slick," a term Mantle and his brothers in vodka, Billy Martin and Whitey Ford, liked so much they began calling each other Slick. In time the incorrigible rascal Martin—"A mouse studying to be a rat," in Red Smith's phrase—would be traded from the Yankees after a nightclub brawl and years later would say with a laugh, "They said I was a bad influence on Mickey and Whitey. Now they're both in the Hall of Fame, and I'm not. Who was bad for who?" And then on Christmas Day 1989, after drinking all day, Billy Martin died in the wreck of a truck on his way home, the bills for his life having come due.

Mickey Mantle never expected to pay. Or, to say it more precisely: Mickey Mantle never expected to be around when the bill collector came looking for him. He lived with a sense of approaching death. Because his father, grandfather and two uncles had died of lymphatic cancer, all before the age of 42, Mantle came to believe he would be dead soon. Unable, or afraid, to confront his fears and share them with his wife and children, he lived a hollow life that seemed to be what Hemingway had in mind when he said, "Whatever makes you feel good is good." Which, for Mickey Mantle, came down to baseball, women and booze, a combination first revealed by a Yankee teammate, Jim Bouton, whose book, "Ball Four," praised Mantle for his boyish charm and warmth to his teammates while suggesting he might have had an even more spectacular career if he had slept more and bellied up to the bar less. To the inevitable cries of outrage, Bouton referred critics to a television commercial in which Mantle and Ford debate a beer's attributes—more taste? less filling?—with one Hall of Famer saying, "I only drink on special occasions," the other answering, "Yeah, like after every game." All of it so much boys-will-be-boys fun until a year ago when Mantle's weary, worn and woeful face showed up on a magazine under the headline, "I Was Killing Myself," a confession to alcoholism. All those good times he had as an American hero, too bad, he said, that he didn't remember most of them.

On that bedroom wall in 1956 was another photograph, a picture of Marilyn Monroe, whose name, so much like Mickey Mantle's, came with its own soft suggestions, no harsh consonants, hers a suggestion of silky whispers and hers, like his, in the end misleading. Not long before her death at 36, perhaps done by barbiturates, perhaps intentionally, she wrote in her dressing room notebook, "What am I afraid of? Why am I so afraid? Do I think I can't act? I know I can act but I am afraid. I am afraid and I should not be and I must not be." Always part of her, fear moved in Marilyn's nights just as it did for Mickey, who once had a dream in which he could hear the public-address announcer saying, "Now batting, Number 7, Mickey Mantle," only Mantle was outside the stadium, the doors locked, the fences and gates locked, Casey and Billy and Whitey all looking for him, waiting, and he can't get in. A recurring dream, night after night, a dream of failure, of banishment, maybe even of death.

Today he is in a hospital, a man who inspired us with his work, who brooded over too many drinks that he would soon be dead. By getting off the booze, too late but off it nevertheless, he has done the brave thing of confronting the life he created. And give him this: Mickey Mantle has taken responsibility, he has sought to blame no one else, and he has asked forgiveness from his loved ones. Such is the stuff of real heroes.

CHAPTER 12

You Never
Quit

One step at a time

The BALL PARK

His father took the boy to the ball park and the boy whose name was
Steve Palermo saw a wonderful place. The ball players were so close. He could
hear their voices. If they moved toward him only a little, he could almost
touch them.

This was 1961 at Fenway Park in Boston. The boy was 11 and even today,
all these years later, he remembers two ball players in their snowy white uniforms. They were rookies, boys themselves. They played catch on the first-
base side and Steve Palermo could hear the baseball hit their gloves. Their
names were Carl Yastrzemski and Chuck Schilling.

When suddenly a ball bounced loose. And Steve did what boys do at the
ball park.

He leaned over the low railing at Fenway park and scooped up the
loose ball.

He looked at it in wonder and cradled it in his hands, the way you care
for a precious thing. It was a real big-league baseball. He told his father he
would put it on the mantel at home. He rubbed his hands around the ball, as
if by touching it he could learn from it. He would never take this ball out of

the house.

Boys often make promises boys can't keep. This doozy lasted six days. Someone got up a game at the corner and little Stevie took along the big-league ball. A week or two of this and the boys had knocked the cover off the ball. So Stevie wrapped white tape around the exposed gray yarn and in time that tape turned dirty and fell apart and the genuine big-league baseball was history.

The father took the boy to the ball park so many times that in 1976 it was the boy's turn to take the father. By then Steve Palermo was a big-league umpire. He worked his first game at Fenway Park. That day, he took his father with him into the umpire's dressing room above the Red Sox clubhouse. And when it came time to walk to the field, Vincent Palermo stood at the top of the stairs.

"Dad, come on," the boy umpire said.

Amazing. That's what the father would say years later. Amazing that his boy was in the big leagues. This was Fenway Park. The father said he stayed at the top of the stairs because it was a moment he wished would last forever.

It was two years later, in the 1978 playoff game, when Bucky Dent of the Yankees hit a home run to left field and broke Boston's heart. Vincent Palermo had a question for his son, the third-base umpire that autumn day in Fenway.

"How," he wanted to know from Steve, "could you call that ball fair?"

"Dad, it was 20 feet from the line," the son said.

"But how could you call it fair?"

Boys and their fathers come to Fenway Park and, in the summer of 1991, a boy maybe 11 years old put his ball glove on the railing along the first-base side. He had printed his name on the glove: ETHAN KERR.

Suddenly, an umpire snatched the glove away.

"Is there an Ethan Kerr here?" the umpire shouted.

"Me," the boy said.

"You have any identification? A driver's license?"

The boy shook his head no.

"How do I know you're Ethan Kerr?" the umpire said as he walked toward left field carrying the boy's glove.

Ethan Kerr called out, "My father's here, he'll tell you."

And Steve Palermo gave the boy his glove and the boy noticed something right away. He opened the glove and there it was. The umpire had given

Ethan Kerr a baseball. A real big-league baseball. The boy held it in his hands. It was precious.

• • •

The SIDEWALK

Before it happened, Steve Palermo had become a great umpire. Still a young man, 41, he worked a baseball game as smoothly and enthusiastically as anyone ever had. He moved with the authority of a man born to his work. Smiling, he talked to players, fans, ground crews, anyone who would listen and (thinking here of Earl Weaver) some who wouldn't. It was Steve Palermo's world and he loved it.

His first mentor, Joe Linsalata, told him good umpires are like boxers. You get down. You move. You jab. You get out of there. Palermo says the challenge is to be perfect. For every can of corn, you get out there as if it's the toughest play you'll ever call. The rules are 15 percent of the job. The game is what matters and rule 9.01(a) says, "The umpires shall be responsible for the conduct of the game ... "

The first time he was paid for umpiring, Palermo, then 13, got $2 a game five times a week. He hadn't umpired in five years when someone asked him to help out in a Little League All-Star game in his hometown of Worcester, Mass. That day, an umpire scout handed the kid a business card and set in motion events that would take Palermo to umpiring school and, at age 26, to the big leagues.

Palermo worked Dave Righetti's no-hitter in 1983. He was behind the plate when the '83 World Series ended. One autumn day, he ran under Dent's fly ball. He once took a Nolan Ryan fastball on his hip and cursed the catcher, who in turn cursed Ryan for crossing him up. Though an old umpire told Palermo a good umpire could miss 12 ball-and-strike calls in a game, Palermo said, "If I miss 12 calls a month, I'd jump off the World Trade Center."

It's the heat that Steve Palermo likes. "Give me the heat of a big game," he says. Larry Bird wants the last shot. Steve Palermo wants to be behind the plate when the game means the most. He went jaw-to-jaw with Earl Weaver so many times that on his living room wall there is an oil painting of Palermo in full rhubarb with the man he calls "the militant midget."

For Palermo, the umpiring has ended, perhaps temporarily but maybe forever. It ended in gunfire the morning of July 7, 1991.

The shooting happened near closing time for Campisi's Egyptian

Restaurant in Dallas. At 1 a.m., after working a Texas Rangers game, Palermo sat with four or five buddies.

As bartender Jimmy Upton opened a door to leave the restaurant, he saw four young men attacking two waitresses. One woman fell under the weight of her mugger. Upton shouted into the restaurant, "The girls are being mugged."

Everyone piled out. Palermo, restaurant owner Corky Campisi, former Southern Methodist University defensive lineman Terance Mann, and three other men took off. For three long blocks, they chased the muggers down East Mockingbird Lane. As he ran, Palermo had thought: "This might not be the smartest thing we've ever done."

But they were into it. Their friends had been attacked. The muggers had made it personal. Palermo kept running

The chase came to an end in front of Mrs. Baird's Bakery at 5630 E. Mockingbird Lane. Mann tackled one thief. The other three had vanished.

Then, as Palermo stood on the sidewalk outside Mrs. Baird's, the umpire noticed a car come up from behind the crowd.

He saw three men in the car.

He saw one raise his hand.

He shouted to his buddies, "Lookout, he's got something—a gun."

Palermo heard five shots. He remembers the sounds. Four quick explosions. Then one more.

A .32 caliber bullet entered Palermo's right hip and cut a path through his body before exiting the left side. Along the way it hit the umpire's spinal column, fracturing a vertebra. It also left the spinal cord frayed. He was, at that instant, paralyzed from the waist down.

Jimmy Upton saw Palermo on the sidewalk outside the bakery. He thought the umpire was dead because he lay there so very still. Coming closer, he saw Palermo's eyes were open and he heard Palermo say, "I've been shot. My back." The umpire tried to roll over on this side to relieve the pain.

But Upton, knowing the danger in moving a patient with a back injury, wouldn't allow Palermo to turn over. He put his chest against Palermo's. He slid a hand under the umpire's back. There he felt moisture and didn't know what it was until he withdrew his hand and saw it covered with blood.

Palermo said, "Jimmy, my legs are hot. My back is hot."

Upton said, "Just lay still, Stevie."

Palermo saw ambulance lights turning red against the night. He saw police cars there. "Maybe I'm going to die," he said.

Upton said, "There won't be no dying done here. We ain't got time for dying here."

· · ·

The POOL

Steve Palermo and his wife, Debbie, live 10 minutes from the Mid-American Rehabilitation Hospital in Overland Park, Kan., a suburb of Kansas City. Monday through Friday, she drives him there for therapy that begins at 9 a.m. in a pool with water warmed to 92 degrees.

The first week of December, five months after the shooting, Palermo sat on a ledge in the pool while therapist Joy Hermesmeyer did her work. A little smile decorated his dark good looks when he said, "Torture time."

Hermesmeyer stood in the pool, took Palermo's right foot in her hands and raised the leg high to stretch the hamstring muscle. She did this for 10 minutes with each leg while Palermo clenched his teeth against the pain.

He wants to be well again. And now. "I am an impatient patient." He has said he will walk again and he will umpire again. Laughing, he calls the therapists "terrorists." He wants to walk. "And I don't mean walk OK. I don't mean walk acceptable. I want to walk great."

A doctor told him it was a good thing the bullet came from a .32 caliber gun. The way it passed through his body, Palermo would be dead had the bullet been a millimeter thicker.

So if giving up your body to terroristic therapists is not as nice as working third base at Fenway, there is this to be said for it: It is better than being dead on a Dallas sidewalk.

During the trial that put the shooter away for 75 years, Palermo described what the gunshot did: "I felt myself going slowly to the ground, melting into the pavement. Sort of a warm numbness came over my legs. I touched them and it was like touching a limb of a tree. There was nothing there."

His first week in a hospital, Palermo could not move either leg. He had movement only in two toes of his right foot. When a doctor told Debbie Palermo that her husband would never walk again, the bright and beautiful young woman—a bride less than five months at the time—told the doctor she wouldn't deliver any such mistaken news.

She said to the doctor, "You go tell him that." The doctor told Palermo it was "highly unlikely" he would walk.

In September, Palermo said his paralyzed lower body made it feel like he has a suitcase inside him. Everyday acts of living became so difficult that he despaired at the prospect of taking a shower.

In the months since the shooting, Palermo has made progress. The progress comes in increments so small as to be invisible day by day. The umpire is often left exhausted and frustrated. At those moments, Debbie Palermo adds up the increments and tells him the total is "unbelievable progress." She even made up a sign that reminds him, "Inch by inch, life's a cinch."

One of those inches of movement came early in December. Palermo sat on the pool ledge and told Hermesmeyer about a pain along his right shin bone. "A shot," he said.

"Steady pain at all?" Hermesmeyer said.

"A shot."

Pain means the nerves, once traumatized into paralysis, are back at work in some way. Which is good, or, as Palermo said with a wince of pain, "A bad good."

The morning of the shooting, Debbie Palermo got a telephone call at 4 a.m. By 8 o'clock, she had flown from Kansas City to Dallas and stood at her husband's bed in Parkland Hospital. In the five months of therapy, she has been with him all but two days. Steve Palermo said people seem to think he's a hero. He says if there's a hero here, it's Debbie.

"Steve's in a hurry," she said that morning at the pool. "I'm afraid he's going to try too much too soon and break an arm or something. That'll set him back from where he is. And where he is now is not where he is going to wind up. He has to measure himself against the time he could move only two toes, not before that. He'll get where he wants to get. It just going to take time."

The pool comes first every morning. Joy Hermesmeyer is there smiling. She says, "The idea of therapy in the pool is that anything the patient can do in water, he will be able to do on dry land." Her tone shifted from instructive to gently chiding as she looked at Palermo and said, "I don't know that Steve believes that yet."

In the water, Palermo did hard work. While sitting, he did 100 leg kicks sideways across his body, 50 with each leg. Then he did 100 leg lifts with a small float strapped to his ankles. Then five walking laps of 16 steps each way across the pool, balancing himself with floats under his hands while

Hermesmeyer followed him with her hands touching his hips for support. Then he did three laps with no floats at all, simply treading water with his hands for balance.

This took 90 minutes. It was a tedious grind of slow motion. Palermo's steps in the pool were ungainly. His knees floated too high and his reaching steps had no certainty about their destination until his feet bumped against the pool floor. He moved like a man in the dark trying to pick his way silently across a floor covered with toys.

He moved slowly.

Inch by inch.

And then he moved with no help at all. No floats. No therapist's hand. It was movement as beautiful as it was ungainly. Here are a reporter's notes: "At the end, Joy isn't touching him at all. She's like a mother who has taken her hands off her boy learning to ride a bicycle. He's free now. He is walking. Steve bites his upper lip. He is single-minded. Eyes are focused on where he's going. No smiling, no talking. Walking takes his full attention. Now Joy hustles to catch up. She's almost blushing she's so happy."

On July 7, he could move two toes. Three months later, he could walk by using hand crutches and full braces to support his legs. Then one day in October he asked a therapist to go outdoors with him because he wanted to do a test. He asked her to go 22 steps away. He held both crutches in his left hand. Then the righthander threw her a baseball.

It was his only bullpen work before saying yes to Commissioner Fay Vincent's invitation to throw out the first ball for the 1991 World Series. Palermo just wanted to be sure he wouldn't bounce it in there.

• • •

The GYM

Mid-America's gym is busy shortly after lunch. Therapists work a patient's body until it can do heroic things. Such as stand up.

A therapist sat across from an old man on one of the larger platforms used during exercises. The therapist tossed a balloon toward the old man and the man reached up, tapped the balloon back toward the therapist and broke into a smile.

A young man named Casey gathered a crowd of patients in a corner of the gym to watch his video. He watches it everyday.

The grainy tape first shows Casey as a rock 'n' roll drummer lashing at the drums so quickly the sticks become a blur. Then he is in bed, eyes open but seeing nothing. A car accident crushed his left side. Doctors said he would never come out of the coma.

But on the TV screen he sits up and bats a balloon back to a therapist. Then he is walking carefully, his left side still weak. The crowd saw all this on the video that ends with Casey seated behind a drum set. He beat the drums slowly, smiling at his good work.

Steve Palermo applauded and said, "Bravo, Casey. Bravo."

Casey said, "They told me I'd be a vegetable. And they told me I'd never have any function in my left hand. I want to see that doctor and say, 'How's this for function?'" At which point, Casey raised a finger of his left hand and laughed out loud.

The Mid-America gym was full of damaged people. A child tried on an artificial arm. A woman lay strapped against a tilt board. A tall young man in a wheelchair wore a steel frame around his head—a "halo"—to stabilize his broken neck.

These people had their damage in common. They also shared hope. Palermo said, "They can look at X-rays of your spinal cord and they can do MRIs and they can tell you about the regeneration of nerves. But they can't take a picture of your heart. They don't know how big your heart is."

As if to measure his heart, the umpire looked around at Debbie and therapist Bobbi Arp and said, "Today, you guys are going to see a paraplegic do a new trick."

The walking Palermo has done since July 7 was accomplished with the help of hand crutches and full leg braces. There would be no leg braces this day. For the first time since he found himself running down Mockingbird Land in Dallas, Palermo asked his legs to work without steel supporting them. "I'm going out there naked," he said.

And he walked, using only hand crutches.

With Debbie beside him and Arp behind him, Palermo walked maybe 50 yards out of the gym and down a hospital corridor.

Back in the gym, he sat down on an exercise platform, tired and hurting in the very best bad-good way.

Debbie tousled his hair and kissed him and when he said nothing, she said with excitement in her voice, "Stevie, are we excited?"

He sat silent, his eyes closed, his head bowed.

She tilted her head to look at him and said, "Sort of?"

He said nothing.

"It's there," Debbie said to her husband. "You just have to get it stronger."

They embraced and he brushed a tear off his cheek. At last he said, "That's the best walk I ever took."

Then he said, "Cut 'em all down," meaning he wanted to get rid of any full leg braces still around. From now on he would need only a small brace to support his left foot, in which nerve damage causes the foot to fall forward.

Palermo next moved to the parallel bars. The routine is to walk between them and hold on for support and balance. But on this glad day he soon became bold.

First he walked while pressing the backs of his hands against the bars. When the therapist Arp moved closer, Palermo shooed her away. "If I fall," he said, "I'll fall all the way."

From across the room Joy Hermesmeyer saw Palermo doing his new trick. The pool therapist called to him, "I'd scream, but you'd probably fall." Which prompted Palermo to take the backs of his hands away from the bars. Holding nothing, touching nothing, he teetered for a moment. Then he walked two steps, three steps, four. A reporter made a note here: "My palms are sweating."

Out of the parallel bars, Palermo, with Arp touching his hips, moved toward Debbie. Then he asked the therapist to let go. He stood in the middle of the gym with no crutches, no bars to grab should he begin to fall, no braces helping, no one touching him.

And at 1:42 p.m. December 5, Palermo walked $2^1/_2$ steps on his own and put his head on his wife's shoulder. At this victory, they wept.

Bobbi Arp said, "So what do you think?"

Palermo said, "It's coming, it's coming."

Debbie Palermo ran her hand across his forehead. "What do you think? That I've been lying to you all this time?"

It was the umpire's best day since July 7. He also walked using only a cane. He once took the cane by the wrong end, swinging it like a golf club, and said he could stand well enough to go hit some chip shots with his buddies at Wolf Creek Golf Club.

Then Palermo looked across the gym to a window through which he could see the Kansas prairie. With delight in his voice, he said he knew what he wanted to do next. "I want to get a running start, jump through that window and fly."

• • •

HOME

Therapy is hard and cruel and exhausting. Progress gives an inch today and takes back half of it tomorrow. A patient's abiding fear is that it's all to no end, that there's only so far the body can go even if the spirit is willing. In those moments of doubt, it helps to know that people care.

At home in Overland Park, Debbie Palermo has a file of 3,000 letters from people who care. One of those letters came from a young boy who lives in Boston.

Steve sat in an easy chair under the oil painting of himself and Earl Weaver. He had the boy's letter in his hand. It began, "Tuesday, May 14, 1991, the Red Sox beat the White Sox, 4-1, in 9 innings …"

The letter was from Ethan Kerr. He didn't know if Steve remembered that day in May. But the boy did. The umpire had been a nice guy. He had given the boy a real big-league baseball. So Ethan wrote the letter thanking him. He also enclosed a card on which he wrote, "Hope you get better soon, Steve."

She still sees blue sky

NOVEMBER 22, 1999

Rebecca Veeck, 8 years old, went to Cooperstown to see her grandfather. Looking at a photograph of Bill Veeck with Larry Doby, she took off her sunglasses and asked, "Which one is Grandpa?"

Mike Veeck knew it was a matter of light and shadow. His daughter is losing her sight. Her eyes were slow to adjust to the room's brightness. Black was white, and white was black. And, if for only a moment the colors were the same—"Which one is Grandpa?"—Mike Veeck recognized that moment. "A lovely thought," he said.

He took his daughter to baseball's Hall of Fame because her grandpa earned a place there, and he wanted her to see it while she can. At home, she had seen pictures of her daddy's daddy. What a man Bill Veeck was, robust and roaring in laughter, even about the wooden leg replacing one lost in war. Just two things to be afraid of, he said: "Fire and termites."

"Look, Daddy, Grandpa's got two feet," Rebecca Veeck said at Cooperstown. The old man she had seen in pictures she now saw as a young man. The wizened face was unlined. The little girl saw her grandpa for the first time with two feet. She saw him with Larry Doby, who came from the Negro National League to play for Veeck's Indians.

Now a Hall of Famer alongside his old boss, Doby came to Cooperstown with Rebecca and her father, because of all the wonders Bill Veeck did as owner/president/marketer, what he did best was look at black and white and see those colors as the same.

Doby saw Rebecca see her grandfather, and he heard her ask, "Where's the exploding scoreboard?" Bill Veeck's ballparks sparkled with circuses and fireworks. Rebecca's question and laugh resonated with Doby: "She's like a chip off the old block. You see it in her, the same qualities that her grandfather had."

It's the family trade. Rebecca's first baseball job was to recline in her bassinet until called on; then she'd sit up and say hi to folks entering her daddy's ballpark. She was not yet talking when she first sang, "Take Me Out to the Ball Game." At 6, she handed out schedules and announced lineups.

In 1917, the sportswriter William Veeck Sr. wrote articles telling Cubs owner William Wrigley how to run his forlorn organization. Wrigley hired him. Until his death in 1933, the reformed writer nudged the Cubs toward respectability.

Then his son, a college graduate without a job, went to work for the Cubs at $18 a week as an office boy reporting to Phil Wrigley, the son of the man who had hired his father.

Bill Veeck and his father had intended to start a small-town newspaper. But during the Depression, an $18 salary was a powerful lure. Veeck soon discovered he loved the world inside a ballpark. For 50 more years, he taught us to love it.

Happily, Mike Veeck is his father's son. Would anyone other than a Veeck train a half-ton pig named Hambino to deliver baseballs to the home plate umpire? Offer a free vasectomy to a lucky man at a Father's Day game? Celebrate "Two Dead Fat Guys Day" on August 16, the date on which Babe Ruth and Elvis Presley died?

He was able to do such fun and foolishness because he did it for a good boss: himself. With ownership interests in five minor league teams from South Carolina to South Dakota, Veeck, now 48, calls himself "a minor league guy. I'll go to my grave a minor league guy."

He forgot that for a minute. In October 1998, he took a major league job as vice president of sales and marketing for the Tampa Bay Devil Rays.

That same month, Rebecca went in for an eye examination and couldn't see the big E on the chart.

"We thought she was goofin' because that's the kind of fun kid she is," Veeck says. "But we found out she'd been living in shadows her whole life."

The diagnosis was retinitis pigmentosa. How long Rebecca will see, no one can say, but the disease often moves rapidly.

One Sunday morning this spring, Rebecca said, "Daddy, look at the sky. How blue."

Veeck had worked eight months of marathon days trying to sell baseball to a Florida audience not buying. He also had worked for another reason. "But you can't work hard enough," he says, "to forget you're this afraid."

So when your daughter, going blind, has to remind you how blue the sky is, it's time to be a daddy. This summer, Veeck quit the Devil Rays and now wants Rebecca to see everything. She saw Grandpa at Cooperstown. Soon she'll see Death Valley, the Grand Canyon and Yosemite.

Veeck and his wife, Libby, talked to Rebecca about making her story public. She said no; kids already made fun of her sunglasses. She changed her mind when her parents said bringing attention to The Foundation Fighting Blindness might help other children.

Recent tests show Rebecca's eyesight improved a little, the deterioration slowing, though still inevitable. Researchers hope that medicine, gene therapy and even computer-chip implants someday will restore vision to patients with Rebecca's disease.

"I treasure this time with Rebecca," Mike Veeck says. "I'm a different person than I was a year ago. While I suffer fools easily because I am one, I no longer am able to see the loss of 20 Devil Rays season tickets as 'a failure of tragic proportions.'"

The baseball man says he now knows what's important. He knows what makes him cry.

Getting back in the box

JUNE 15, 2000

On April 29, a year and six days later, college baseball player Anthony Molina stepped into the batter's box for the first time against the team that did it. "Emotional," he said, and his coach said, "It's amazing, how far Anthony has come." Pinch-hitting with two out and two on in the last inning, Molina could win the game. "I wanted to beat them because of what they did to me."

The ratzenfratzing truth is he grounded out. The blessed truth is he came to bat at all. He came to bat a year and six days after he might have been killed in an act of baseball terrorism.

It was April 23, 1999. A lefthanded hitter leading off the game for the University of Evansville (Ind.), Molina walked from the third base dugout around Wichita State's catcher. The catcher took warmup pitches from Ben Christensen, a major league prospect whose 95-mph fastball helped him win 21 of 22 college games.

As Christensen threw, Molina stood on the first base side of home plate. He was 24 feet away. We know it was 24 feet because investigators later measured the distance from the plate to the bloodstains.

Molina's memory of how the blood got there: "I put on my batting

234

gloves, got my helmet, got my bat, took two or three swings and began to walk around the back of the catcher. I stopped to let a pitch come in, then I went on to the other side and saw him throw two or three more."

Then Molina looked away, toward first base.

At that moment, the third baseman/catcher's vision was 20/10. He was a .310 hitter who had played baseball since age 8 and wanted to be a big-lea-guer. All that would change in the next moment, for as Molina turned his head back toward home plate, he became the victim of an act so con-temptible it's sickening.

The Evansville coach, Jim Brownlee: "After Christensen's fifth warmup pitch, his catcher calls for a slider, and Christensen makes a quarter-turn to his left. I'm thinking, 'What's he doing?' Anthony had his head down, and I'm seeing Christensen turn toward him, and, damn, he lets it go. Then Anthony's head comes up. The ball gets him square in the face. He never saw it."

A sledgehammer against the eye. That's a doctor's description of the damage. A fractured left eye socket. Twenty-three stitches. The first test result of Molina's vision after surgery: 20/400, legally blind.

As to how the Wichita State pitcher came to throw at an unsuspecting player 24 feet from the plate, the Wichita explanation is absurd. Here it is: Because Molina was "timing" Christensen's warmup pitches and Wichita State's pitchers are taught to brush back any hitter doing that, Christensen intended not to hit Molina but to send him a message.

Whatever the intent, the act was savage. Even Christensen realized it. He told a Wichita Eagle reporter, "All I could think about was if that ball would have been a little bit to the left, or a little bit to the right, I could have killed him."

On his 1955 arrival in the American League, cutthroat pitcher Sal Maglie warned Ted Williams not to indulge in his habit of standing just outside the batter's box and swinging in time with warmup pitches—or he'd throw at his head. Two years later, Tommy Byrne did just that. Williams biographer Ed Linn called it "the first time—in all probability—that a hitter had even been brushed back before he even came to bat."

But the Byrne precedent, iffy on its own merits, doesn't justify throwing at a hitter who's not at the batter's box edge (24 feet away) and isn't timing pitches (not even watching them).

After four surgeries, the vision in Molina's left eye tests at 20/60. Today, wearing glasses, he plays despite a permanent retinal detachment that leaves a blind spot in the center of his vision in his left eye.

"If you're two feet away from me, the blind spot covers your entire face," Molina said. "Ten feet away, all I can see is your feet."

The blind spot affects Molina more in the field than at bat. "It's a depth-perception problem. On balls I dive for, left or right, I'm OK. But a ball straight at me, it's hard to judge the speed and hops." His only concern about another eye injury also has come in the field: "On a double-play ball, I lost the shortstop's throw in his white cap. It hit me in the arm."

Through 47 games this spring, Molina hit .285 with three home runs. He played second base, caught some and has been Evansville's designated hitter in a good season that should earn the team an at-large invitation to the NCAA Tournament. It's a trip that would come, most likely, after the Aces face Wichita State for the Missouri Valley Conference tournament championship.

Ben Christensen may become a star. The Cubs' first pick (26th overall) in the '99 amateur draft, he is 3-6 in parts of two Class A seasons. He hasn't spoken to Molina since the incident, and Molina dismisses a Christensen letter of apology as "sounding like lawyers wrote it."

This may be Anthony Molina's last season. "It's hard to swallow, that it's about over. I'm not giving up on pro ball, but, realistically, I don't see it happening. Maybe I'll coach."

He'll remember this spring. Without using Christensen's name, he says, "Even though he did that to me, I wasn't going to let him get me down, push me around. I'd do what I want to do."

So, a year and six days later, he came to bat.

CHAPTER 13

World Series

The Fall Classic

Little boys who would be men dream of the World Series.

The World Series is men who would be boys.

It's hot dogs and The Star Spangled Banner. It's the Yankees beating the Dodgers again. It's Reggie Jackson sending baseballs into the Mr. October night and saying, "You can love me or hate me, but you can't ignore me."

The World Series is Bob Gibson pitching a seventh game and Kirby Puckett leaping against the center-field fence. It's Kirk Gibson dragging his heroic bum of a body around the bases. Babe Ruth pointed to center field one World Series day and Jackie Robinson stole home and Brooks Robinson caught everything Johnny Bench hit.

It's the Oakland A's of Charlie Finley punching each other out, and it's the Pittsburgh Pirates singing, "We Are Fam-a-lee." Every October we come to another World Series, another chance to be a kid with our first baseball glove. Another baseball season older and still we remember Mel Allen on the radio and Red Smith in the papers. The World Series is both memory and anticipation, each made better by the other's existence.

Willie Mays turned his back to home plate in the 1954 World Series, and the World Series turned its back on Ernie Banks forever.

It's Connie Mack in his gray suit.

It's Pepper Martin firing up the Gashouse Gang.

It's Grover Cleveland Alexander fighting off a hangover.

Tommy Lasorda says three words, and they're musical and almost heavenly the way he says them, certainly said with such devotion they should be printed by The Sporting News in capital letters: "THE FALL CLASSIC."

The Fall Classic is grainy black-and-white film on which we see, thousands of times, Don Larsen getting Dale Mitchell on a called third strike for a perfect game in 1956. Al Gionfriddo goes to the wall in center, Sandy Amoros goes to the line in the left, Ron Swoboda lands on his belly in right with the ball somehow in his glove.

There's always a World Series. An earthquake and its fires didn't stop the games. Neither did gamblers in 1919. Baseball played through both World Wars, Korea and Vietnam. Woodrow Wilson left the White House to throw out the first ball of a World Series. Franklin D. Roosevelt said to keep playing because we need dreams as well as guns. The Cubs haven't been in the World Series since the season we dropped the atomic bomb.

Open "The Baseball Encyclopedia" to any page. Turn to the E's. It's George L. Earnshaw, Michael A. Easler, Rawlins J. Eastwick, Zebulon V. Eaton, C. Bruce Edwards, Howard Ehmke, Horace O. Eller. They all played in the Fall Classic and they would talk about it forever and their names would go in the record book, men who made real the dreams of boys.

Almost nobodies Mark Lemke and Brian Doyle, Al Weis and Billy Martin became somebodies in the World Series.

The World Series is shoe polish off Nippy Jones' spikes and it's Casey Stengel letting a sparrow loose from under his ballcap and it's Bill Lee saying he received pitching instructions from another planet. It's Bill Buckner befuddled by a ground ball and Mickey Owen chasing a third strike and Lonnie Smith forgetting how to run.

The World Series is fun. The pressure is off. It's Sparky Anderson hugging everyone he sees. It's an old ballplayers reunion. We hear war stories, lies and other truths as they should have been. We heard Casey Stengel say, "That guy we got in right field that's got the crooked arm that hits lefthanders good, he's going to be OK if he finds his way to the park enough." And everyone knew what Casey meant.

It's Pete Rose, Joe Morgan, Johnny Bench and Tony Perez demanding greatness and getting it.

It's Carlton Fisk dancing down the first base line, leaning, shoving the air, hoping.

It's Minnesota-Atlanta 1991, the best ever.

The World Series is the chill of the year, October nights after summer days, the resolution of a contest that began in the spring, a contest that ties generations together, as Steve Garvey said in 1984 after his playoff home run put San Diego into The Fall Classic: "It is rare enough to be part of history, but it is rarer and even more special to know it as it is happening—to consciously revel in the tradition and love the moment for what it is."

The World Series tells us the world is in fine working order, and we should put aside our troubles for a minute to love again the best game there is. It's the best game because it speaks to our hearts. We grow up knowing what it feels like to play this game. We know it so well we don't so much know it as we are, in some wonderful way, made to understand that the game is part of our being. We don't have to explain it to each other; we all feel it the same way. And we share it without being asked to share it. This is love.

Bill Millsaps, a wonderful Virginia sportswriter, knows how this love touches sons and fathers, and he'll tell you about the events of October 8, 1956.

That day the stern Tennessee school principal William Millsaps rapped on a classroom door to interrupt a class in progress. He demanded that young William Millsaps Jr. leave the class. When the boy, frightened by the circumstances so brusque, asked his father what was wrong—is Mother all right?—the principal Mr. Millsaps said to be quiet and just come along.

Millsaps the elder and junior went to the principal's office. They marched through the secretary's anteroom, the father stonefaced silent. They were in the principal's private office when Mr. Millsaps said, "Billy, shut that door behind you." Then he said, "Sit down, son, and watch the television. You won't believe what Don Larsen is doing to the Dodgers."

As Series go, '91 is one to remember

NOVEMBER 4, 1991

The World Series of 1991 stands alone. There is no need to thumb through record books. No need to ask historians for perspective. Anyone lucky enough to have seen this one knows what it was. It was baseball as good as baseball gets. It's just too bad the Twins and Braves quit so soon.

Commissioner Fay Vincent said to Ted Turner, "Why don't we play all winter and make it the best of 90?" Atlanta's little hero Mark Lemke said, "I wish this season would never end."

One soft and beautiful autumn night, the Orlando baseball poet Russ White sat in the upper deck along Atlanta's right-field line. He heard the fans, as one, sing low and sweet an Indian hymn. He saw diamonds in the sky above him. He saw Steve Avery on the diamond below. Pretty sure he wasn't in Iowa, Russ White asked, "Am I in heaven?"

For a week and more, to baseball folks, the answer was yes, spoken loudly. Minnesota and Atlanta, last-place teams a season ago, had been transformed, as if by divine touch, into champions who gave us a World Series so good that it can be called the best ever.

About such bold judgment there is room to quibble. The Hall of Famer Johnny Bench quibbled about some poor baserunning and flawed fielding.

242

"The fans were the best thing of all," Bench said. He liked the hankies and tomahawks. As for the games, he said, they were not so well played.

One begs to differ with the distinguished Mr. Bench. His Cincinnati Reds of 1975 created a classic Series. Oakland's dynasty began in the '72 Series that gave us six one-run games. And who didn't like it in '55 when Brooklyn's beloved Bums finally beat the Yankees?

All were good Series. But none, it says here, ever had all the right stuff of this one.

"Every pitch, every strike, every ball, every inning—everything mattered in every game," said Terry Pendleton, the Atlanta third baseman.

"Tomorrow," said Minnesota's Kent Hrbek, "I'm going to the doctor to fix my ulcer."

Never in 87 years had a World Series given us three games decided on the last pitch. This one gave us not three such games but four.

Five games were won by one run and that run scored in the home team's last at-bat.

Two games were won by sudden home runs, lightning bolts of drama. And two nights in a row, a baserunner's gambling sprint and wonderful slide carried home the winning run a heartbeat ahead of an outfielder's throw. Never before had any team won two nights in a row in its last at-bat.

We saw three runners tagged out at the plate by catchers so resolute they accepted collisions and rose from the dust to do it some more. Dan Gladden of Minnesota, spikes Ty Cobb-high, knocked over Greg Olson. The catcher was seen standing on his left ear, an exclamation point turned upside down. Did Olson straighten up with his fists balled, looking for a fight? No, he simply rose and handed Gladden his cap. This is the show. It's hardball up here.

We saw 16 home runs, at least two in each of the first six games. Someone should look that up to see if it has ever been done. (It hasn't.) In Game 5, Atlanta scored 14 runs, the most ever by a National League team. The Braves that night racked up a record 34 total bases. That's two more than the Yankees of '28 managed with Babe Ruth and Lou Gehrig.

We saw players who may be in the Hall of Fame someday, and we saw why. What Kirby Puckett did to Ron Gant in Game 6 was astonishing. Willie Mays outrunning Vic Wertz's long fly in '54 was no more sensational and certainly less meaningful than Puckett's flight to Gant's line drive.

Jack Morris, of the thick and villainous red mustache, rendered helpless Atlanta's good offense. He went 10 innings to win Game 7 and threw more effectively the later the hour became. Someone asked him afterward how much longer he could have pitched and Morris allowed himself a little smile.

"A hundred and 12 innings," he said.

Atlanta couldn't score against Morris in the eighth after putting men at second and third with none out. Minnesota loaded the bases with one out in the eighth and couldn't score. In the ninth, the Twins had runners at first and second with none out—and couldn't score.

As Pendleton came to bat in the 10th inning, Minnesota catcher Brian Harper said to him, "Why don't we just quit and call it a tie?" Pendleton laughed aloud and then grounded out to shortstop, the last out of Atlanta's season.

Minnesota would win it in their part of the 10th, doing it with a hit delivered by an obscure infielder named Gene Larkin. He'd driven in only 19 runs all year. He'd been to bat only three times in this Series. Perfect.

It was perfect because for a week and more, in this day of the jaded millionaire slugger, we saw the pure heart of baseball, a kid's game.

Greg Olson loved it. The Atlanta catcher is no one's fool. He understands his worth. In April, after all, he was not Atlanta's starting catcher.

"This year could be the last year when I know I'll be an impact player in a World Series," Olson said one sweet afternoon. He spoke to his ghost writer who took notes for "Greg Olson's Diary," appearing in the Atlanta Constitution. The pay: $100 a piece. A guy making minimum wage takes a buck wherever he finds it.

"So I'm having fun right now because I may never have this chance again," Olson said. "I enjoy baseball, period. I can't tell you with a straight face that it's a job."

We might grouse about the Metrodome. It distorts the game as surely as the designated-hitter rule distorts it. Lonnie Smith may be roasted for what some will call a baserunning mistake in Game 7, but he deserves the benefit of our doubt. If Pendleton says it's hard to see the ball against the white roof, it's hard to see it. Smith did the careful thing, waiting until he saw the ball bouncing, and Atlanta still had men at second and third with none out. Not Smith's fault. Blame it on the Dumbdome.

Otherwise, it as a Series made fascinating by the ways it thrilled us. Even now anyone who saw it can see it still: Puckett on the run toward left center. Gant's shot is out of reach. Surely it is out of reach. But Puckett is on the run. He catches most everything that stays inside Minnesota's borders. He is on the warning track. He gathers his stubby little self for an Air Puckett leap. Bumping high against the wall, he snatches the baseball out of the air.

A night later, Puckett is off the ground again. His Twins have won the World Series. Chili Davis has Puckett in his arms. Davis has lifted Puckett high above the celebrants clamoring around the pitcher's mound. Puckett throws wide his arms. His cap is in one hand. There is on his face a little boy's smile of pure joy.

Another chapter, not an end

NOVEMBER 2, 1992

Looking like Buffalo Bill at the ballyard—his hair long, wild, yellow; his mustache tipped in tight curls—the "Shoeless Joe" author W. P. Kinsella stood by the cage before Game 6 of the World Series and offered himself for Fay Vincent's old job. Give him insurance, move the desk to Palm Beach and he'd do anything the owners wanted—right after he opened the Hall of Fame to Shoeless Joe Jackson and invited Pete Rose back.

As a child on the lonely plains of western Canada, Kinsella knew major league baseball only by reading The Sporting News sent home by his father, a minor-leaguer in Florida. So he knew the 1940s heroes and understood box scores before ever seeing a game, that on the new-fangled invention television, a 1950s time so long ago, he said, that "dinosaurs were still around." But here he was, at a World Series for the first time, hired by baseball to write for a commemorative book, and W. P. Kinsella sounded like a man who wanted it to never end. He said there is a timelessness to this game. No clock says it's over. We might play forever, a hundred innings, a thousand. A timelessness and a lovely mythology: The field of play is so expansive, the foul lines running away from each other to embrace the whole of the universe, that the game invites myth, even demands it to fill the dreamy spaces.

Its sinners forgiven, its mistakes forgotten, the game as healer of our hearts, baseball came to midnight of Game 6 on a wonderful Southern autumn night and brought up to bat a man who in a year moved from the shadows of exclusion to the bright lights of a World Series with his team needing a base hit from him to tie the game in the last of the ninth inning.

Otis Nixon, that man, missed last September's pennant race and last October's World Series because he twice tested positive for drugs and was suspended. A .297 hitter with 72 stolen bases, those important games, Nixon watched them on television with other patients in a rehab clinic.

Eight teams wanted to sign Nixon when he finished rehab. Only Atlanta, he said, cared about him as a person dealing with the pain and shame of an addiction so evil it demanded attention when attention surely meant discovery, exposure and punishment. "Everyone else just talked about how much money they'd pay me," Nixon said. "The Atlanta people asked how I was doing personally. How I felt. What could they do to help."

Certainly, Atlanta's $ 2.7 million offer was as good as anyone's. But only Atlanta also offered a helping hand. It touched Nixon to see help from the people he had disappointed most. This season, at age 33, hitting .294, stealing 41 bases, playing center field sensationally, Nixon repeated his good work—and near midnight of Game 6 he stood at the center of a World Series, his team utterly dependent on him.

There were two outs in Atlanta's ninth inning. Toronto led by a run. Men on first and second. Nixon at bat against Toronto's best relief pitcher. No balls, two strikes. One pitch away from defeat. The ballpark hummed with the electric thrill of not knowing. This was Otis Nixon's moment in what he called "my 'wish' year, the year God gave me a second chance. Because of the way it went last year, I wanted to be at the plate. I wanted to be the guy." Nixon's body is a kid's, tall, thin and whipcord strong. His face is an old man's, all cheekbones, jawline and haunting eyes. The eyes left no room for doubting him when he said, "I don't think anyone wanted this as bad as I did."

On Tom Henke's 0-2 fastball, at midnight, in bright lights surrounded by darkness instead of last year's darkness surrounded by bright lights, Otis Nixon slapped a line-drive single to left field. It scored the run that tied the score 2-2 and when Atlanta could do no more in that inning, Nixon went out to center field and lifted his cap to thank fans cheering his work.

What a World Series: Toronto wins all four games by one run. Devon White does Willie Mays, and Pat Borders is Yogi Berra, Kelly Gruber hits a home run and hits his chin. Dave Winfield is no longer Mr. May. The SkyDome suggests the 21st century's possibilities, as does victory by a team outside the United States. Atlanta steals the most bases in 83 years. Toronto hits as many home runs as any team ever.

Even the U.S. Marines, who carried the Canadian flag upside down in Atlanta, came out of this World Series a winner, thanks to a graceful apology orchestrated by baseball, the Toronto ballclub and the Marines. Before Game 3, the SkyDome announcer said the Marines had "requested the privilege of again carrying the National Flag of Canada." This time the maple leaf pointed straight up. Everyone was touched by the moment. They also hoped the poor Marine who made the original mistake would soon be done with his four kajillion punishment push-ups.

Almost 1:45 in the morning and Otis Nixon stood at his locker. "We could still be out on the field if I had got that bunt down where I wanted it." There is no clock to end baseball's wonders. Innings spin out a thread of gold that can stretch forever. Almost 1:45 in the morning and Otis Nixon said, "Nobody wanted it to end."

In the bottom of the 11th inning of Game 6, Atlanta needed one more run to tie it, one run to stretch time. The game that gives us W. P. Kinsella's sweet field of dreams first gives us truth, the truth so perfect it seems fiction. Here came Otis Nixon to the plate again, with two out, this time with the tying run at third base.

On Mike Timlin's second pitch, Nixon tried to drag a bunt toward first base. He is baseball's best bunter. But the pitch came too near him and he caught it on the end of the bat. The bunt died too soon. The pitcher threw him out. Toronto's happy men piled atop each other in celebration. Otis Nixon walked the the Atlanta dugout, his head held high.

Measuring up in the face of heartbreak

NOVEMBER 1, 1993

This World Series, memorable for its hitting, had been over for an hour when the Philadelphia doughboy, John Kruk, tipped a beer between his furry lips and said to third-base coach Larry Bowa, "Come down to Atlantic City."

Bowa said he might just do that. He'd think about it.

"Gonna be there three, four days," the first baseman said. "Be fun."

The Phillies had been out-toughed by Toronto. So now Kruk had a plan. He said he'd take a month off and just lay in bed.

John Kruk hits you line drives. He picks up a ground ball. What you might not know about Kruk, and what you should know, is this: The guy can flat play. Watch him on the bases. Every pitch, he checks the outfielders. Not even Rickey Henderson, a Hall of Fame runner, is as meticulous as the scruffy Kruk looking for an edge.

Kruk said he'd take a month, lay around, soak up a beer or three.

"Same thing I did all year," he said.

A smile then. Smiling through the heartbreak. Kruk's words: "It's heartbreaking, but what can you do? It's over." The Phillies' last two losses were victories there for the taking. In one, they led by five runs in the eighth inning. In the last one, they moved from four runs behind to one ahead only to lose in the ninth.

The man in the corner didn't smile. He hurt too much. Mitch Williams sat on a stool at his locker in Philadelphia's clubhouse. They pay him to do a hard thing and he had failed. They pay him to pitch with victory there for the taking. Those heartbreakers, he'd lost them both.

He'd lost the last one after Kruk came to him on the mound. Kruk came to him in the ninth inning. The Phillies led by the one run. Now it was up to Williams to finish it off. He'd been the man all year. Without Williams, the Phillies go nowhere. With him, they're in the World Series. Now Kruk came to him, a run up, needing three outs to get to Game 7. Kruk said to Williams, "No way we're going to lose this game."

But lose it they did, losing to a home run that sent Joe Carter dancing, Joe Carter on air, Joe Carter disappearing into two dozen teammates at home plate, disappearing into the whiteness of Toronto's uniforms at the instant Mitch Williams disappeared into his dugout's shadows, walking alone, alone from the diamond's shining center into the darkness.

Now Williams sat at his locker in his undershirt. There's a tattoo on his right shoulder. It's a Tasmanian devil and the words WILD THING. Yes, he pitches like a man with his hair on fire. But no. Nothing wild about Mitch Williams now. He hurt.

He talked about it. He came to his locker and talked to reporters. He didn't hide from the pain.

"Ain't nobody walking this Earth that feels worse than I do," he said. Loser of Game 4, not used in Philadelphia's Game 5 victory, Williams talked about the night after Game 5.

"About 2:30 in the morning, I went out to put some stuff in my truck," Williams said. "That's when I saw the cop in my driveway. I asked him what he was doing there. He said, 'Didn't they tell you?' I said, 'Tell me what?' "

Someone had called the Phillies. Someone threatened to kill Williams. The police spent Game 5 with Williams' family. They watched his fiancee and her family. Without telling him, they watched Williams himself.

The threat made no difference in Game 6, Williams said. It didn't affect the way he pitched. He simply pitched badly. He just didn't get the job done.

A sick society. Williams used those words. Just a sick individual. He got along fine with Philadelphia fans. This is one sicko. It's a game played for enjoyment, he said, and if you take that enjoyment away, some people react differently. Some people pick up a phone and talk pain onto you.

Only one of Philadelphia's many pitching failures but the most obvious, Williams stood up to the pain: "Ain't nobody going to make me hide from what I've done. I'm proud of what I've done. There ain't nobody going to make me feel worse than I feel myself."

We learned a lot of things in this World Series. Toronto's bats are the best ever in October, so good that Tom Boswell of The Washington Post said with incredulity, "Look at these numbers." Toronto's nine guys, in career postseason play, have hit .322. Prorating the numbers to a 600 at-bat season, the average Blue Jay hits his .322 with 16 homers, 87 RBIs and 36 stolen bases. Nice player to have in October.

We learned to lust for interleague play. Anyone who doesn't see Robby Alomar and Devon White in person isn't seeing all of baseball's beauty. We learned: Curt Schilling is a superstar in the making; Pat Gillick and Cito Gaston do sensational work softly; and Lenny Dykstra in the postseason is what Barry Bonds wants to be.

It was long past midnight in the Philadelphia clubhouse. Mitch Williams had showered and left, walking alone to the team bus. John Kruk looked around. "Turn that camera off?" he asked. "You, too," he said, nodding at another television man. "I need to take a drink." He lifted a cool beer. "This is my offseason now."

Another smile. What's not to smile about? Out of all the baseball teams in the world, he said, the Phillies were second-best. Hey, Ernie Banks is in the Hall of Fame and he never got in a World Series at all. "I won't be in the Hall of Fame," Kruk said, "but I've got six World Series games. And I had a helluva time."

This one's for you, Bud

September 26, 1994

There are good reasons for what we do and there are the real reasons.

The imp Muhammad Ali liked to tell a story about Abraham Lincoln. One night, Ali said, the old president enjoyed himself more than enough in the company of good Kentucky bourbon.

"Next morning," Ali said, "ol' Abe rubbed his eyes and rubbed his head and looked around and said to his wife, 'I freed the who?' "

The lords of baseball closed down the game for what they declared are good reasons essential to financial survival. The real reasons, in one man's opinion: They did it for the macho glee of it. They did it to show they could strut as cockily as any kid wearing his cap backward. They did it to prove again who lives in the big house. Little else explains why the owners' acting commissioner, Bud Selig, would bend fact so far as to say all 28 teams face financial catastrophe. That is ludicrous. Hardly more ludicrous, though, than Selig's repeated reference to his side's negotiators as "the Dream Team."

Here was a baseball man using a basketball analogy as if 125 years of his own game had given him no language sufficient to express his pride in negotiators who did nothing and did it for a long time.

All a reasonable person can hope is that Selig woke up the next morning and said, "I called off what?"

The lasting sorrow here, beyond any loss of the World Series, is that Bud & His Nightmare Boys have made the game smaller, if not in reality, certainly in spirit.

Practically anyone who has walked into a major league stadium has been in awe of the people, the place and the game. For some of us romantics, that feeling of awe is gone—perhaps forever.

Despite the lessons of baseball's robber-baron history, we looked upon ballparks as cathedrals of a sort, vessels of the human spirit. Not now, not for a while anyway. The owners have reminded us again that ballparks are cash registers for their personal use.

And now, in the mad tradition of burning the village to save it, the owners have torched the World Series on the premise that baseball is about to go broke, an argument threadbare for a century and patently absurd today.

Baseball sold more tickets for more games for more money in 1993 than ever before. It is a $3 billion growth industry with a dozen cities lusting to pay $125 million each to get in the big leagues. Never has baseball been more competitive, seldom has it been so vibrant. Were there interleague play, were there creative marketing, were there a partnership of owners and players, baseball would truly be in a golden age.

Still, Bud & His Nightmare Boys insist the game is hurtling toward the darkness of a financial abyss.

As it happens, and not so coincidentally, Selig's Milwaukee team may be one of the few truly in distress. As it also happens, there is a solution to his distress: Don't shut down baseball, just sell the team for, guessing here, $75 million more than he paid for it.

Or Selig could do what owners did in Atlanta, Cleveland and Baltimore. They cut payrolls, found good players and built ballparks. Now they're making money in markets not much different from Milwaukee.

All it takes is talent and imagination. Of course, some folks living in the big house don't have those necessities. They prefer a monopolist's system guaranteeing success. Thus, the 1994 salary cap/revenue sharing proposal, which, by the way, shows that owners trust no one, not even each other.

Teams agreed to share revenues only if everyone agreed to use the divvied-up money to pay players. That's why the cap scheme demanded that all payrolls be at least 84 percent of the average.

The incredible part of this is that most fans blame the players for the mess, when it's the owners' doing. And they did it while operating as this country's only billionaires' industry given immunity against antitrust laws protecting taxpayers from the dictatorial excesses of monopoly businesses.

U.S. Sen. Howard Metzenbaum of Ohio believes baseball owners have more power than executives in any other industry. Metzenbaum says, "If the CEOs of the auto industry, for example, had the same immunity from the nation's pro-competition laws, they could eliminate competition from imports, raise prices in lock step and even divide up the country—dictating that only Fords could be sold in New York, Chryslers in Chicago and General Motors cars in Los Angeles.

"... Consider what the owners have done for us lately. They have inflated ticket prices, blackmailed cities for tax breaks, controlled TV coverage, blocked expansion and provoked the players to strike."

Basketball, football and hockey players seldom strike because they can play while lawyers argue. But baseball owners use the antitrust exemption to stand immune to such litigation. The players' only recourse is a strike.

Baseball's immunity originated in a decision by the otherwise brilliant Supreme Court Justice Oliver Wendell Holmes, who in 1922 ruled that baseball was a sport, not an interstate business. Congress 60 times has considered ending the exemption. But romance, tradition and other soft-headedness have always prevailed.

Now more than ever it is obvious that Congress should act; now more than ever it is obvious that the owners cannot be trusted to deal fairly with anyone.

We should remember words once spoken by Jerry Reinsdorf, who owns the Chicago White Sox. He said baseball is a business that should be run "for the owners, not the players or the umpires or the fans."

The night the lights went out in Georgia

What a thing baseball has. What a thing. We only need October to remind us. Baseball has what football and basketball will never have. It has October when it's hard to breathe. Make it a day in May and it's just another baseball game. Make it a night in October and you remember it forever.

It's 10:21 on a chilly October night, a night with diamonds dancing in the dark, those diamonds flashbulbs glittering, fans wanting a piece of this moment to hold in their hands.

Baseball does this. No other game, only baseball brings us to a moment when every breath is done at a cost. Only baseball in October gives us a story whose silences are as thrilling as the thunders.

You can have Michael Jordan in the air. You can have Emmitt Smith on the ground. They're fine and mighty and they move us to wonder at what they can do. What they cannot do is what only baseball does. When baseball comes to October, we feel heartbeats in our fingertips and we remind ourselves to take a breath, a deep one.

We see Atlanta's big man bringing ninth-inning heat to the Clevelands with the world championship for the taking. We see the big man and we know the possibilities: One mistake, it's tied; one hero's swing, it's tied.

Almost by instinct, for we learn this child's game without knowing how we learn it—by instinct, we know the weight of the moment.

The world championship. Who would have thought it? This is Atlanta, once woebegone, Ted Turner's baseball toy, which once had a blind pinch-hitter (but only in one eye), Atlanta for whom Joe Pepitone refused to play because he had misplaced his new toupee.

Mark Wohlers, the big man, has the ball in his glove. He takes off his cap, a nervous habit, and runs his pitching hand across his hair. He puts the ball in his hand, showing the split-finger grip to the hitter, and now he lets his arms fall free and loose and almost casually, the big man loving the heat and bringing the heat.

"It's what you dream of," Wohlers says later. Closers live for the moment when they are gunslingers moving down dusty streets with all eyes on them. "You want the ball then."

You want it when the world championship is there. You want it when your team is a dynasty in full flower: three league pennants in four full seasons; three or four Hall of Fame candidates on the roster; an extraordinary minor league system built by a wealthy and zealous organization; a front office that sees diamonds where other folks see coal.

You want the ball, if you're a closer, when the men in front of you have done wonders. Greg Maddux pitched a two-hitter to open the Series. This night Tom Glavine allowed only one hit in eight innings before telling manager Bobby Cox he should come out. He had thrown too many bad pitches in the eighth inning, pitches that worked maybe because luck was on the pitcher's side on this night to remember.

It's 10:23 and Wohlers brings heat to a Cleveland hitter who can only foul it weakly to the wrong field. One out.

It's 10:26, the count 1-and-2 to a pinch-hitter, Wohlers daring the enemy to handle his best breaking stuff as well as the 96 mph fastball. The hitter manages only a lazy fly to center. Two out.

On a day in May, with other things to do, fans head for the exits when it comes to two outs in the ninth inning. On a night in October, with nothing more important than a third out, fans stand and shout and stomp their feet in thunderous anticipation of the drama's denouement.

It's 10:27. The umpire wants a look at the baseball, so Wohlers flips it to him, underhanded, and the umpire, satisfied, tosses it back to the big man. In May, these nuances are nuisances. In October, they bring into the drama anyone who ever held a baseball and wondered where it might go if thrown.

With the ball in his hand, Wohlers turns his back to the Cleveland hitter. He scratches at the mound's dirt with his left foot. Now he faces the man he must beat, and now his arms swing up from his sides, and now diamonds dance in the night again, flashbulbs glittering, everyone wanting to go to a scrapbook with the grandchildren and say, "All these years later, it's like it's happening now. Look at my arms. Goosebumps."

In the night, Ted Turner would stand on the infield grass and pose for pictures with his ground crew. He would put the world championship trophy atop his head, a goofy thing, a wonderful thing. We smell champagne in the clubhouse and we feel champagne and we hear an old Atlanta scout, Paul Snyder, whose work helped build the team: "I'm weak in the knees, is how I'm feeling."

We see the center fielder Marquis Grissom. The 14th child of 15 born to parents who grew up picking cotton half a century ago, Grissom grew up playing ball 10 minutes from the Atlanta ballpark. This is the stuff of a boy's dreams. "And my boy," he says, meaning the boy on his shoulders, D'Monte, 3, "is going to play his ball here, too."

We see Bobby Cox, who was the Atlanta manager 17 seasons ago, a season after a 61-101 year, a manager saddled with players who couldn't play, who made that outfit respectable only in time to be fired by Turner, who at the firing news conference said he really admired Cox: "If I hadn't just fired Bobby, I'd hire him."

In time, Turner found a way to do just that. And we hear Cox in the champagne clubhouse saying, "Sure, Tommy Glavine has pitched that well before. Every time out in '91. A machine."

It's 10:27 and Cleveland's hitter has put up a flyball toward left center field. And now the ball is falling, and now diamonds dance in the night, the falling ball a tiny dot to be pointed out on fading photographs to grandchildren asking how the great night happened.

What a thing baseball has. What a precious thing.

Torre's blessed Yankees

NOVEMBER 4, 1996

Who'd have ever thought it, a Yankees team we could like?

But here it is midnight.

We're leaving Yankee Stadium where the Yankees have won the World Series for the first time in 18 years.

And all is well.

Passers-by wave from automobiles and shout their happiness.

We decide to take the subway downtown.

Amazing thing, we're on the No. 4 train leaving the 161st Street station.

And the train is filled with kind and gentle folks, each and every one mellow and smiling. (Except for a young man who seems to have celebrated himself into a strap-hanging state of unconsciousness.)

All of which prompts a question.

This is New York?

Even Reggie Jackson has a warm-and-fuzzy look. The Hall of Famer from the Yankees' glory days of the late 1970s is now a muckety-muck in owner George Steinbrenner's stable of revolving muckety-mucks. Jackson comes to the Atlanta clubhouse. He wears a Yankees cap and carries a cigar and beer. He shakes hands with Braves pitcher John Smoltz, who says, "Tell

Andy Pettitte he did great. That last game, it'll boost his career."

Jackson says, "I know you know what you're saying," and then, with a fraternal nod of respect, he moves on.

Who'd have thought it, Reggie Jackson a beneficent sage?

Once upon a time, we scribes scribbled our Yankees stories with pens fashioned from razor wire.

Now we tickle the keyboards with feathers.

How could we do otherwise?

You gotta love Yankees manager Joe Torre. In him is the essence of baseball, a kid's game that can be a man's life. He was an immigrant's son tagging along with his big brothers, Rocco and Frank, on Brooklyn's sandlots in the 1950s. Quickly a major league player, it yet took Torre 33 years to get to a World Series, 18 as a player, 15 as a manager. He held the record. Most major league games played and/or managed without being in a World Series. More than 4,200 games.

Fired by the Mets, Braves and Cardinals, Torre started this season in the last manager's job most any rational man wants, the Yankees'. But if he knew anything about the job, this is what he knew first: It was home. He also knew the part-time fool Steinbrenner is a full-time zealot in pursuit of victory. And he respected Bob Watson, the new general manager, who once played for him.

Together, the three men created a Yankees team unlike any in two decades of Steinbrenner control. They're world champions. Nothing new there. The new part is, they're people you could invite into your home without asking the cops to drive by occasionally.

Strongman Cecil Fielder at first base; rookie Derek Jeter at shortstop, second-year pitcher Andy Pettitte and his mentor Jimmy Key; 28-year-old center fielder Bernie Williams, and the sweaty-capped closer John Wetteland—they're stars who bring dignity to a team once called "the Bronx Zoo," a collection of perversities, contrarians and egomaniacs that transformed Yankee Stadium from cathedral to asylum.

Reckoned to be a middling team this season, the Yankees became champions when Pettitte became a dominant pitcher, the American League's certain Cy Young Award winner. The rehabilitations of Dwight Gooden and Darryl Strawberry, while incomplete, were remarkable enough to win a dozen games and more. Perhaps as important, the fallen stars set a tone of sacrifice and commitment that pervaded the Yankees clubhouse.

"We just kept coming back," Bernie Williams says. "This club, despite everything, wouldn't take no for an answer."

By "everything," he meant the usual. Steinbrennerian rages. Threats of resignation. A $20 million pitcher relegated to the bullpen. A pitcher with an aneurism that might have killed him on the mound. Gooden's no-hitter followed by his movie deal followed by his dead arm followed by Steinbrennerian rage.

These things, Joe Torre pretty much ignored. Once a kid in a man's game, he's now a man in a kid's game. He wanted to work in New York. But if the owner didn't want him, he'd go somewhere else. Big deal.

He worried more about his big brother who took him to the sandlots so long ago. Frank is 64. He played in the major leagues ahead of Joe, seven seasons in all, was in the World Series with the Milwaukee Braves of 1957 and '58. By this summer he'd had three heart attacks. Heart disease had killed the Torres' brother, Rocco. Doctors said Frank needed a new heart.

So, for 72 days this summer, he waited in a New York hospital.

He waited for someone to die whose heart he could have.

He waited and watched his little brother, Joe, manage the Yankees past mighty Cleveland, past the Baltimore Orioles (with an assist by Jeffrey Maier) and into the World Series. He watched and made telephone calls about strategy and lineups. He made calls and talked ball when Joe came to the hospital.

And when the Yankees came back to New York with a 3-2 lead in this World Series—by winning three games on the road, winning one after falling behind 6-0 through five innings—then came the best news of Joe Torre's season.

Doctors had found a heart for his brother.

On a day off, they found a heart.

"How do you think it goes from here?" Frank Torre asks a nurse wheeling him back to his room after a preparatory X-ray at 4 a.m.

"We have the best doctors in the world here," the nurse says. "The operation will go just fine."

"I mean the Series," Frank Torre says. "You think we can beat Maddux and Glavine if we have to?"

"Why don't we worry about that tomorrow?" the nurse says.

On the morrow, Frank Torre has a new heart. That night, Joe Torre managed the Yankees to a world championship.

Who'd have ever thought it, the blessed Yankees?

Maybe this is rock bottom

NOVEMBER, 1997

Defending Jimmy Hoffa, the superlawyer Edward Bennett Williams invited boxer Joe Louis to sit near the defense table in hopes that black jurors might notice the champ and draw the proper conclusions. As a bonus, EBW knew the tactic would irritate the U.S. attorney general, Robert F. Kennedy, who had guaranteed Hoffa's conviction. "Or I'll jump off the Capitol dome," RFK said.

Well.

Upon Hoffa's acquittal, Williams mailed Bobby a note. He wrote, "You may need this." The note accompanied a parachute.

I'm thinking of EBW because of baseball's despair. For $12 million in 1979, to his great joy and constant consternation, he became the owner of the Baltimore Orioles.

Too soon by far, he despised baseball's leaders. A players strike threatened his first season. I asked what he thought of Bowie Kuhn, then the game's commissioner. He said, "Kuhn would screw up a two-car funeral."

Almost 20 years later, that impression persists, perhaps even more profoundly melancholy. Could today's gentlemen get even one car to the graveyard?

Imagine Bud Selig driving.

261

Selig: "Who's got the map?"

Don Fehr: "We're voting on whether or not to give it to you."

Richie Phillips: "Touch me, I torch the car."

Wayne Huizenga: "If the city would buy the graveyard and put up a stadium, I'd wear this seasick-green sports coat 24 hours a day."

Don Ohlmeyer: "Just get us there and back before Seinfeld."

It's easy to make sport of baseball. And it's sad to know it's easy. Bob Verdi, the Chicago Tribune sage, said, "Why is it that if Jacksonville and Carolina get to the final four of the NFL playoffs, it's a great thing—but if the Indians and Marlins get to the World Series, it's a bad thing?"

It's so bad that Ohlmeyer, a muckety-muck with NBC, which is one of baseball's biggest business partners, said he wanted a four-game sweep so as not disrupt the network's Thursday night lineup.

It's so bad that Selig, acting as commissioner, said TV ratings would have been better with the Yankees and Braves, an observation repeated so often that Jim Leyland, the Marlins' manager, said, "It makes me puke."

After Game 3, Selig knocked his own product. Ugly, he said, of the 17-walk; six-error; 4-hour, 12-minute; 14-11 game. "Through the whole game, I felt the 'Unfinished Symphony' had a better chance of being finished before that game ended."

His criticism included slow play: "We need the umpires to get the hitters in the box and make the pitchers pitch. To have the pitcher circling the mound waiting for a message from God and the batter stepping out of the box after every pitch is nonsense."

More evidence that baseball people have lost faith in their game came from Huizenga, the Marlins' owner, before Game 6: "It's more important to us to get a new stadium than it is to win the World Series."

Huizenga spoke of the long run. Absent a new stadium, he thinks the Marlins are dead fish in south Florida. No doubt survival comes first. But to say it during a World Series? To diminish the importance of what should be the game's crown jewel?

Maybe this is rock bottom. Maybe a forgettable Series distinguished by ennui and anger—redeemed by the game's inevitable magic only at the end—will move baseball's leaders to do something constructive about the World Series.

They should:

• Take less TV money and play day games. Rex Hudler, the Phillies' veteran utility man, said, "Sure, play in the daytime. Players want the fans to enjoy the games. What's a winner's Series share, $270,000? For some guys, that's an every-other-week paycheck. We'd take less money."

• Penalize pitchers and hitters for dawdling. The rules exist now. They only need to be enforced.

• Call the strike zone as it's defined, a vertical rectangle, not the horizontal mail slot that leaves beleaguered pitchers so frustrated they circle the mound, praying to God for more Eric Greggs.

• Teach the casual fan, as Earl Weaver put it, "This ain't football. We do this every day."

When Leyland gave the Marlins a day off before Game 6, his guys had played 207 games, spring training through playoffs. Small wonder they might be too weary to be their best. Late in October, playing in snow, playing past midnight, the wonder is not that a game lasts three hours—the wonder is that an Omar Vizquel yet can do beautiful work, as in the sixth inning of a Game 6 victory.

The shortstop took three running steps and dived to his right, flying, to put his glove around Charlie Johnson's sharply hit ground ball. He then rose and threw out the Marlins catcher, ending the inning when a two-run single would have reduced the Indians' lead to 4-3. "The most important play I've ever made," Vizquel called it.

Marquis Grissom becoming Willie Mays against the wall. Darren Daulton still rippin' ropes. Sandy Alomar ascendant at last. Chad Ogea twice a wonder/befuddlement. Bobby Bonilla dragging himself to work. Gary Sheffield a hitting machine.

Those images go in my memory book along with a story the likes of which you hear only at a ballpark, this one suggested by the old Indians hero, Bob Feller, a Hall of Fame pitcher who 50 years ago brought serious heat. Asked about Marlins reliever Robb Nen's 102 mph fastball in Game 1, Feller harrumphed: "My changeup."

Tim Kurkjian, the TV idol at CNN/Sports Illustrated, once stood in against Feller during a minor league promotion. Kurkjian, laughing: "He's a hundred years old! Throwing 40 mph! First two pitches, I crack 'em. Base hits. So what's he do? Starts throwing me breaking stuff off the plate! If you hit him, you got a certificate. But at the bottom, in big letters, it said, 'The aforementioned slugger realizes that had he faced Mr. Feller in his prime, the result would have been different.'"

An extraordinary Joe

NOVEMBER 2, 1998

In the spring of this glorious baseball year, the inglorious George Steinbrenner wondered if anyone had ever gone 162-0. "He said it kiddingly—I think," said Joe Torre, the Yankees' gentleman manager. But on the chance The Boss expected perfection, Torre delivered it. At 125-50 with a World Series championship, the Yankees achieved the baseball equivalent of Miami's undefeated 1972 NFL season. We'll be our grandchildren's dim memories before we see such a baseball thing again. So good were these Yankees that even the most rock-ribbed Big Red Machine man said, "Hmmm, time to rethink?" Maybe Morgan, Bench & Rose had an edge offensively; even that is now uncertain. And there's no argument about the game's most important element, pitching. These Yankees leave those Reds in the shade.

As wonderful as Sparky Anderson was—his Stengelesque genius fit a Cincinnati clubhouse filled with egos waiting for the next train to Cooperstown—Joe Torre has done work all but unimaginable. By skill and manner, Torre helped create and sustain a selfless team in an era when selfishness is exalted. And he did it while winning 125 games, in New York, for the Yankees, for Steinbrenner. Zounds.

Torre put this complex idea simply. "There's an inner conceit here," he said of his players. "We know we're good, and that's enough. We don't have to push it in anyone's face. We don't spike the ball."

It's a far better thing they did. They worked. "Twenty games over .500, 30 over, 40, they never took a day off," Torre says. "That's something you cherish." And that is no accident, says Dusty Baker, the Giants manager and once a teen-aged teammate of the veteran catcher Joe Torre: "People feel comfortable around Joe because he lets them be themselves—as long as they're working to get better."

Maybe more than anything, Torre's equanimity mattered in the clubhouse and with Steinbrenner. "Joe is a calming influence," says Gene Michael, the Yankees' director of major league scouting. "We thought he'd be good with George in that he doesn't panic—not that George makes people panic." (A raised eyebrow here.)

Torre's peace is that of a warrior who has fought all the battles. "I've hit .240 and .360, and I've tried every bit as hard at both ends," he says. Pitcher David Cone says, "Professionalism, that's what Joe's about." Such is Torre's dignity that the kid shortstop Derek Jeter is given to calling him Mr. Torre.

So, on a seat so hot it has scorched the bottoms of 13 long-gone Yankees managers in Steinbrenner's time, Torre has been able to win two world championships in three seasons without once leaping over a desk to compress The Boss' larynx.

And who'd have ever thought it? "CLUELESS JOE," the New York Post screamed on Torre's hiring three winters ago. Fired by the Mets and Braves, Torre wandered in the wilderness of TV commentary for six years before the Cardinals hired him in 1990. Five years later, given the gate, Torre might have been done as a manager—except an old friend asked, "Do you want to manage the Yankees?"

It was Arthur Richman calling. Steinbrenner's senior adviser, a baseball lifer, Richman had been in the Mets' front office in Torre's time and roomed with him on the road. Richman had considered Tony La Russa, Davey Johnson and Sparky. But La Russa cost too much, Johnson had a job lined up and Sparky was reluctant to leave retirement.

So, Torre. "Joe'd turned down our offer to be general manager," Richman said, giddy and champagne-dripping the night the Yankees changed the order of baseball history. "Then I asked about managing. Right away the papers were critical: 'They've hired a guy who in 35 years has never been to a

World Series as a player or as a manager.' George got nervous and I told him, 'If I'm wrong, why don't you fire me?' "

Gene Michael says the Yankees didn't hire Torre because his manner fit the players' personalities. "We're not that smart," he said. Along the way, Torre has done a couple of smart things; he replaced nettlesome Ruben Sierra and Charlie Hayes with good guys Darryl Strawberry and Scott Brosius. One or two bad apples out of the barrel, a clubhouse becomes a nicer place.

It becomes a Torre place. A lunch story may explain what sort of place that is. It happened in the spring after the Yankees had won the '96 World Series in Torre's first season. At a diner somewhere in New York, Torre sat with his wife, Ali.

"Joe was stressed and wasn't being himself," Ali Torre says. "I asked what was wrong and he said—well, how to put it? He didn't want to appear 'too relaxed,' like he wasn't working hard enough to keep winning.

"I told him, 'That's crazy.' He'd always worked hard and he'd always enjoyed it, too. But he wasn't enjoying it then. I said, 'I don't know who you are right now. You just have to be yourself.' "

From that day on, Torre said, "I didn't care what people thought. I was going to enjoy this job."

That he has done, even before Game 4 of the World Series when he stood with a jokester soliciting sound bites for television's David Letterman show. Quoth the Letterman doofus, "Joe, who're you rooting for?" Without so much as a raised eyebrow, Torre responded brightly, "The Bulls. Yes. I'd like to see the Bulls win again."

The Yankees' skilled workers

NOVEMBER 1, 1999

Snow covered the blood in December 1944. Six months after D-Day, his army in retreat across the Rhine, the madman Adolf Hitler still sent tanks and men on an offensive from Germany into the south of Belgium. The offensive became the Battle of the Bulge, and in that snowy hell "we were actually surrounded by the Nazis," the great old lefthanded pitcher Warren Spahn says.

All these years later, Spahn sat warm in a glittery hotel. Sandy Koufax had said major league baseball's All-Century team would be no team without Warren Spahn as its lefthanded pitcher. How many games did Spahn win? Three hundred sixty-three. How many years did he pitch? Until he couldn't. And wouldn't you have pitched forever if you'd made it out of the snows of Bastogne? "I don't think the Germans even knew they had us surrounded. They certainly didn't take advantage of it, thank God, or I wouldn't be talking to you now. Thing is, we didn't trust anybody, even men in American uniforms. The Germans were stealing uniforms, boots, rifles, dog tags. And some of them could speak English well."

So the Americans developed a code they used to tell good guys from bad guys. The code included a wonderfully American question. "Anybody we didn't know we'd ask, 'Who plays second base for the Bums?' "

And if there came no answer?

"If the German wasn't a baseball fan," Spahn says, "he was dead."

Warren Spahn here. Willie Mays in the next room. Bob Gibson saying, "Koufax wouldn't throw me a fastball. I'd hit it. Threw me nothing but hooks." Brooks Robinson saying Pete Rose doesn't belong in the Hall of Fame if he bet on baseball games. Across the ballroom, Yogi Berra says, "These Yankees, this year, they're like our old teams. They all pull together. They're having fun."

Talking baseball at the World Series. Talking with the immortals. Now Yogi: "In my 17 (full) seasons, we never had a fight in the clubhouse. We'd even have our own meetings. We'd tell Casey (Stengel) later. We'd get together and say, 'Hey, guys, we need a new wing on the house.' " Meaning they wanted another World Series check.

There are no such money concerns for today's players, for whom a World Series check is tip money, but Yogi insists these Yankees are the '50s Yankees all over again.

"I do think that, I do," he says. "They play the game right. They make the bunt, they make the cutoff, they make the right play. They're baseball players."

And there is the beauty of this World Series. To say these Yankees are baseball players is to confirm the skilled worker's commitment to a craft worth such a worker's passion. In Boston this October, steely-eyed manager Jimy Williams said of his steely-eyed shortstop Nomar Garciaparra: "He's a baseball player. Every day he comes to play baseball." These Yankees work with a simplicity and attention to detail that always identifies the true craftsman.

We should remember Paul O'Neill's at-bat in Game 1. A lefthanded hitter batting .190 against lefthanded pitchers this season, he came to an eighth-inning, bases-loaded, no-out, game-tied, infield-in moment when the game could be won—and he stood in against the Braves' action-hero reliever, John Rocker, a lefthander who brings incinerating heat.

But O'Neill is a professional hitter who gave Rocker none of the help the kid needed in his first, adrenaline-running World Series appearance. So the count went to three balls, one strike—a hitter's count, and yet even here O'Neill had no Mr. October imaginings of glory.

"Lefthanders aren't going to make their living against Rocker," he says. "I just wanted to put the ball in play." That is, be a baseball player. Hit it somewhere, anywhere, and force the Braves to make a gut-check play. On a Rocker fastball, O'Neill did it—a ground ball to the first base side. Nothing heroic, as even O'Neill would admit later: "If the ball finds a hole, we win. If they turn a double play, we might still be playing."

O'Neill's ground ball became a single driving in two runs. "We got a break," he says. Yes, the Yankees got a break when the ball bounced between the first and second basemen. But they created the circumstances that made the break possible. Atlanta's infield was in, increasing the chances of a ground-ball single, because the hitters preceding O'Neill had done everything right to score the tying run and load the bases, forcing the Braves into the high-risk defensive maneuver.

Chili Davis is the Yankees' designated hitter. He's also a baseball player who has been places and seen things. When he sees Paul O'Neill drive in the winning runs of a World Series game, he sees the moment as definition of the 1999 Yankees.

"Nobody on this team is thinking he needs to be the star," Davis says. "But we trust each other to step up when someone needs to step up." So O'Neill, all but helpless against lefthanders this season, stepped up against one of the game's most formidable lefthanders. And afterward said not one word intended to raise himself to heroic proportions. "Paul is not a Barry Bonds, he's not always in front of a camera," Davis says. "He just wanted to play."

Oh, one more thing. Back to Koufax's favorite lefthander, Warren Spahn. Someone asked the tough old bird, 78 years old now, "Who did play second for the '44 Bums?"

Spahn started to say a name, then hesitated, then admitted he'd forgotten, so a writer whose father also came home from Belgium looked it up. The Dodgers' second baseman was Eddie Stanky.

There's no crying in baseball

NOVEMBER 6, 2000

Al Leiter fell. The Mets' pitcher fell reaching for the silly little ground ball. He fell on his hind end, as if in a hurry to sit down only to miss the chair. Another foot this way, the ball so close, he'd have grabbed it, and everything would have been all right.

But now he could only hope someone else could field the silly squib. And surely they would, a ground ball rolling slowly a foot from the pitcher's reach.

Leiter had made a good pitch, a change-up so good that the Yankees hitter, the journeyman Luis Sojo, scraped the top of the ball and created a silly, bouncing, rolling, hopping squib that maybe once in 10,000 times amounts to anything.

Such a long, hard night. Midnight now, Leiter's face drawn tight at the lips and eyes. The pitch to Sojo was his 142nd. He'd quit on hard stuff and gone to changing speeds and locations. He'd given up only five hits to a Yankees team eager for the one more victory that would give it a third straight world championship.

"Anxious, gut-wrenching games," the Yankees' Paul O'Neill called this subway drama in five acts, and Leiter says of the Yankees, "Every pitch against that lineup, you're grinding."

Leiter's good pitch to Sojo, a master's pitch, produced a little ground ball that this time, this once in 10,000 times, eluded Leiter and passed a foot left of second base headed into a no-man's land beyond two diving infielders.

Anywhere else, the squib was harmless, the inning over, the runner at second left there, a 2-2 tie going into the last of the ninth inning. But Sojo's silly ground ball rolled under all the gloves and into the outfield grass. And Leiter, in the dirt, propped up on his hands, his eyes fixed on the ball rolling away from all the grasping hands, was helpless after doing so much all night.

The day before, Leiter spoke to Bobby Valentine. The last three years, the 35-year-old lefthander built a 46-26 record for the Mets. But 10 times in his career he had started postseason games, somehow winning none. Now the Mets needed a victory to move this World Series to a sixth game.

"You can leave me in for 150 pitches," Leiter told Valentine, maybe 40 over the usual limit.

For another manager in another place, Leiter once threw 166 pitches in midseason. For three weeks after, he brushed his teeth righthanded. "Who knows what that guy was thinking?" Leiter says. "But with Bobby, I told him, 'I've got four or five months to rest.'"

He would leave only when carried off on his shield. Even with two Yankees on in the ninth, Valentine let Leiter face Sojo. "He'd earned the right to win or lose it himself," the manager says.

Only after Sojo's squib caused two runs to score did Valentine replace Leiter. He left to a standing ovation and sat in the dugout head down, face in his hands, spent, weeping. His friend and teammate, John Franco, says, "Al gave us his heart and soul."

These are disintegrating Yankees, eroding before our eyes. Yet now they have won a third straight world championship, four of the last five. And they have reason to call themselves the best team of all time.

They just might be, if we add up the five years and let this one count for only a little. But this .540 season, the ninth-best finish in Major League Baseball this year, is cause to argue that the 2000 Yankees are the worst team ever to win a World Series, though the .525 Twins of 1987 were ninth-best in the standings as well.

It also can be argued that the fifth-best team in the A.L. standings beating the fourth-best N.L. team would be seen as nothing special had it not involved both New York teams in a reprise of those glorious Yankees-Dodgers days when the world was young.

So argue it.

Here the preference is to remember Al Leiter in defeat, a man larger than Roger Clemens in victory. "Pitching for the team I grew up watching, it can't get much better than this," says Leiter, a Jersey boy.

Three nights earlier in Shea Stadium, Franco stood with Leiter and stared up at two big stars in the sky and decided, in Leiter's words, the stars were their fathers "having a beer, watching us have fun."

An hour after the Game 5 defeat, Leiter hung at his locker answering reporters' questions. Not easy, no fun. New reporters showed up every few minutes, asking questions asked by earlier reporters. Leiter answered them all, some with a smile, making eye contact, standing tall.

He said the Yankees were better. "Not much better than us, but enough," he says. Wasn't Luis Sojo's hit just lucky, a 15-hopper up the middle that gets two runs? "I'm convinced that with good teams and good players, lucky stuff happens," he says.

One pitch from ending the ninth, a 2-2 slider called a ball, Leiter then walked Jorge Posada and gave up a single before Sojo came to bat. "I'm upset about what went on in the ninth. I wanted to be able to finish it."

How upset? "It was the most emotional time I've had as a pro. Maybe in Little League, I got more emotional, I don't know. I was a kid then," he says.

He laughed with us at that, and someone asked if he had cried on the bench.

"You know the line in the movie, 'There's no crying in baseball,'" he says.

"But did you cry?"

"I'm not telling you." Smiling.

"Did you?"

"No." But he knew we knew, and he smiled, and that made it all right for all of us to smile with him.

We did.

We felt better, some

The morning after Game 4, the hotel maid who had come to New York from Puerto Rico said her son was 7 years old and loved baseball and went to bed the night before without knowing what happened. So she told him, "The Yankees win," and he was happy, and as she told the story she asked, "Who do you want to win?"

There was a Yankees cap in a chair by a desk, and the man pointed to it. He might have said he'd bought the cap because now, if only for a moment, it represented more than a city's team, it represented an idea. The idea was, if you got knocked down, you got up.

"Of course, the Yankees," is what he said, the baseball team now an idea.

• • •

In the hour after Game 1, in the Diamondbacks' happy locker room, Mike Morgan's story began with his parents 17 years old, one thing leading to another leading to their baby boy.

They dropped out of school. They got in the car, and they drove out of California across mountains and desert to Las Vegas. They carried the baby boy named Mike in a five-gallon bucket and made him comfortable by surrounding him with sponges. A laugh here: "The first 'car seat,'" Mike Morgan says.

273

Mike Morgan is baseball's human atlas. In his crinkly, smiling face is a map of the game. The relief pitcher has worked in four U.S. time zones, in Canada, on both coasts, from top to bottom, in the heartland, in the desert. He has worked for 22 professional teams, 12 in the major leagues; no other athlete in any sport has played for as many major league teams. Another laugh: "Have arm, will travel."

Such an arm it is, all but impervious to the erosion of muscle and tendon that comes to most human body parts. At age 42, Morgan is in his 21st big-league season. He's the only active player left over from the 1978 season; he's only the ninth pitcher to work in four decades, and he's only the fifth pitcher with more saves after age 40 than before. "This thing is rubber," he says, raising his right arm. "I'll pitch 'til I'm 50—the white Satchel Paige."

A starting pitcher until the last two seasons, Morgan has been so good for so long that he has lost a lot of games for middling teams. Seven seasons he won 10 games or more; 11 times he lost in double figures. At 140-185, he leads active pitchers in defeats. He's now an eighth-inning specialist getting the game to the closer.

And now, a World Series. His first. "The only other time I played for a championship was 1981, in Double-A ball, in Nashville. We lost to Orlando and Frank Viola, 2-0. I got clipped with another of my 'L' shutouts. But I tell you, this is different, this World Series. Back in Nashville, we didn't have all this media. I think we had one photographer, and he went to 7-Eleven and bought a disposable Kodak. This is the big time here."

His voice was a boy's, giddy, words piling on each other as he remembered his World Series debut, the eighth inning of Game 1: "Man, I was ready, 10 pitches, ready, and the umpire tells me, 'Two more minutes, throw some more.' And I'm going, 'Throw more? I'm ready. I'm saving these bullets for the guys with bats in their hands.'

"It hit me when I looked up in the stands to see my family. I've never done that, ever. I'm thinking, 'What am I doing, looking up in the stands?' I looked for my wife of 21 years, our two kids, my niece, my nephew, my mom. Her name's Nellie, she's a little thing, barely 4 feet tall, 80 pounds. I thought I saw her with tears in her eyes."

Facing the three-time defending world-champion Yankees—he worked for them in 1982—Morgan pitched a perfect inning: "A little splitter, a little hammer, a slider in, a heater out. Three quick outs. It was a rush."

When the 17-year-olds, Henry and Nellie, made their home in Las Vegas all those years ago, Henry Morgan went to work setting tile. In time he took the boy Mike with him, teaching him the trade, how to work the grout and tile, $4 an hour. Mostly, though, the father wanted the son to play all the games.

The Morgans started early.

"From 6 years old, Henry's boy was good," Henry's boy Mike said. A great day came a week after high school graduation when Mike Morgan, 18, made his major league debut with the Athletics. The 17,157 spectators included the man he calls Pops.

Last November, out of telephone reach on a hunt in the back country of Utah, Morgan saw his wife, Kassie, driving through snowdrifts. She'd come to tell him about Pops' heart attack. Before and after surgery, Morgan held his father's hand. Eight days later, Henry Morgan died.

He was buried wearing his boy Mike's Diamondbacks jersey.

When the Diamondbacks won the NLCS, they returned to Phoenix at 3 in the morning. Even at that hour, Mike Morgan began driving north. He would go to the cemetery to tell Pops. But an hour out, exhausted, Morgan called his brother in Las Vegas: "I asked Larry to go out and give a knuckle to Pops' grave."

Now Morgan stood at his locker and said it was wonderful that his mother, his wife, his children had seen him, after all these years, in a World Series. "But Pops had the best seat of all," he said, "a reserved seat in heaven watching his boy play ball."

• • •

Twenty years ago, from Peru, the husband and father Mario Luna came to New York because he knew he'd do better there than in Lima. On Sept. 11, 2001, he was working, driving his taxi, when the first tower came down, and a sheet of aluminum clattered against his car's hood, and he turned on the windshield wipers to scrape away ash falling from the sky.

A month and more later, after Game 5, Mario Luna said, "This little island, something happens on the East Side, it changes something on the West Side. It is like a body, where everything is connected. Now the Yankees, they win again. So everybody, this morning, we feel better some."

We feel better some.

Perfect.

Walk a mile or so from the firehouse at Canal and Allen streets to the intersection of Broadway and Fulton. From there you can see the disfigured ribs of the steel skeleton once hidden by the tower's beauty. The sight is hell-ish. Leaving, take the subway north, past midtown, into the Bronx, to 161st Street. There, Yankee Stadium.

There, find Tino Martinez. The first baseman came to New York five years ago. "The Yankees," Martinez says, "are what baseball is all about."

Ruth and Gehrig, DiMaggio and Mantle, Jeter and Clemens, Larsen's perfect game, Maris' 61—and now and forever more the home run by Tino Martinez, a home run so wonderful that at least one rabbi, as we shall see, suspected divine intervention.

Martinez hit the home run with a man on base and two out in the last of the ninth to tie the game. Only once in 98 years had the Yankees tied a World Series game with two runs in the ninth, and that was 62 years earlier. The further wonder is, Martinez meant to do it.

He went to bat, two runs down, his team about to lose a third game, to lose it in Yankee Stadium, and he went up intending to hit a home run. He said, "I looked for something I could turn on and take a good, strong hack at it." First pitch, gone.

Such a moment, an earthquake of joy.

Soon enough came another Yankee home run, followed by another the next night to tie that game in the ninth inning with two outs—events so improbable as to prompt Rabbi Ephraim Z. Buchwald, director of the National Jewish Outreach Program, to write a letter to The New York Times:

"The events of recent days raise some ponderous theological questions: With so much going on in the world, why is God spending so much time with the New York Yankees?"

Or with baseball, for that matter.

Improbably, implausibly and all but impossibly, the Diamondbacks won Games 6 and 7, Mike Morgan in the bullpen at the end, "praying I wouldn't have to pitch," and he didn't, for Luis Gonzalez dumped a single to center to defeat the previously unbeatable Mariano Rivera.

"God Bless America" is beautiful, as all the flags are beautiful, and in the weeks since September 11 they have been a balm and a blessing, make no mistake. But in an October, even this October, or maybe especially this October, few things speak more clearly of our national character than a plain, simple, glorious baseball game.

That, we'll remember forever, just as we'll remember firefighters and police officers in dress uniform. We'll remember how ineffably sweet it sounded to hear "God Bless America" as preamble to "Take Me Out to the Ball Game." We'll remember the Yankees, like little boys wishing to be their heroes, wearing FDNY and NYPD caps.

We'll remember all those games where folks got knocked down and got up.

We'll remember, too, that for a moment, one sweet moment, we felt better some.

CHAPTER 14

September 11, 2001

A firefighter's story

OCTOBER 22, 2001

A half-hour out, on the train from Washington to New York, you see the city's skyline. There's the Empire State Building. Then, as always, your eyes move to the right, south, to the bottom of the island, where the towers used to be. There's a hole there, a hole in the city, in our hearts. To walk down Broadway, to where the towers were, to where ash is yet in the air a month later, is to feel the emptiness of disbelief.

This is war, not games. But games are part of the story. The Mets and Giants came to work wearing firefighter and police officer caps. The Rangers' captain carried a firefighter's helmet onto the ice. Every seventh inning, we sing "God Bless America." So let's talk to Frank Tepedino, who is part of both, the war and the games. He says, "This for The Sporting News?"

Yes, sir.

He laughs. "Good. The last time I was in The Sporting News, I was 0-for-1, a strikeout against Don Sutton."

Frank Tepedino is one of those old major league baseball players you might never have known. He was 19 years old and on the Yankees' bench the day Mickey Mantle hit his 500th home run. A banjo-hitting first baseman (.241, six homers), he played parts of eight seasons with the Yankees, Brewers and Braves. The day Hank Aaron hit his 715th, one Brave showed up on the videotape identified by his really long sideburns. "Me," Tepedino says.

A generation later, on September 11, 2001, Frank Tepedino was at home on Long Island when killers flew airplanes into buildings. Seeing it done, here's what Tepedino did. At his home in Hauppage, he piled into a car with his son and two other New York firefighters. He drove toward the danger, four hours to the city: "You never saw so many emergency vehicles. And all going to the same place."

For 20 years now, as a member of the salvage-duty New York Fire Patrol, Tepedino has worked out of a Greenwich Village firehouse five minutes from the World Trade Center's towers. That day in September he began 24-hour shifts of rescue and recovery alongside firefighters whose every step suggests a professionalism breathtaking in its purpose and commitment.

On that day, Bobby Cox remembered Tepedino. The Braves' manager was once Tepedino's roommate and later his manager in the minor leagues. Cox says, "I thought, 'Holy cow, Frank's fire station is right there. He'd be in the first or second bunch there.'"

It was 10 days later, at Shea Stadium, in the world's greatest city, when Cox came into the visitors' dugout, looked up, and shouted, "Teppy!" His old friend was alive. And Bobby Cox did what every American wants to do: He hugged a hero. Tepedino had come into the city to see the Braves and the man who in 1973, managing the Yankees' Class AAA team in Syracuse, wouldn't answer a question.

"Bobby always taped the lineup card to the light tower, so I look at it and I'm not in the lineup after going 4-for-5 the night before," Tepedino says. "I go, 'Skip, what's going on?' Bobby says, 'You can't play because you can't get hurt. And the deal might not go through, anyway. Come to my room at 4 in the morning, I can tell you then.'"

At 4 a.m., Cox told Tepedino he'd been traded to Atlanta. "I said, 'Oh, that Richmond ballpark's too big.' Bobby said, 'Not Richmond, you're going to join the big team.' Then he drove me to the airport."

For 20 years and more, Tepedino stayed away from ballparks, as old players often do. But when the Yankees reached the World Series in 1996—against Atlanta—Tepedino's sons asked if he knew any way to get tickets. Well, what's a dad to do? Ever since, when the Braves come to the city, Cox makes sure the Tepedinos have tickets.

Because the Braves-Mets series came so soon after the attacks, there was talk of switching the games from New York to Atlanta. Cox would have none of it. He played for the Yankees, coached for them, loves New York. On September 21, when his team came to the world's greatest city, Cox walked to Ground Zero, where a policeman invited him behind barriers to say hello to rescue workers. Later, Cox told reporters, "The Braves are a lucky team to be here."

Lucky to be there?

Where killers flew planes into buildings?

Where who-knew-what might happen next?

Yes. Lucky. Lucky to be in the world's greatest city. Lucky to be playing games. The games say life can be terrible and frightening, and yet we live life the way we want to, not the way killers would have us live.

We've played games through wars before. We'll play them through this one.

"Baseball is like the flag," Frank Tepedino says. "It brings us together. It's what America is all about, competing, winning. It's the best of what this country is. What we've been through at the World Trade Center with the rescue and recovery operations wasn't just about firefighters and cops. It was everybody. It was contractors, electricians, carpenters, plumbers. And it was baseball, too. This was about America."

Index